Education and Empire

Naval Tradition and England's Elite Schooling

David McLean

British Academic Press

LONDON • NEW YORK

Published in 1999 by British Academic Press
an imprint of I.B.Tauris & Co Ltd
Victoria House, Bloomsbury Square, London WC1B 4DZ
175 Fifth Avenue, New York NY 10010

In the United States and Canada distributed by St. Martin's Press
175 Fifth Avenue, New York NY 10010

ISBN 1 86064 295 0

A full CIP record for this book is available from the British Library.
A full CIP record for this book is available from the Library of Congress

Library of Congress catalog card: available

Typeset in 10/11pt Palatino by The Midlands Book Typesetting Company,
Loughborough.
Printed and bound in Great Britain by WBC Ltd, Bridgend.

CONTENTS

ACKNOWLEDGEMENTS

This book has been published with the aid of a grant from the bequest of the late Miss Isobel Thornley to the University of London. I am grateful also to my wife, Eva Gordon, for her invaluable critical observations as well as for her contribution to the final text.

INTRODUCTION

"Revolt of the boys at Greenwich school

On Friday a very alarming disturbance broke out in the Upper school of the Royal Asylum, Greenwich. It appears that Lieutenant Rouse, R.N., one of the officers and directors of gymnastics, had (it is said, without the sanction of the superior authorities) restricted the intercourse between the boys and their friends, which so irritated the pupils that they commenced a general row, smashing the windows with slates, rules, brickbats, and other missiles, and breaking upwards of 1000 panes of glass. Five of the ringleaders of the disturbance have been placed in confinement. A strict investigation is going on under the orders of the Governor, Admiral Sir Robert Stopford, K.C.B., before Captain Huskisson, R.N., one of the principal officers of the institution. There are nearly 800 boys, the sons of commission and warrant officers, in the Upper school, and many of them are 15 or 16 years of age, who, on a former occasion, expelled the police by a volley of stones, etc."

The Times 24 January 1843

Journalistic licence was not unknown in the British Press in the mid nineteenth century and *The Times* proved itself to be as adept as any at fuelling the imagination of astonished readers. There certainly was rioting by boys at the institution mentioned, though no attempted repetition such as was falsely reported on 28 January. After that, the story was never continued. The Greenwich Hospital Asylum sank back gratefully from this unwelcome exposure into its comparative obscurity.

Behind this isolated report, however, lay a bold and deliberate experiment in British education. It was not the subject of contemporary publicity and, but for the rioting in January 1843,

vii

most of its details would never have been recorded. The experiment involved every facet of changing practice in teaching and school administration. It thus illustrates a period which, many scholars have asserted, was crucial in the history of mass education. Writing in 1972, T.G. Cook observed that although it is not difficult to discover what was intended as good practice in early-Victorian schools, 'what is not so easy is to find much exemplification of what actually did go on.'[1] That is certainly true: historians, of course, are always at the mercy of surviving documentation and very few institutions have left us any insights into their daily routine and organisational problems.

The Greenwich Asylum incorporated educational practices common at both private and elementary schools in the 1840s and is therefore a major point of reference for comparable study. A unique set of records preserved by the Admiralty, combined with those in private collections, illuminates the national debate about education in the early-Victorian years and highlights a remarkable clash between the philosophy and practice of idealistic reformers and the constraints on change imposed both by the reaction of long-serving teaching staff and by what was realistically achievable with the resources available. At a time of rapid and important change in the provision of popular education in Britain we can assess for the first time what really did go on – and in schools which were, in fact, among the largest in the country.

1 • EDUCATION IN EARLY NINETEENTH CENTURY BRITAIN

The early nineteenth century witnessed radical and unprecedented changes in society in Britain, the driving forces for which were the explosion of population and the accelerating pace of industrialisation. A population of 6 million in England and Wales in 1751 had surged to 9 million by 1801 and to 18 million by 1851. Textiles, iron, coal and mineral extraction, and the expansion of Britain's international trade had transformed an essentially agrarian economy into one which was different in kind from even the more prosperous regions of western Europe. Concomitant with these changes was rapid urbanisation, which increasingly shaped the national culture and produced sprawling communities typically dependent on the fortunes of specific economic enterprise. In 1801 one third of Britain's population was urban, though only London had more than 100,000 inhabitants. By 1851 half the nation's population lived in towns, most of which had done little to provide adequate accommodation, sanitation or education for their largely impoverished residents.

The great cities were the pride of early Victorian economic achievement but at the same time they were an omnipresent reminder of the social depravity which, if unchecked, might yet subsume all that respectable opinion held dear. Violence, crime, moral baseness and an ignorance of Christian precepts and civil obligations were all manifestations of the destitution prevalent in urban Britain. Individuals themselves were blamed. Poverty was the failure of will and character; sobriety, integrity, persistence and honest toil would enable every God-fearing man to overcome even the greatest adversities and to take his place as a useful contributor to the common weal according to the legacy of his birth and the limits of his ability. But by the mid-nineteenth century there was growing doubt expressed that this philosophy held the answer to Britain's burgeoning social problems. Almost

1

50 per cent of the population was below the age of 20 throughout the period 1821 to 1841 and by 1851 about 25 per cent of the population was under 10.[1] For a large proportion of British children, unschooled and undisciplined within the industrial slums, self help was an incomprehensible message and an implausible means of escape from hereditary degradation.

Population expansion, in any case, had far outstripped educational provision in the new industrial regions by the early nineteenth century. Church and charity foundations, and local voluntary effort, had stemmed the descent into illiteracy in some areas, but in most they were simply overwhelmed by the pressure of numbers and the absence of school buildings. The same was true in parts of London where great numbers of wretched and untended children entered lives of vice and crime neglected both by parents and by society at large.[2] Even where charities existed they were often either incapable of adapting to new social conditions or else infested with malpractice which invariably impaired the proper distribution of resources. Attempts to change the law respecting charity administration usually failed on account of the expense entailed or the lack of any serious political interest in educational matters. Legislators believed that tending to the destitute was not the job of government. Furthermore, even those who championed the spread of education among the lowest levels of the population were often of the view that the state had no proper role to play in their religiously inspired and morally uplifting work. In this, they reflected public opinion at large. As late as 1861 a school inspector who had toured most of eastern England reported categorically that 'with regard to government interference with education, the feeling, as far as I have been able to test it, is almost unanimously against such interference.'[3]

Nonetheless, by the 1830s the improvement of society through legislation had become a pervasive theme in British politics. Parliamentary and municipal government, the Poor Law, factory conditions, the Church and taxes on newsprint were all subjected to the zeal of Whig and radical reformers eager to assert the will of a representative House of Commons over bastions of aristocratic and ecclesiastical privilege. Where zeal was lacking, pragmatism often came to the assistance of change. A society, most of whose members lived below the threshold of poverty, was not likely to prove stable or enduring. What was denied the masses by gracious concession might later be demanded amid scenes of bloodshed and disorder; social and political tensions were better regulated by judicious efforts to address identifiable grievances rather than a strict insistence that public order was the only function of the state and that it must always be upheld. In 1839, however, Thomas Arnold, then eleven years headmaster at Rugby, still warned a friend that insufficient in this spirit had been done. 'People are not enough aware of the monstrous state of society,' he recorded. The masses were 'poor, miserable, and degraded in body and mind, as much as if they were slaves,' he continued, and yet with an ability to combine together for industrial action and political protest which made them far more dangerous than slaves could ever be.[4] Cheap popular literature also brought to the common man a greater awareness of his plight and fostered too his willingness to fight for improvement. Far better, reformers urged, that by the extension of rudimentary schooling which would instil both useful knowledge and a respect for civilised values the impact of revolutionary propaganda might be nullified and future generations given the means with which to render service to God and society.

Arnold's world was, of course, removed from the squalor of the lower orders. The public schools of Victorian England catered for the aristocracy and the wealthy professional classes and, like the ancient universities, were acclaimed as great national institutions which guarded through the generations traditions of Church and state. This was the domain of classical scholarship where chapel dominated a boy's spiritual development and where transgression of the rules and expectations of domineering masters and bullying prefects was often met with savage physical assault. Education here was remote from ordinary life and was never intended to meet the needs of an industrial economy. The sons of the landed classes, of clerics, of lawyers and of eminent medical and literary men were schooled in Latin, Greek and Euclidean mathematics with barely any concessions to English, history, geography, science or modern languages. It would be their lot to preach, to teach and to govern and defend the nation and its empire. The codes of conduct learnt and the discipline imparted would, in many cases, count for far more than any knowledge acquired.[5]

In the 1850s Eton, Harrow, Winchester, Rugby, Westminster, Shrewsbury and Charterhouse had a combined total of 2,500 pupils. In Britain, by then, there were 3 million children of school age of whom, it was calculated, well over 2 million were attending day schools.[6] Yet the line between privilege and poverty was not neatly drawn, for there was a variety of schooling available to families of modest means. Since the sixteenth century endowed grammar schools had educated a wide spectrum of the nation's youth and had provided opportunities for entry to the universities and professions for the academically gifted in their localities. By the late eighteenth century, though, the grammar school sector was broadly in decline. Population changes meant that the schools were no longer serving substantial communities. Their endowments were frequently abused or otherwise diminished in value, their buildings were decayed and the classical education which the statutes of most such schools dictated was less attractive to an expanding commercial class. Improving transport made it easier for respectable families to send their sons beyond the local market town.[7]

Different types of school had also emerged by the late eighteenth century. Academies which provided for the religious scruples of dissenters from the Anglican Church, and their secular equivalents which likewise emphasised a wider curriculum, appealed increasingly to the middle classes who were willing to pay for what they perceived as a more practical education. By the early nineteenth century many of the major towns had at least one such establishment, often eclipsing the old grammar school and even drawing clientele from local gentry families. Science, mathematics, English, writing, geography and modern languages were the staple of their teaching; most pupils would need to make their own way in the world, as had their fathers before them. New Anglican schools were set up to respond to the challenge of these academies. In London and the larger cities there was no shortage of demand for day-school places for fees of up to £10 per annum and an entrepreneurial schoolmaster with an eye for the developing market could make a handsome living from plying his trade. Providing boarding facilities would make him richer still. Proprietary schools, run for the benefit of subscribers, added to the choice available to the more prosperous middle classes.

For the poor, the enterprise and philanthropy of others offered the only hope of educational opportunity and even this was not much in evidence at the start of the nineteenth century. In 1845 Her Majesty's Inspector of schools in northern England observed that 'it has been the practice to look upon the lower classes as machines, rather than men.'[8] Too much learning, many argued, would spoil the quality of their labour and encourage both unrealistic aspirations of improvement and undesirable expressions of grievance. Nonetheless, an interest in popular education did become fashionable in the early nineteenth century. The Royal Commission chaired by the Duke of Newcastle which investigated working-class education in the late 1850s was pleased to report 'the surprisingly rapid progress of elementary education in this country since the beginning of the century.' Sixty per cent of the nation's elementary school children could read, write, calculate and comprehend the tenets of the Christian faith 'well enough for the purposes of their condition in life.'[9] That this was so reflected well on the work of Sunday schools throughout the land and of the two largest national bodies which sponsored popular education: the Anglican National Society for Promoting the Education of the Poor in the Principles of the Established Church, founded in 1811, and the non-denominational British and Foreign Schools Society, founded in 1814.

The Sunday school movement, created by Robert Raikes in 1782 and spread by the enthusiasm of Sarah Trimmer and Hannah More, was teaching over 300,000 children to read by the 1800s. Classes held in Church buildings were conducted by volunteers on a non-denominational basis. A million children were enrolled in Sunday schools in England by 1831 — about 50 per cent of working class children between the ages of 5 and 15.[10] The National and British societies carried on the pioneering work of the 1790s by Andrew Bell and Joseph Lancaster, both of whom had raised money by impressive royal, aristocratic and ecclesiastical patronage to pay for the construction of schools in areas of deprivation and, where voluntary effort would not suffice, for the employment of teachers trained in their model establishments in London at Baldwin Gardens and Borough Road. Along with dame schools, those of mechanics institutes, ragged and industrial schools, and others founded by impressive charitable donations, the followers of Bell and Lancaster contributed significantly to the spread of popular literacy.

The distinctive feature of the National and British schools was the monitorial system of mutual learning whereby older or more able children instructed by rote all the others. It was cheap to operate and allowed one competent master to supervise a whole school of several hundred pupils. The schools also had elaborate systems of rewards and non-violent punishments to encourage good behaviour and regular attendance. These were innovations which made mass education possible; the techniques of Bell and Lancaster remained in vogue for a generation. However, not all reformers were impressed. In 1816 the philanthropic industrialist Robert Owen told a Parliamentary Select Committee that his educational system at New Lanark now employed one headmaster and ten qualified assistants for 700 pupils and that monitors with their mechanical drills had simply not been sufficient for imparting knowledge or broadening minds. In time, many of the shortcomings were more widely revealed. Children teaching other children had obvious drawbacks for discipline and the academic content of lessons. Monitorial instruction also required that the school be held in one large room under the nominal supervision of the teacher: the noise and disorder thereby created was in itself an impediment to effective learning. The monitors were frequently unhappy with their duties and their parents complained that they gained nothing by school attendance. The end product in many elementary schools was an appalling state of ignorance. HMI for the Midlands region in 1845 was staggered to discover that 'hundreds of children taken from the highest classes of our National schools should be incapable of telling me *the name of the country in which they live.*'[11]

Problems in running schools for the needy went well beyond techniques of instruction. Education was not compulsory and as late as the 1850s over half the children attending the National and British schools did so for less than 100 days per annum. Nor were these elementary schools free of charge. Fees of one or two pennies per week were collected from the children, which placed a burden on large families and effectively excluded the destitute. The National and British schools catered for the deserving poor who would make family sacrifices for the betterment of their children. 'Part payment by the poor in every case enhances the value of the thing purchased,' a clergyman informed the Newcastle Commission. 'In no case should education be gratuitous, except the parents are in receipt of parochial relief.'[12] Giving something for nothing was not compatible with the ethos of early Victorian England; nor should the poor be deceived into believing that charity, from whatever source, could ever be other than an aid to their own endeavour.

Such attitudes were reinforced by the fact that many working-class parents did not take naturally to the idea of educational advance. Some were suspicious of its benefits: others preferred the income of two or three shillings per week derived from their child's labour or else the baby-watching service which enabled a mother to work. But even when parents were encouraging, the pennies paid by irregularly attending children for only three or four years was an insufficient financial base for operating a school. Local benefactors, landed or commercial, would often subscribe to the erection of a building and take their places on the management committee and, amid much fanfare, at the opening ceremony. Routine costs, maintenance bills and a teacher's salary, however, appeared less glamorous and many schools in deprived areas soon became dilapidated and ineffective. Too often clergymen found themselves the agents of educational provision by giving their time to teach, badgering more prosperous parishioners for financial support and, ultimately, by assisting from their own stipends. Not surprisingly, many of them took a keen interest in how the local school was organised and in the religious and moral attitudes of its teacher.

'Are our elementary schools doing their work?', asked HMI for the north of England in 1846. His answer was that 'they are not doing all that such institutions ought to do, but all that, as they are, can fairly be expected from them.'[13] It was a widely held opinion among those involved with popular education. By the mid-nineteenth century criticism of this essentially voluntary system was not uncommon. An inspector in central England lamented the quality of schooling in 1844. In Norfolk it was observed that the mechanical instruction in reading, writing and scripture provided 'is not in fact education, or anything more than its unformed, undeveloped germ.' 'If the legitimate educator does no more than this,' he warned, 'there are those who will do more — the Chartist and Socialist educator.'[14] A colleague visiting south Wales and the West country also found school children of the mid 1840s still ill-educated and undisciplined: 'A band of efficient schoolmasters is kept up at much less expense than a body of police or of soldiery,' he reflected.[15] Even those who pressed for better academic provision remained mindful of the social function which universal schooling must also deliver and that this, in fact, was its ultimate justification.

'To anyone who has ever tried to teach children to think, to reason, and to understand, it must be obvious that there is a great art in it.'[16] Therein, as one learned visitor to a training college succinctly observed, lay many of the problems of early nineteenth century education. In large measure, teachers were untrained and often as ignorant as those with whom they laboured. The aged and infirm, drunkards, bankrupts and the generally incompetent all qualified for a livelihood which commanded little respect from society since, for most practitioners, it held out little prospect of adequate remuneration.[17] Of course, it varied greatly according to the master and the school. At the famous public schools annual stipends of £1500 ensured considerable comfort for the ordained graduates from Cambridge and Oxford whose task it was to educate the upper classes. Headmasters at these schools were paid £4000 or more per annum. For most masters, even in the privileged sector of private education, salaries of £200 or £250 after years of service were the norm. In the small private and preparatory schools which served the less affluent middle classes, and which proprietors habitually maintained with every conceivable economy, payment might be between £40 and £80 per annum.

Elementary school salaries naturally fell into this category. A qualified master might earn above £50 a year with accommodation provided but, as the Newcastle Commission was reminded, 'a man whose services can be obtained for a moderate stipend is often one whose character will not bear close investigation.' A schoolmistress would likely earn no more than £30 per annum. 'The profession, as a profession, hardly exists,' another witness to the Commission complained. 'It is a complete refuge for the destitute.'[18]

Conditions of employment matched the levels of remuneration. Although headmasters at large schools and sole masters at many of the small endowed grammar schools enjoyed tenure of appointment, most teachers lived a precarious existence subject to the whims of those in authority over them. Arnold at Rugby and Edward Thring at Uppingham at least recognised the frustration of their colleagues by holding regular staff meetings but even popular and progressive headmasters seldom surrendered any of their autocratic powers. Teachers in all types of school had little protection from peremptory dismissal whether from a head, a school committee or an assertive parish priest. In many schools staff did not wish to stay long and many men left teaching if a better opportunity in life arose. In the expanding economy of early and mid-nineteenth century Britain those with literacy and a competence with numbers were always in demand as clerks, company secretaries, accountants or, from the 1830s onwards, employees of the railway companies. HMI for Scotland, in his 1845 report, expressed surprise that there were any teachers at all for the elementary schools on his tour.

One further problem for such teachers was their ambiguous social status. In the worst districts and in rural villages a master, with his basic education, would likely be an isolated figure. He would influence the minds of children from the working classes and, given his own humble origins, might help articulate the grievances of their parents. This was not lost on conservative opinion which remained unconvinced that the benefits of popular education would outweigh its disruptive effects. For the Bishop of St. Davids, in 1859, a large body of schoolmasters trained to spread secular education 'would prove a very dangerous element of society.'[19] Some years earlier Lord Wharncliffe, as Lord President of the Council, had been asked to rule on the provision of accommodation for teachers in rural areas. It should be provided as a supplement to the teachers' meagre stipend, Wharncliffe decided, but the schoolhouse should be 'by no means too large, so as to exalt him too much in the scale of society.'[20] A school inspector of long service later remarked on the dissatisfaction felt by many masters that they were not accepted as professional men. 'It is rather a morbid desire to be a gentleman too soon, I think,' was his conclusion.[21] Toiling among the masses and possessing an education sufficient merely for that purpose certainly did not propel a man into polite society.

Education, of course, reflected the hierarchy of status and wealth in nineteenth century Britain. By and large, children were sent to schools where they would mix with those of comparable backgrounds regardless of whether the education received merited the expense incurred. Where money was tight parents usually still preferred to find what was necessary for a dame's or small private school rather than face the stigma of their offspring receiving charity. 'Even in humble life, there is something in the *exclusiveness* of a private school which recommends it to our aristocratic English nature,' HMI for northern England discovered in 1845.[22] Ordinary people appeared to understand instinctively that there was much more to schooling than simply imparting knowledge. The result, perhaps, as Matthew Arnold suggested to the Newcastle Commission, was that 'our middle classes are nearly the worst educated in the world.'[23] For as long as schooling was regarded essentially as a reinforcement of social aspirations, even among the respectable working classes, this was likely to remain a valid opinion. One of Newcastle's assistant commissioners summed up the prevailing attitude: 'there is a feeling of *caste* in this country, which goes down to the roots of society.'[24]

As was widely comprehended, the schools of the National and British societies had limited ambitions which seldom transcended basic writing skills and religious knowledge. One of their functions, HMI for Birmingham confirmed in 1841, was to teach humble children to make the best of life's tribulations and to meet death with tranquillity. 'It would be a great mistake to point out to children instances of persons raised by successful industry, or by remarkable talent, to dignity and wealth, as illustrating what education may do for them,' he cautioned.[25] To do so would invariably raise expectations doomed to disappointment. Five years later a colleague restated the principle in terms of the practical application of education to the lower strata of society: those destined to be mechanics should be knowledgeable in their trade and those destined for farm labour should have some acquaintance with agriculture. 'In short, that every man should know his own business can be fraught with no peril to the interests of Religion or of the State.'[26] By contrast, most private schools, however modest, offered to turn unprepossessing boys into young gentlemen. It was a seductive appeal even to families whose resources gave them no right to think in those terms.

* * *

Promoters of mass education took a keen interest in developments abroad where, it was commonplace to insist, better practice had developed. The English had only to travel north to find in Scotland structures of, and attitudes to education which made it both more suited to an industrial age and more universally available.[27] Reformers also toured the continent to study German, Dutch, Swiss and French provision and usually returned with glowing, if somewhat fawning, accounts of the superior training and intelligence of foreign schoolmasters and the perfect order in their schools. The Prussian state, indeed, had made education to the age of 12 compulsory since the mid-eighteenth century. The Dutch legislated for a national education system in 1806. In Holland every town with 10,000 inhabitants was also required to build scientific and industrial schools. France, Austria and Switzerland also had technical schools in profusion. After 1837 the Massachusetts School Board in America provided an example of rate-supported and compulsory popular education. But education by coercion was all too much for a large strand of opinion in Britain, antipathetic to the power of the state and sensitive to the freedom of the citizen to regard the schooling or otherwise of children as a private family matter. Besides, statistics seemed to show that continental legislation made no practical difference since the early nineteenth century saw ever more children in England and Wales brought into the educational net. In 1803 the ratio of day-school pupils to the total population was 1 in 17.5. This rose to 1 in 11.25 in 1833 and 1 in 8.36 in 1851. By 1858 the ratio was 1 in 7.7 — not as impressive as the 1 in 6.27 in Prussia, but better than 1 in 8.11 in Holland and 1 in 9 in France.[28]

Continental education was usually spared one of the most divisive features of provision in England — religious sectarianism. Divisions between Anglicans and dissenters dominated the development of early nineteenth century schooling. The latter resented any rights or privileges enjoyed by the established Church and insisted on conscience clauses in all regulations concerning the teaching of religion. Many Anglican clergy held steadfastly to their creed in the National schools which in the smaller towns and rural areas were the only schools available. When tax-payers' money was distributed to support the work of the National and British societies after 1833, religious teaching was elevated to a still higher plane of controversy — particularly since the National Society secured over 70 per cent of government grants. Were dissenters now to subsidise the Church of England so that their children could be taught its doctrine in the National schools? Anti-Church and anti-state sentiment became, at times, bound up together; by the 1840s the only acceptable solution for the more passionate non-conformists was voluntaryism whereby every religious community provided from its own charity for its own children. Jews and Catholics, wherever possible, built their own schools too. The common enemy of all was secular education — something proposed only by a handful of broadminded pragmatists and political radicals. Voluntaryists took their stand on the principle of religious freedom. 'Freedom of education is but one portion of national freedom as a whole,' they bellowed, 'and it is at once intimately connected with all the rest, and absolutely essential to their preservation.'[29] Churchmen, educational reformers and politicians debated the place of religion in education and the role of the state with undiminished fury throughout the nineteenth century. Meantime, as one of Newcastle's assistant commissioners reported wearily in 1861, 'the generality of parents seem to be utterly indifferent to the sectarian character of the school, their only anxiety being to ascertain the value of the secular instruction.'[30]

The encroachment of the state upon the provision of popular education was to prove relentless. In 1833 the Whig administration allocated £20,000 to help with the building of schools. The sum rose to £30,000 per annum in 1839, £40,000 in 1841 and £75,000 in 1845. Thereafter government spending on schools and on the provision and training of teachers increased exponentially. The government grant for education stood at £125,000 by1848, £260,000 by 1853 and over £800,000 by 1859. Spending public money required a monitoring process. In 1839 a Committee of the Privy Council on Education, chaired by the Lord President and to include the Chancellor of the Exchequer and Home Secretary, was set up to distribute the grant. On 26 August 1839 Dr J. P. Kay (later Sir James Kay-Shuttleworth) was appointed to be its full-time Secretary.[31] Value for money had to be guaranteed. A government inspectorate was thus created in 1839 so that schools in receipt of tax-payers' money could be visited regularly and assessed for their effectiveness.

There were only two inspectors in 1840 and even their permanent status and salaries were not confirmed until 1841. By 1858, however, HMIs numbered 30 with an additional 16 assistant inspectors on the payroll. Three years later the corresponding totals were 36

HMIs and 24 assistants. By 1860 the original Committee of Council with its one official had grown into what was effectively a government department of education with a staff establishment of 127. Even some of those closely involved were disturbed by the process. Harry Chester, an assistant-Secretary in the Committee of Council office in the 1840s testified to the Newcastle Commission that 'the system of placing the education of the country under the control of a department of the political government appears to me to be vicious in the extreme.' 'It is a very great evil,' he warned, 'that the government should be the body to direct the education of the country.'[32]

Impressive as some of the statistics revealing the growing power of the state to direct the nation's education might appear, and virulent as its opponents undoubtedly were, government in fact remained remote from many of the daily realities of elementary schooling in mid-nineteenth century Britain. The Committee of Council in London sent out HMIs and collected their reports, corresponded over grant allocations to encourage local enterprise where appropriate, supervised a handful of teacher-training colleges and, of course, presented the copious papers to Parliament which have since become the enduring record of early-Victorian popular education.[33] But there were many other influences on educational thinking and practice. Ideas about children were changing, both in Britain and on the continent where Swiss and German experimentalists caught the eye of those who espoused progressive opinions about the individuality of the child and its need for kindness and sympathetic understanding. By the early nineteenth century there was indeed a growing literature on educational principles and techniques, much of it written by men with practical experience. John Evans' *Essay on the Education of Youth* was published in 1799. William Johnstone's *Result of Experience in the Practice of Instruction* appeared in 1818 with the author claiming that he had read 'much of what has been written on education.' Moses Miall published his *Practical Remarks on Education* in 1822 which attempted to collate useful tips for would-be educators. These works all advocated a liberal education for the young; early specialisation was to be avoided and cramming or rote learning was not conducive to the proper development of intellect. Children should understand the things they knew. Explanation and illustration should therefore play an important part in teaching.[34]

Within the public schools, Thring at Uppingham was the most notable exponent of individualism. Thring believed that every boy had the potential to succeed at something; the function of a good school was to bring out the qualities in the average, or below, and not merely to revel in the achievements of the academically able.[35] Such values did reach down the social scale and found expression in the Minutes of the Committee of Council published in 1841. 'The tyranny of schools commences when any unreasonable effort is required,' it was decreed.[36] Learning should be enjoyable and not regarded by children as an incomprehensible imposition to be endured. To the majority of masters in mid-nineteenth century Britain these suggestions seemed impractical. Boys in particular needed discipline and the surest means of securing that lay with the rod or cane. Even those who boasted that they could run schools without corporal punishment did not always live up to their own ideals.

Renowned as several famous nineteenth century heads were for the thrashing of boys, and brutal as many private and elementary masters proved to be, discipline nonetheless had become a contentious issue by the 1830s. Thring claimed: 'I have never struck a boy and I will never permit a boy to be struck.'[37] Few of his contemporaries at the public schools shared these sentiments. In the private school sector in London, however, there appeared to be a larger market niche for liberal values. University College school considered its dispensing with corporal punishment sufficiently attractive to many parents as to publish the fact in its original 1830 prospectus. It was not uncommon for private academies in the suburbs to advertise that pupils were treated with kindness and, as one claimed in *The Times* in 1835, discipline was maintained 'without recourse to corporal punishment.'[38] King's College school likewise renounced the rod. Government inspectors generally took the line that a good elementary teacher could control his class without it, but reserved its use for some of 'the wretched, uncultivated and almost brute-like occupants of some of our boys' schools' when all else had failed.[39] Most HMIs agreed that 'that school is ill-managed in which the moving principle is terror of the rod.'[40] One declared bluntly that 'punishment is in itself an evil' and later waxed poetically that 'love melts almost all hearts, effecting that which no harshness can ever accomplish.'[41] For many hard-pressed masters in the urban slums the operative word was 'almost'.

Greater recognition of the individuality of the child and of the role which schooling had to play in the development of character was reinforced by the work of educational innovators across Europe whose ideas had become common currency in debate in Britain by the mid-nineteenth century and whose schools were visited by enthusiastic reformers. In Switzerland, Friedrich Froebel was creating schools where children felt respected and appreciated as part of their communities. Lessons were devised and taught which matched the children's level of understanding. Philipp von Fellenberg ran an industrial school at Hofwyl, near Berne, designed to spread a practical education among the lower classes. His use of gardens, farms and workshops was much admired. In addition, the curriculum included music, drawing and a knowledge of the natural world acquired by walking tours. His principles became well-known in England via his disciple, Lady Noel Byron, who founded a school based upon them at Ealing Grove in 1833. His assistant at Hofwyl, Jacob Vehrli, also set up his own school at Constance and rapidly gained a reputation for training peasant teachers to propagate a basic but useful education among their own class of society. For Vehrli and von Fellenberg, a school was essentially a family bound together by natural affection and mutual respect. Problems with discipline and the need for punishment featured little in their writings.

Two names stood out among Swiss innovators as the best known in Britain. One was Mulhauser in Geneva who published a comprehensive manual on teaching writing skills and whose success in spreading literacy was widely acclaimed in Switzerland by 1831. In 1841 the Committee of Council took the step of 'placing the method of M. Mulhauser in the hands of schoolmasters as an example of a constructive method of teaching to write.' Formerly, the Committee of Council admitted, 'young children were required to perform the complex before they were able to accomplish the simple.'[42] Mulhauser, in essence, broke down letters into their component shapes so that a child could see how words were composed rather than merely copy them uncomprehendingly. At the Ealing Grove school this method was in use by 1842 where it was found by one of HMIs 'to economise time and improve the handwriting.'[43] The second name was Johann Pestalozzi, revered by some Englishmen as the father of progressive education in the late eighteenth and early nineteenth centuries. Pestalozzi's inspiring humanity placed the close relationship between teacher and pupil at the heart of the educational process. Fear was the enemy of learning: it destroyed all interest and confidence in a child. Trust and mutual affection, as if between a child and a parent, was the natural bond which every master should aim to establish. Through the example of the teacher the child would develop a moral code and come to know the difference between right and wrong.

Like Mulhauser, Pestalozzi believed that children had to be taught to think and should understand what they were learning.

While Mulhauser's chief contribution lay in teaching them to write, Pestalozzi had focussed on the processes of mental arithmetic which enabled the calculation of fractions through the use of numerical tables. This sharpened the mind and facilitated abstract thinking. 'The authority of Pestalozzi's teaching is acknowledged in Holland, Switzerland and some parts of Germany,' the Committee of Council noted in 1841.[44] Pestalozzi had demonstrated what could be done with simple peasant children when severity was removed from the classroom and when schooling became part of youthful curiosity. By the time of Pestalozzi's death in 1827 his name was a byword for enlightened thinking and sustainable achievement in European education.

One strand ran throughout the fashionable canon of school reform in the early nineteenth century — the importance of the personal tie between professional teacher and impressionable pupil. The ethos of the past had been that a master's duties ceased when the lesson ended; moral and social attitudes among the young were not a scholar's responsibility. The growing middle class in Britain expected more from those to whom their children were entrusted and to whom they paid their fees. The poor had lesser expectations but it was clear that elementary schools in many areas must, perforce, perform a social function. Touring the government-assisted schools of the Durham coalfield in 1846, HMI witnessed the ignorance, depravity and drunkenness prevalent in so many of the homes from which the pupils came. 'It seems plain that, until a rightly-educated generation of parents has been raised up,' he concluded, 'the poor child's best home is its school.'[45] A colleague confirmed this in the same year: 'the whole time allowed out of the life of a poor child for its school days is all too short, and it is daily decreasing. Nothing can be expected to be done, unless the most powerful of the resources which the schoolmaster has at his command be brought to bear upon every moment of it.' A child should not be 'tossed about', moving from one teacher to another as it passed through a school, the inspector continued.[46] Only by knowing pupils from the moment they entered until they left could a teacher correct faulty developments of character as they became apparent. This was an impressive vision of schooling in which every teacher was a well-trained enthusiast and every child receptive to the exemplary moral and social behaviour constantly displayed. Reality, of course, was often far removed. Reporting on the Northumberland and Durham region in 1840, HMI lamented that 'I never found in my conversation with the masters that they felt it to be their duty to endeavour to form the characters of the children, or to lead them to think, or even to convey to them instruction apart from the routine.'[47] There was much work to do if the principles of the new educational philosophy were to be realised in the common classroom.

One important barrier to change was the constraint of resources, both human and material. Reformers attached importance to supervision beyond the schoolroom but this was hard to practice if there was nowhere available. Lancaster had urged the construction of a playground since it 'attaches the children to the school', even though the monitorial system which both he and Bell had been so successful in introducing into elementary education in no way required an intimacy between teacher and pupil.[48] After 1840 it was the policy of the Committee of Council to vet plans for school construction with an eye to land being available for recreational facilities. The master of a school in a run-down area of Bethnal Green remarked in 1842 that the playground, under his direction, provided frequent opportunities for moral training. It was there that he discovered 'the evils which I have to remove.' But for the playground most of the children would be 'exposed to the contagion of the public streets,' he concluded. 'The playground, therefore, is one of the most useful parts of the institution.'[49] In the cities space was frequently a problem — especially so in London, as the Newcastle Commission was informed in 1861. Nevertheless a playground was the 'uncovered schoolroom', an assistant commissioner reported, 'for there the formation of character goes on even more decisively than in the schoolroom strictly so called.'[50]

Supervision by the teacher was also to extend to simple domestic tasks. At an institution in Islington in 1847 HMI was impressed with the washing room where masters oversaw the boys' daily ablutions. Attendance at the spacious communal bath encouraged a special bond between teacher and pupil, he affirmed: 'the habit of frequent immersion in cold water being of the highest importance in a sanitary, and even in a moral, point of view.'[51] But there was much more to the role of the master as spiritual and intellectual mentor than playgrounds and cold baths. The role called into question the size of classes and even the design of the school itself. The large open schoolroom was no longer adequate. A close relationship between the teacher and the members of his class required a separate room — 'a silent room', one inspector insisted in 1846, 'a room in which no other voice is to be heard than his own, or that of the child whom he is at any moment examining.'[52] What, then, was the proper size of class so that this relationship might develop? In the early nineteenth century, even in schools for the wealthy where classroom teaching by a proper master existed, sizes of 70 or more were not uncommon; best practice on the Continent tended to set 80 pupils as an upper limit. Reformers proclaimed that this was too many. Another HMI wrote in 1846 that 'no teacher, whatever his excellence may be, can *truly educate* above 50 children — can instruct them in school and watch over them during the hours of recreation — can inform their minds and influence their hearts.'[53]

The shortage of human resources was succinctly explained to Kay-Shuttleworth at the Committee of Council in July 1842. Standards were slowly rising in schools for the masses: books were more plentiful, useful subjects were taught beyond the basic skills in communication and even drawing and singing might be found in some government-assisted elementary schools. But there were now insufficient teachers since monitors were useless other than for the most basic tasks. Of 66 schools recently visited in and around London, only 3 had teacher-pupil ratios of less than one in 100. This was simply not compatible with the duties of teachers such as the Committee of Council itself endorsed.

The educational literature of the early nineteenth century also included tracts on the theory of teaching. Again there was a flow of ideas from Europe; German writers especially debated didactics and focussed on methods of teaching and the internal arrangements of schools. Among theorists the Socratic method, whereby questions for examining children were arranged in logical sequence, was much in vogue — but should it be pursued synthetically or analytically? Such abstractions figured far less in debate in Britain. 'On the question of the best mode of organising schools, the Committee of Council have wisely occupied a neutral ground,' one of HMIs pronounced with relief in July 1842.[54] There was in fact no need for educational thinkers in England to steep themselves in tortuous introspection. For many of them, David Stow in Glasgow and John Wood in Edinburgh had already shown the road ahead.

Stow was a merchant and Sunday school teacher who opened a normal seminary for the training of elementary teachers in 1824. He extended it in 1832 and by 1838 operated an establishment with up to 18 classrooms in which his budding masters laboured with waifs from the city streets. Wood was a lawyer who founded a sessional school in the 1820s which operated along lines similar to many of Pestalozzi's ideas about stimulating the individual intelligence and understanding of children. Wood too trained teachers. Stow was perhaps the more imaginative: he saw the teacher as moral and social trainer, gave as much importance to work in the playground as in the classroom, and preferred oral instruction directly from the teacher to the use of books. He also developed the gallery method whereby the different groups in the school receiving simultaneous training from a master or assistant were brought together for communal lessons on subjects such as scripture or those requiring physical demonstration. As the fame of both men spread, their schools received a steady stream of visitors from across the border. Beyond supplying competent teachers, Stow offered a vision of effective elementary education based on precepts dear both to the liberal conscience and to pragmatic reformers.

Inevitably there were sceptics. New ideas were never uniformly welcomed and even those who pressed for improvement in education did not always agree on the means to be adopted. Thomas Arnold advised a friend in 1835 that 'experience seems to point out no one plan of education as decidedly the best.'[55] One of HMIs in 1846 cautioned the Committee of Council that 'we are yet in the infancy of our knowledge and experience in such matters, and that something a great deal better will soon be devised.' 'What we appear to want now, is the free action of thought upon education,' he reflected, 'and that public interest which is the result of such action — the collision of system with system, and method with method.'[56] Some of his colleagues were less restrained in their remarks. From the north of England one inspector poured scorn on the current fashion for ideology in education. 'We blame masters, and we blame monitors, and we punish children,' he wrote dismissively in 1845: 'we find fault with methods and systems, and rooms and situations; but we often leave untouched the tap-root of all the evil — the parent.'[57] Another colleague in East Anglia ridiculed the obsession with progressive modes of teaching. Throughout Essex and along the Suffolk coast in 1845 he found 'women who have not been regularly trained and have no systematic methods of teaching, contrive to make young children read, repeat the Catechism and easy hymns, in much less time, and more effectively, than is common in schools of much higher pretensions.' New methods were usually designed to bring a marginal benefit to older children, he concluded, but could have a disruptive effect on the progress of instruction, especially in larger schools. 'It should make us take care when we introduce new methods, that we keep up the rate of attainments of the younger children.'[58]

These arguments continued throughout the 1840s and beyond. By the late 1850s educational theorists were under attack for the impracticality of many suggestions made in the past and for the ease with which they pontificated regardless of experience and any sense of realistic expectations. A clergyman from Colchester advised the Newcastle Commission in 1859 that education was becoming too removed from the wishes of parents and the needs of their children. 'Simple methods in every way, and plans that are every way less expensive, more contentedness with what is *practically possible*, and less of the theoretic, the ostentatious and the ideal,' he continued, 'seem to be the great things that we now require.'[59] Others inveighed against 'mere theorists, who talk, but do nothing.'[60] In his evidence in January 1860, old Harry Chester expanded on his fears for the future of education now that the state had assumed so prominent a role. 'The army of educational functionaries, already great, will be raised to an extent which will prove too unwieldy to be efficient, and too influential over the education of the nation to be regarded as constitutional or safe.'[61] In truth, however, much of the damage of which Chester warned was already done. The pattern and structure of education in Britain had changed during his own career and particularly so during the 1840s.

* * *

With increasing public spending through the Committee of Council and with a network of HMIs checking on every school in receipt of state assistance, the 1840s saw the beginning of a national education system in Britain. By the 1840s, too, education had emerged as an issue of universal concern and was no longer the preserve of interested Churchmen and philanthropists. Arguments over whether it was useful or necessary to provide schooling for the lower orders of society were effectively finished. Elementary education was generally accepted as an essential corrective to misinformation and subversion and an indispensable agent of social control.[62] This did not apply only in the cities: village schools were being built in rural areas as landed families assumed a greater obligation.[63] 'A sense of the responsibilities attached to property is happily, year by year, gaining ground in the country,' an inspector optimistically noted in 1845.[64] Another concluded, in 1847, that 'public opinion now recognises that education is not a privilege to be graduated according to men's social condition, but the right of all.'[65]

Bound up with these changing attitudes in society was the question of what was actually meant by popular education. 'What formerly were looked upon as the *ends* to be secured by the institution of popular schools, are now beginning to be regarded as simply instruments for attaining a far higher and nobler object,'

HMI for the north of England recorded in 1848.[66] Basic reading and writing skills were no longer sufficient goals; instead, in the 1840s they came to be regarded as the starting point for proper schooling. Secularisation was also underway. Not only did political radicals campaign for less emphasis on religious teaching in government-supported schools and a greater concentration on what they judged to be useful knowledge, but by 1840 even the National and British societies, and many clergymen, had reached the conclusion that the Bible should not be employed as a reading primer and that scriptural study needed to be placed in a context sufficient to enable proper respect. Throughout the 1840s Manchester was the source of much reforming opinion which pressed for the development of a publicly funded national system of education in Britain, the curriculum of which would not be sectarian or Bible-based but reflect instead the new orthodoxy of political economy.[67] In the 1830s and 1840s a more secular education indeed became realistic due to new forms of inexpensive, non-denominational school literature, much of it produced under the auspices of the Commissioners of National Education in Ireland. Philanthropic experimentalists such as William Ellis in London and George Combe in Edinburgh founded and supported schools for the poor in which secular curricula were taught.

Working class unrest associated with the rise of Chartism after 1838 gave a greater urgency to debates about the extent of elementary education necessary and what the nature of that education should be. In 1841 the Poor Law commissioners reported on the training needs of pauper children in the nation's workhouses. Ragged schools also extended rudimentary educational provision. The Ragged School Union, formed in 1844, operated what were effectively refuges for destitute children, many of whom lived on the streets of the large cities and who could never provide even the few pennies per week necessary to attend the other religious and charitable schools. Legislation in 1844 increased the onus on many factory owners to provide some part-time schooling for the children they employed. An Act of 1840 assisted some of the old grammar schools to break from the stipulations attached to their endowments and to adopt curricula more in keeping with the needs of the local population. The role of the state in defining minimum standards of provision and practice came to be accepted after 1839. The Committee of Council office in the age of Kay-Shuttleworth was recognised as one of the most rigidly administered departments of government in London. It had to be so. As Matthew Arnold recalled in 1861, 'it has grown up under the broad daylight of publicity.'[68]

Active as the Committee of Council unquestionably was in the 1840s, the secret of much of its success was the cautious and pragmatic way in which it went about its business. Large and highly vocal sections of public opinion were still sceptical about government involvement in education. The Committee of Council's leading opponents among the religious communities played upon the general apprehension of a uniform and stereotyped system being devised. 'But when it has been seen that the 'Government plan' is to enforce no plan whatever, but simply to proffer aid, knowledge, information and incentives to all alike,' one of HMIs reflected in 1848, 'few indeed have been the cases under my own observation in which confidence and satisfaction have not been the result.'[69] In 1847 another inspector praised the achievements of Kay-Shuttleworth's office: 'No-one who has taken pains to observe what has been going on in our schools for the poor will, as I suppose, fail to recognise during the last seven years a happy progress in the right direction.' Schools had better buildings, better curricula and access to guidance both from the Minutes published by the Committee of Council and from the inspectors who operated under its authority. Above all, he concluded, no-one in the 1840s could fail to be struck by 'the rise which has taken place in the attainments, qualifications and character of our teachers.'[70]

In 1837 there were three establishments in England which trained teachers: in 1847 there were more than 20 and by 1850 around 30.[71] It was perhaps in the area of teaching standards and practice that the greatest advances in education were made in the 1840s. A profession was beginning to emerge from the unregulated ranks of those who judged themselves fit to instruct the young. Touring northern England in 1846, HMI was pleased to report that the training of both men and women for their duties was much improved on what he had found two years before. In 1844 only one in every 3.5 men and one in every 6 women teachers were adequately trained: now the ratios were nearly 50 per cent and over 25 per cent respectively. The inspector of the Chester Diocesan Training College in 1844 reported enthusiastically that 'the standard of elementary education is rising so rapidly and the number of efficient educators so fast increasing, that already those of inferior skill find great difficulty in obtaining employment.'[72] The status of the qualified teacher in society was modestly rising. An enduring contributor to this was the Committee of Council's Minutes of 1846 which effectively scrapped the old monitorial system in state-assisted schools and introduced a paid system of pupil-teachers with Queen's scholarships available for the more able and committed to attend a training college.

With the battle for basic literacy essentially won, education in the 1840s became more specific to a child's age and regimented by the stricter timetabling and examination requirements of the expanding curriculum. The gradual spread of more relaxed views on the need for discipline accompanied these changes. 'The reign of terror, if not altogether passed away, is at least on the wane in our schools,' HMI reported from Scotland in 1842.[73] In 1848 a colleague from the north of England remarked upon 'the general abandonment of corporal punishment and the application of order and moral suasion to accomplish what was once only attempted by severity.'[74] Books, equipment and better buildings were now creating the right environment for the proper training of the child. In East Anglia by 1845 the old enormous schoolrooms of the monitorial age were no longer being constructed. An inspector added that he no longer found new buildings ill-lit and ill-ventilated as had been the case with so many erected in the past.

In fact, the tide of educational change in the 1840s was not confined to schools for the masses. In the public schools, too, the ethos of the master as friend and mentor to his charges was replacing the former role as gowned and cassocked scholar insensitive to anything but the well-learnt classical lesson. As in many of the endowed grammar schools, the curricula of the public schools were expanding — albeit at a slower pace. Accommodation and domestic arrangements for boys at many of the great schools also began to improve after 1840. Written examining became more common in schools which catered for the middle classes; one attender at King's College school in London in the 1840s recalled years later how regular examinations had proved a strong stimulus for work and how all his contemporaries 'acquired a fatal facility for answering questions on paper.'[75] The list of schools founded for the growing middle class market tells its own story of educational innovation: Cheltenham in 1841, Mount St. Mary's and Eltham College in 1842, Marlborough and the Liverpool Collegiate in 1843, Rossall in 1844, Brighton College in 1845, Ratcliffe, Taunton and Radley in 1847, the Woodard schools of Lancing and Hurspierpoint in 1848 and 1849 respectively, and Bradfield College in 1850. Across the whole sector of education in Britain the census conducted in 1851 revealed that of the nation's 46,042 schools, 22,214 had been created since 1840.[76]

Giving evidence to the Newcastle Commission in 1859, the rector of Maiden-Newton in Dorset was in no doubt that, from his own parochial experience, the spread of education had changed the nature of society. 'Since a day-school was first instituted in 1842,' he reflected, 'education has done more to civilise the inhabitants and to prevent outward acts of impropriety or breach of law.'[77] From London a police constable reported that over 30 years of education had made the worst areas of the city safer. The cultural gap between the mass of children and their foul-mouthed and brutal parents was there for all to see. Thanks to elementary schooling 'the generation of savages was passing away.'[78] Writing in 1844 a rural dean confirmed from Cambridgeshire how most of the sick whom he visited were acquainted with the precepts of the faith and how he 'never met with such instances of ignorance as were common some years ago.'[79] In 1859 the prebendary of Lincoln recorded a moral improvement in society due to educational advance. 'There is certainly less vulgarity and coarseness, less rudeness and violence at our feasts and statutes, our fairs and markets,' he noted. 'There is more good taste in dress and general behaviour.'[80] Other witnesses complained that much still needed to be done for the training of teachers and for the intellectual level of the education which was offered. But as one such critic was obliged to concede, there remained 'the incontestable fact that advances which a few years back we should have regarded as impossible have now been made.'[81] The 1851 census showed that most children in England and Wales were receiving some measure of day-schooling. Indeed, so great was the transition underway that one of HMIs in 1846 expressed his fear that public interest in popular education might soon wane under the impression that sufficient had already been done to fit the bulk of children for the humble tasks which lay before them.

2 • THE GREENWICH SCHOOLS IN 1840

The armed services were not obvious participants in the national debate on education in the nineteenth century and seemed perhaps unlikely to provide the setting for an important experiment in reform in the 1840s. That they did so was due largely to the fact that the Royal Navy had long maintained charitable schools at Greenwich which were administered by the famous naval hospital. More widely, the navy, like other branches of state service, the civil professions and the world of commerce had a natural concern for standards of recruitment — particularly for its officer class. But even common seamen and dockyard workers needed training and elementary knowledge, and if such was not available in the coastal towns then the Admiralty was reconciled to making its own provision. Portsmouth, Chatham, Plymouth, Pembroke, Woolwich, Deptford, and Sheerness all had schools for their dockyard apprentices by the 1840s. 'The object is not to confer the best possible education on a portion of the lads who might become naval architects,' one senior officer observed, 'but to give to the apprentices of all trades in the dockyards such a degree of education as shall fit them to become useful and well-principled men as working artificers.'[1] More randomly, assistance in school construction was given where opportunities arose. In 1844 the vicar of Greenwich received a donation from the hospital towards the cost of a local school and a vicar in Northumberland received a gift of land owned by the hospital on which to provide elementary education for the children of his parish.

The naval schools at Greenwich had distinct histories and characters.[2] The Upper school traced its origins to 1715 when a school had been established for the sons of commissioned and wardroom officers. The Lower school was an amalgam of two bodies: the Royal Naval Asylum, founded in 1798, which moved to Greenwich in 1805, and the school of the hospital at Greenwich with which it was united in 1821. Under the terms of an endowment of £40,000 from the Lloyds Patriotic Fund in 1806 the Asylum had agreed to accept pupils as nominated by the fund committee. That commitment was transferred to the Lower school in 1821. The Lower school recruited from farther down the social scale than the Upper school and took the children and orphans of distressed families of petty officers, able seamen or sailors from the merchant navy where the father's naval record, either in terms of length or suffering incurred through active service, merited such a reward. Since 1801 the army had also run a school, the Royal Military Asylum at Chelsea, on similar principles for the education of boys between the ages of five and ten.

In 1821 the Lower school contained 600 boys and 200 girls. The Upper school was smaller with only 200 boys. Seven years later the Admiralty changed this balance when it removed 200 places for boys from the Lower school and redistributed them to the Upper school. This naturally increased the powers of patronage enjoyed by those senior naval officers who had the right to present boys for entry to the Upper school, where no service record by the father was required, while making entry to the Lower school much more competitive. The Upper school took boys at 11 and taught them till the age of 15. There was a basic test for entry in which minimal attainments in reading, spelling and arithmetic were stipulated. The Lower school, by its regulations, took pupils as young as nine though as its waiting list increased by virtue of diminished places its age of entry rose accordingly. By the early 1840s the Lower school had as many as 800 boys on its waiting list all of whom were eligible under formal requirements. There was no educational test for admission. The Admiralty gave preference to orphans from the homes of impoverished service widows: 300 such cases were begging entry in 1842. It also restricted admission to only one child per family. Wherever possible, enquiring parents were advised to seek the patronage which might gain entry to the Upper school. The hospital authorities made no secret of the fact that 'the education there is superior.'[3]

Free elementary education for the offspring of seamen was a means of promoting loyalty to the service among the lower ranks. But the navy, and hence the tax-payer, received a return on its charity. The schools trained boys for naval careers; a strong sense of discipline was instilled in their young minds by drilling and by the routine of service life, and, for the more able, the practical skills of navigation were conveyed by an academic diet weighted heavily towards mathematics. For boys entering the seafarers' profession, bedding and clothing provisions were issued on discharge from the schools. Boys were encouraged, indeed expected, to prepare themselves for life at sea. Girls who left the Lower school in the 1820s and 1830s were seldom proficient even at domestic toil. Most could read and write tolerably and had learnt to sew by the age of 14, though the skills required for cutting out clothing and knitting were usually absent. They cleaned and folded laundry in their school houses for much of the time: the more intelligent and presentable among them might look forward to a position in domestic service.

The schools claimed status as a great educational institution partly because their catchment area was nationwide. All children boarded, even the 10 per cent or so whose families lived in Greenwich. Most came from the great seaports and made the journey to Greenwich by coach or wagon for the start of the new school year every September. Once arrived, there would be no return home until the 6 weeks of vacation in the following summer. The Governor of the hospital, however, had licence to allow 14 days of leave at Christmas which was normally done for the children who lived locally. Visitors were allowed on the first Wednesday of every month, and every Wednesday and Saturday were half-day holidays when recreation on Blackheath was usually permitted. Dormitories for up to 200 occupants accommodated the children at night where they slept in the presence of two of the resident drill-serjeants. It was the task of these men, invariably retired military personnel and under the orders of a Lieutenant Superintendent, to check and supervise the daily routine of hygiene, gymnastic exercises, parade drill and out of class recreation. Before 1841, only in school itself did the children come under the direction of academic teachers. Each school had its own headmaster with 3 or 4 undermasters and assistants.

By the standards of the day Greenwich was a large institution: its pupil numbers exceeded those of the residential public schools. The largest of them, Eton, housed an average of about 600 boys in the early nineteenth century. The schools of Christ's Hospital educated about 1,200 children in the 1850s. King's College school taught about 500 boys in the 1840s; the school at University College took about 340. The Royal Military Asylum accommodated just under 500 boys in the mid-nineteenth century. The most successful proprietary school, Cheltenham College, housed 303 boys in 1845, while those in Leicester and York had about 100 in the 1840s and that in Wakefield taught about 150. Leeds grammar school educated 211 boys in 1845 while that at Uppingham educated only 63 in 1850. Elementary schools, particularly in rural areas, were usually smaller. Battersea village school stood out as large with 260 children in 1845 and the normal school at Borough Road admittedly took almost 400 pupils. Most schools for the poor, however, had less than 100 members.

Similarities existed with some other charitable schools. There were five hospital schools in Westminster which together educated 230 children from endowment incomes totalling about £7000 per annum in the mid-nineteenth century and with comparable admissions procedures based on patronage and sponsorship. The Drapers' Company also operated the Green Coat school for about 100 sons of needy watermen, fishermen, soldiers and sailors in east Greenwich. In addition to its similar size, Christ's Hospital provided a further comparison: it also taught a mathematically based syllabus to prepare some of its boys for apprenticeships at sea. In fact, mathematical and navigational teaching was not uncommon in schools in the major ports or in London. The grammar schools in Dartmouth and Rochester, for example, prepared boys for maritime careers as did many smaller private schools in coastal towns where masters had themselves often been at sea as navigators or as instructors aboard ships. The Upper school at the Greenwich hospital certainly saw itself as a prestigious supplier of sound mathematical and nautical education and aspired to produce young gentlemen, fit by their academic training and their respect for discipline, to serve and in time to command in the name of their sovereign in the world's foremost fighting force.

For the Lower school, comparisons were rather less flattering. The nature of its intake made the Lower school appear more akin to the large pauper union schools to which some of the London boroughs sent their destitute children and which were run by contractors in large suburban premises. When the Poor Law commissioners reported on the training appropriate for such institutions in 1841 they touched on many of the issues concerning discipline and teaching methods which were also coming under review at Greenwich. The Board of Guardians of the West London Union established a school at Edmonton where much attention was given to industrial occupations. The Stepney Union ran a similar school at Limehouse. The best-known and largest of these pauper union schools was at Norwood where around 1000 children from east London were accommodated for the purpose of useful instruction and elementary education. Norwood was managed by Frederick Aubin, not himself a teacher, and regularly inspected by the Committee of Council which looked upon the establishment as highly suitable for educational experimentation. Norwood was an obligatory port of call for all educational reformers in the 1830s and 1840s. Before he was offered the position with the Committee

of Council, Kay-Shuttleworth had worked with the local Poor
Law commissioners at Norwood in 1838 and he continued to visit
the school in 1839. François Guizot, when French ambassador in
London, much admired Aubin's efficient discipline of so many
children — most especially Aubin's interest in seafaring skills
and the way in which he trained the boys in sailors' exercises.
For Kay-Shuttleworth, whose ultimate ambition was to bring all
the schools of government departments, prisons and the Poor
Law commissioners under the Committee of Council's supervision,
a likeness with the Lower school at Greenwich was easily drawn.

Whether the tax-payer received value for money from the
Greenwich schools was difficult to judge. The cost of maintaining
them amounted to about £8000 per annum in the early 1840s, to
which the bill for teachers' salaries contributed little more than
10 per cent. In the context of state expenditure on education this
was a sizeable sum and the Committee of Council was always
ready to remind the Admiralty of the generous treatment of its
schools at a time when provision from the public purse was
meagre and, in any case, did no more than match local private
subscription. The navy argued that international maritime
supremacy did not come cheap and that a nation which basked
in the glories of its naval tradition and commercial dominance
would do well to think about where future generations of suitably
trained and educated junior officers and navigators in all areas
of seafaring were to come from.

In the early nineteenth century the Admiralty certainly had the
better of the argument. In November 1842 the hospital bursar
wrote confidently that 'many of our boys bound to the merchant
service are now commanding ships — with great respectability.'[4]
But by this time the schools were beginning to experience some
difficulty placing their pupils. In the two year period after
1 April 1840 495 boys left the schools; 91 entered the Royal Navy
while a further 154 joined the merchant service. The schools kept
only first destination returns: other boys undoubtedly went to
sea after a brief employment at home. But the figures, however
interpreted, were not impressive and worsening career prospects
seemed undeniable. The bursar addressed the issue in March
1843: 'the applications for berths have so multiplied of late years
that premiums are now very generally offered and expected in
the merchant service,' he judged, 'while for the navy, the Admiralty
have long since declined taking any of our boys except such as
at the annual examination in June might be selected for very
superior attainments.' It was worse perhaps for the boys of the
Upper school for whom expectations of a respectable placing were

greatest. 'For the sons of seamen, who are brought up in the Lower school,' he reflected, 'we have less difficulty, as they are often provided for in the coal, coasting and steam navigation home trades, but those are situations which I could not advise for the son of an officer.'[5]

Schools the size of those at Greenwich inevitably had problems with control, regardless of their social standing. Aside from breakdowns of institutional authority, individual misbehaviour could and often did embarrass schools and create tensions with the local population. In 1831 two boys at Greenwich 'brought disgrace upon the whole school' when discovered to have sent a letter of an 'obscene and disgusting character' to a clergyman's daughter.[6] Both boys were severely flogged before being expelled. The rules about letters leaving the schools were then altered so that the author's name appeared on the envelope and letters were submitted to one of the masters. In 1841 one boy was expelled for stabbing another in the arm. A year later another boy was expelled, as his mother was informed, 'for having been repeatedly guilty of misconduct, and recently stabbed two boys.'[7] In the twelve months after April 1841 six boys were either discharged early or expelled from the Upper, and 11 from the Lower school. Before 1841 the schools were regulated by a strict regime of corporal punishment inflicted by the headmasters in the classrooms and by the Lieutenant Superintendent out of school. The birch was applied either over the breech or to the palm of the hand.

The offences for which such punishment was applied reveal in themselves much about daily life in the schools. The most common crime was climbing over the wall and absconding. Other misdemeanours in 1843 were a mixture of insubordination towards authority and boisterousness towards fellow pupils. Being drunk, impudence to drill-serjeants, insulting and hurling objects at a sail maker, climbing through the window into the head's classroom, throwing coal over the wall, stealing meat from the butcher's cart during a delivery to the kitchen, refusing to wash and wilfully cutting a table cloth at dinner obviously merited a beating. Tipping other boys out of their hammocks, pouring water into and applying excrement to hammocks and throwing caps down a privy were also glaring cases for remedial action. In broad terms, though, the schools at Greenwich coped reasonably with the 1000 pupils in their care. Under instructions issued by the Admiralty in 1821 and 1829 the respective duties of schoolmasters and naval personnel were clearly defined and the management of the schools vested in a civil board on which the Governor of the hospital sat. After

1830 overall responsibility for the different aspects of the schools' activities was transferred to the Governor whose job it now became to maintain a balance between the needs of a school and the functions of an institution regarded by its naval staff as essentially a training for life in the service.

Given that nearly all recorded offenders in the schools were boys it was harsh perhaps to close the girls' school for disciplinary reasons in 1841. Nonetheless, there had always been a view that it was not the navy's job to provide for the daughters of sailors nor indeed that there was any advantage from so doing. As problems of control were felt to worsen in the late 1830s one cause was judged to be the presence of so many girls in the Lower school and the particular difficulty of preventing improper contacts with the boys. No amount of vigilance, the superintending officer reported in November 1839, could prevent illicit messages from passing to and fro. Covering up for secret correspondence or unauthorised meetings bred a spirit of lying and hypocrisy in the institution and distracted boys from their work. Moreover, given the long list of boys awaiting entry, converting the 200 places for girls into extra capacity for boys made excellent administrative sense.

The Governor of the hospital added to these pressures with a damning judgment in August 1840. Describing the condition of the girls' school as deplorable, and with attainments by the age of 14 as minimal, he urged the Admiralty that the girls would in fact be better off without the navy's charity. 'Incapable of relieving or assisting their parents, and not amenable to parish relief,' he observed, 'they too frequently become abandoned and finish at an early age a life of misery, which might have been avoided had they been left under the eye of their parents or natural guardians.'[8] The chaplain, masters and naval authorities all agreed. The final blow for the girls' school was delivered in September 1840 when an outside inspection of the Greenwich schools condemned it as an impediment to proper discipline. The head nurse and her two assistants were ineffective in their supervision duties; in any event, the girls were sent home in groups along with the boys and mixed freely in their home towns during vacations. In these circumstances, forbidding meetings on school premises would always fall foul of carefully laid plans. In 1841 the girls were discharged and the Upper and Lower schools reordered such that each now contained about 400 boys.

* * *

The Governor in 1840 was Admiral Charles Fleming. His succinct letter to the Admiralty, dated 7 August 1840, effectively opened a new chapter in the history of the Greenwich schools by exposing officially the utter inadequacy of their provision. Fleming was interested in education and informed his colleagues on the Board of Admiralty that since the schools had been remodelled in 1821 many important changes in the world of education had taken place. The training of children had become a matter of far greater study and concern to society, he continued in authoritative tone; his own investigations had now convinced him that comparable schools offered superior benefits. It was sad to record, Fleming added, but it could very easily be shown that the schools were 'very far in arrear of the majority of such institutions.'[9] More than half the boys in the Lower school could not even read and, when discharged at the age of 14, few were fit to enter service at sea, to undertake an apprenticeship or even to earn a livelihood by any means. Since the Lower school had only two teachers for its 400 boys, Fleming rebuked the Admiralty by saying that it should not be surprised to receive this depressing intelligence. Wherever blame lay, however, the fact was, he concluded, that a great charitable body supported by public funds was producing children fit only for poor relief and hence to become a burden to society.

Faced with such unqualified criticism from so senior an officer the Admiralty felt that it had no option but to turn to the newly-formed Committee of Council for advice. On 10 August Kay-Shuttleworth was requested to supply one of HMIs for a visit to Greenwich and a frank examination of the schools. Kay-Shuttleworth, at this stage, had only two inspectors: the Rev. John Allen, formerly on the academic staff at King's College, London and Seymour Tremenheere, a barrister by profession who had established himself as an authority on educational needs for the working classes. Tremenheere was chosen and duly seconded for Admiralty service. Kay-Shuttleworth was keen to establish an interest for his own department: Tremenheere was to report to the Admiralty but via the Committee of Council, which would keep a copy for reference.

Ambitious as Kay-Shuttleworth unquestionably was for the expansion of the Committee of Council's authority he was also realistic about the obstacles to his progress. In October 1839 he acknowledged that the Committee of Council had not been endowed with any direct powers to regulate the internal organisation of schools but merely with licence to distribute public money largely for the erection of buildings. By his reckoning, charitable subscription had already failed as a means of establishing a national system of elementary education in Britain and the task could only be completed by government agency. No real advance would be made, however, until parishes and towns were enabled to raise local taxes for the purpose. Kay-Shuttleworth was a tireless proponent of popular education and an obsessive administrator within his own department. Upon his success in raising the level of knowledge among the masses, he believed, depended the future tranquillity of British society and an avoidance of the scourges of socialism and revolution. More positively, he professed, 'a well instructed, industrious and religious working class is one of the most fruitful sources of prosperity in peace and security in war.'[10]

Kay-Shuttleworth took up his post in Whitehall at the age of 35 having spent some years as a doctor in Manchester and, since 1835, as a Poor Law commissioner in East Anglia. His views were certainly conditioned by his work with the poor. He also visited Glasgow, where he met Stow, and he returned to Edinburgh, where he had been a medical student, and where he now met Wood at the sessional school. Both men and their schools made a great impression and he corresponded with Stow thereafter. In 1839 he made a six-week tour of France, Holland, Belgium, Prussia, Saxony and Switzerland where again he was excited by progressive curricula and teaching practices in the style of Pestalozzi, Vehrli and von Fellenberg and was much struck by the concern shown by continental innovators for the individual development of children. Back home, he had already demonstrated his enthusiasm for such ideas by helping to reorder teaching at Norwood 'according to the Dutch and Prussian method.'[11] In 1840 he gave practical expression to his belief in the need for better qualified teachers by funding, from private subscriptions and with a good deal of his own money, the Battersea training college which he ran, with friends, until it was transferred to the National Society in 1843.

Kay-Shuttleworth had opinions on almost every aspect of school management. He instructed HMIs to encourage playground construction, he believed that classes of roughly 40 pupils should be in separate rooms and under different masters when a school exceeded 150 children and he considered that corporal punishment was unnecessary in a properly regulated institution. When in 1842 the King of Prussia told him that nothing but Greek, Latin and mathematics should be taught in schools, Kay-Shuttleworth boldly retorted that such an education was 'monastic and unfitted to prepare a modern gentleman to take his place in society.'[12] He acknowledged that religion should have a central place in a child's development but asserted equally that secular instruction should be wide-ranging and that a proper curriculum for elementary schools must include impartial political awareness, the tenets of political economy and rudimentary scientific and technical knowledge. Education must be an elevating experience which would serve in time to lessen the tensions and divisions in society. In this, the teacher was all important. It was he who bound any school together as a family with shared identity; it was he who fostered trust and moral values among the young, especially in residential institutions where the exposure of child to mentor was at its greatest. Kay-Shuttleworth was therefore convinced that residential schools provided the most effective environment for all-round education. Stow, no less, was a great admirer. 'I have to thank you for your long attention to our interests,' he wrote from Glasgow in 1843, 'and to congratulate you on the success of your endeavours to promote the great cause of true education or a training of "the whole man".'[13] Fired by his own reforming vision, Kay-Shuttleworth eagerly awaited Tremenheere's account of what was wrong with the schools at Greenwich.

After a month's examination Tremenheere described his findings in a long report dated 9 September 1840 in which he elaborated on the levels of competence in reading and knowledge evident in all classes. He found the schools arranged in a manner typical of the early nineteenth century. The Lower school met in a room measuring about 100 feet by 30 feet into which were crowded eight classes, each with a monitor and assistant monitor. The headmaster and his one assistant master presided over the gathering. Desks were arranged so that the master and monitor could address each class in the manner prescribed by the Bell system. The four divisions of the Upper school, each with its own master, were assembled in a room of similar dimensions. Again the furniture was 'disposed in a manner resembling Dr Bell's plan.' Even in the Upper school the levels of religious knowledge, history and geography were woeful: indeed, Tremenheere observed, 'those boys who have no ability for a mathematical course leave the school with scarcely any acquirement at all.'[14]

The books employed as texts in the schools amply illustrated Tremenheere's criticism of a limited curriculum, though they were in line with the provision of reading materials in most schools offering an elementary education. The Bible was used alongside Trimmer's abridgements of the Old and New Testaments. Two small reading books issued by the National Society which listed the miracles and parables of the New Testament were also produced for Tremenheere's inspection. Some reading cards were used by the monitors and, as befitted naval schools, a *Life of Nelson* and Goldsmith's *History of England* were available. The Upper school used a book on English grammar and Guy's *Geography*; it also had some maps which were lacking in the Lower school. Equipment was basic throughout — a blackboard, slates and copy books. In the Upper school 80 per cent of all class time was devoted to arithmetic, geometry and the study of techniques of navigation. The text used for this was Edward Riddle's *Course of Geometry and Nautical Astronomy*. Riddle had been senior mathematician in the Upper school since 1821 and, briefly, headmaster until April 1841. There was a library for the Upper school which, Tremenheere noted, gave a reasonable supply of books for amusement and recreation. Depressingly, these were seldom requested and, even when issued, frequently destroyed.

Deficient as their education was, the schools did not appear unduly disorderly in 1840. Such confusion as he witnessed, Tremenheere ascribed to the very crowded state of both schoolrooms. The dormitories were likewise overflowing and inadequately furnished. Ventilation in all the buildings was bad and the means of heating in the dining hall and schoolrooms was demonstrably insufficient. 'The schools are so crowded as very materially to interfere with the process of instruction,' the inspector concluded; neither school could properly accommodate more than 250 boys. As for improvements, more staff would be needed. Two extra masters should be engaged in the Lower and one extra in the Upper school. Desks should be rearranged and accommodation reorganised so as to make way for 'an improved method of instruction.' Each school should receive two further drill-serjeants to supervise the boys in their daily routine, though Tremenheere also stipulated that the masters themselves should play a greater part in out of school activities. Behaviour in hall and in the dormitories would unquestionably be improved by the influence of a schoolmaster: if possible, one master should always be in attendance on the boys.

Tremenheere recommended that the curriculum of the Upper school should be extended to include an understanding of steam engines, the principles of book-keeping and other clerical work. The age of leaving both schools might be raised to 15, or even 16 at the Governor's discretion, so as to allow a boy's strength to develop sufficiently for work on board ships. Boys in the Lower school might also receive more by way of industrial training in the workshops. He did not favour corporal punishment save where the most severe chastisement was required. He referred the Board of Admiralty to the practice at the Royal Military Asylum in Chelsea where discipline was maintained perfectly well by the impositions of extra drill, fatigue duties, deprivation of recreation, rolling flat the school playground and solitary confinement.

Such liberal credentials on punishment were no bar to recommending a greater distinction between the Upper and Lower schools since their pupils came from such different strata in society. Tremenheere suggested that the Upper school should eat separately and with a higher quality of diet. Its boys might also be more distinctive in their dress by means of badges or buttons. All this would help raise the general tone of the schools and, once the girls had gone, to liken them to the nation's other large residential establishments. With regard to the manners, habits and respect for the institution which the boys displayed, Tremenheere was not impressed and believed that for the money expended, the public had a just expectation of a higher level of personal and social accomplishments, such as were instilled at the public schools. The potential existed to raise the Greenwich schools from being providers merely of charitable elementary education to being providers of training which might fit young men for a range of careers. The schools were a 'magnificent establishment' and the opportunities afforded were 'great and commanding.'[15] Tremenheere left little doubt that it was the Admiralty's duty to revive them by introducing a modern system of education.

Weeks passed without any response from the Admiralty. The next move in fact came from Kay-Shuttleworth who, on 1 December 1840, wrote to remind the navy of Tremenheere's services and to point out that the Committee of Council had studied the report carefully. He tactfully offered his department's assistance 'in removing from the schools the defects and abuses described.'[16] The matter was not a priority at the Admiralty where all the talk was of naval action in the Mediterranean and the current Eastern crisis. The First Lord of the Admiralty, the Earl of Minto, confided to a colleague on the Board of Admiralty, Admiral Sir Charles Adam, on 6 December that 'St. Jean D'Acre had certainly driven Greenwich schools out of my mind.' 'But I entirely approve of your suggestion,' Minto assured Adam. 'In case you should have forgotten it yourself, I may as well tell you.'[17] Wary of excessive interference from another branch of government, Adam had proposed an Admiralty committee which would be given the task of assessing the practicality of Tremenheere's recommendations and implementing any necessary reforms. Lord Duncannon, a former Whig Home Secretary and since 1835 First Commissioner of Woods, Forests and Land Revenue would be appointed Chairman of a Greenwich hospital schools committee. Duncannon had also been a member of the Committee of Council since its creation in 1839. Adam then suggested that Lord Dalmeny, a junior government minister attached to the Admiralty, and William Cowper, a junior Lord of the Treasury, should serve. These three would be joined by Sir James Gordon, the Lieutenant-Governor of the hospital. The brief of this new committee would be 'to place these schools on a proper footing, so as to remedy the evils complained of, and to secure those benefits and that efficiency which the public, and the parents and friends of the children, have a right to expect.'[18]

Preoccupied as he was, Minto was obliged to give the Greenwich schools more attention than simply approving the idea which Adam put before him. There was the serious matter of Kay-Shuttleworth's attempt to intrude into the navy's affairs to worry about: to limit the danger of this would require access to credible educational advice from elsewhere which was not readily at hand. Adam had considered that the headmasters of the schools might be asked for their response to Tremenheere's findings, but Minto was not at all keen. 'This would only open the door for a paper war with the Inspector whose report we have,' he replied, 'and besides the answer would be "the want of a sufficient number of masters".' Tremenheere had also touched upon that most sensitive of areas — religious instruction. Even a schools committee chosen by the Admiralty was bound to be alarmed by the shortcomings in moral and scriptural training which had been exposed.

In fact there was disagreement over religious education right from the start. The issue much excited Cowper who was critical of the chaplain, and head of the Upper school since 1834, the Rev. George Fisher, for his inattention to spiritual duties. Minto wrote of Cowper: 'he is I think very wild.' Cowper wanted to dismiss Fisher on the spot and replace him with a more devout clergyman. Minto was no religious zealot and thoroughly disapproved. 'I would have the best headmaster I could procure for the pay, be he layman or parson,' he insisted.[19] Perhaps Fisher had been too relaxed in the past, but it was wrong to make him a scapegoat for failings in the schools for which hospital governors and even Boards of Admiralty were equally to blame. To Minto's embarrassment, Fisher had not forgotten their conversation during the annual visit in 1839: 'Lord Minto expressed an opinion that too great a portion of time was devoted to religious instruction,' the chaplain recollected in December 1840.[20] On reading Tremenheere's report Minto was thus inclined to gloss over the teaching of religion and to focus instead on the suggestion that the schools were probably too large and that given the limits of public funding available the numbers of boys educated would need to be reduced. In general terms, however, the First Lord was encouraged by the suggestions for reform which Tremenheere had put forward and which the Greenwich schools committee would likely endorse. 'When the whole is put upon an efficient system and it is understood that it is something more than a charity lounge,' he reflected, 'I have no doubt people will do their work fairly.'[21]

Duncannon's committee met in January 1841. It interviewed the naval officers at Greenwich who were responsible for administering the schools and concluded at once that all Tremenheere's allegations were correct. Teaching practices were antiquated, the syllabus was too restricted, standards of attainment were abysmally low, and moral and religious training had been seriously neglected. As Minto had anticipated, this last observation provoked a stern rebuke. 'For whatever service these children are intended, their education should be grounded on religious instruction,' Duncannon insisted. 'All instruction must be based on religion. We must recommend an entire change in the system at present pursued at Greenwich, which appears to have sent forth the children into the world almost as ignorant on this subject as on their entrance into the school.' Duncannon saw no conflict between this and the scientific training required for naval life. The schools committee also upheld Tremenheere's views on punishment and his suggestion that boys be allowed to stay on until the age of 16. Most significant for the future organisation of the schools, they also applauded the notion that more masters be employed and that their duties be extended to the supervision of boys out of school. The Admiralty should 'make the masters of each school responsible for the education and discipline of those under them.'[22]

This much was at least acceptable to Minto and was consistent with the Admiralty's concern to restore the reputation of its schools. But there were two further recommendations about which the First Lord was a good deal less enthusiastic. First, Duncannon wanted half-yearly inspections of the schools by an HMI from the Committee of Council. Secondly, he urged Minto to expand the schools committee to include two new members — Kay-Shuttleworth and his good friend, the Rev. Robert Eden. Eden was vicar of Battersea and offered his village schools for teaching practice to the apprentice masters at Kay-Shuttleworth's training college. Together they would be an influential voice in the work of the Greenwich schools committee. Gordon might have stopped this suggestion at the committee but he had been ill and unable to attend the meeting at which Duncannon, Dalmeny and Cowper reached their decision. To have the chief executive of the Committee of Council as a member of the Admiralty's own schools committee and sending in his own inspectors every six months was a dreadful prospect in terms of the power of interference which would be afforded. For all that, Minto was an astute enough politician to recognise a setback when he saw one. The struggle to keep the schools under Admiralty direction would continue despite the blow sustained at the hands of its own committee. On 30 January 1841, and with good grace, Duncannon was thanked for his services and authorised to expand his committee as proposed.

3 • NEW IDEAS AND NEW HEADMASTERS, APRIL TO DECEMBER 1841

The most immediate task in reforming the schools was the appointment of new headmasters. When the girls' school closed its doors for the last time on 31 March 1841 the building which it had occupied became the location for a newly formed Nautical school to instruct up to 200 of the ablest boys. Hiving this off from the Upper school enabled Edward Riddle to be transferred as its first headmaster thereby creating an opening at the Upper school. Riddle had replaced Fisher as head of the Upper school just a few months earlier. The headship of the Lower school was already vacant. It was for the schools committee to recommend suitable candidates. Kay-Shuttleworth was quick to show his hand.

'In selecting a master for the Upper school the committee naturally turned to Scotland, where, during the last 25 years, methods of intellectual instruction have been much more cultivated in elementary and in secondary schools than in this country.' This was a sweeping condemnation of English education but, in making it, Kay-Shuttleworth was convinced that he spoke for the Greenwich schools committee as a whole. He sought a gentleman 'whose acquaintance with these improved methods was assured by long practical service in some school in which such methods were known to be successfully applied.'[1] His attention was drawn to William Graham who ran the mathematical and English departments of the Circus Place school in Edinburgh. Graham was a graduate from St. Andrews. After university he moved to Brechin as a candidate for holy orders where he broadened his study with literary and theological pursuits. Eminent clergymen in Edinburgh and professors at St. Andrews testified to his scholarship. He entered teaching and was for ten years at Circus Place a colleague of John Gibson who, in 1840, was appointed the first HMI for Scotland. Graham had never met Kay-Shuttleworth despite the latter's tours in Scotland; he was, however, highly recommended by Gibson. In March 1841 Graham was offered the post as head of the Upper school at a salary of £285 per annum, an allowance of £15 for coals and candles and lodgings on the premises at Greenwich.

Graham was a stern man with strong and progressive views on the education of children. 'He looks fierce,' a colleague later remarked, though added that 'when punishing he is always cool on principle' and was never observed losing his temper with miscreants.[2] He accepted the job, not for any increased salary nor because he was unhappy in Edinburgh: 'As is well known,' he wrote confidently, 'I occupied the highest status in my profession.' Greenwich did, of course, offer him a headship and, importantly for him, 'a favourable opportunity for promoting, on an extensive scale, an improved and effective system of education.'[3] His mission to take enlightenment to the backward English, Graham set out with his wife on the long journey south.

The appointment of Thomas Irvine to the headship of the Lower school on 12 March 1841 revealed even more the growing influence of Kay-Shuttleworth over the deliberations of the Greenwich schools committee. The two men had met when, soon after his appointment at the Committee of Council in 1839, Kay-Shuttleworth had visited Dublin with Eden and inspected elementary schools. Many such schools were run by the Society for Promoting the Education of the Poor of Ireland which was well known for its model school in Dublin at Kildare Place. Irvine had worked for the Society since 1831 and had been head of Kildare Place since 1834. He was held in high regard by the Anglican clergy and other prominent professional men in Dublin who supervised the school; indeed, many ascribed the reputation of the school itself to the zeal and intelligence which Irvine brought to bear. Kildare Place was especially known for its use of an arithmetic progress roll to chart each pupil's advance from one level of ability to the next. Kay-Shuttleworth and Eden were deeply impressed during their visit. Kay-Shuttleworth reflected that 'the Kildare Place school was better organised and conducted under Mr. Irvine's management than any school on the method of mutual instruction which I have ever visited in any part of Europe.' Irvine and Kay-Shuttleworth kept in touch and met occasionally when the former was in England. These meetings merely served to confirm Kay-Shuttleworth's belief that Irvine was 'a very skilful master of an elementary school.'[4]

On 11 February 1841 Kay-Shuttleworth wrote to Irvine to inform him that since their last communication he had been appointed a member of the Greenwich schools committee, that it was the Admiralty's intention to reorganise the institution and that the headship of the Lower school was vacant. The Lower school had been taught on the 'National system', Kay-Shuttleworth explained, 'which, however, it is our intention to replace by methods of a more intellectual, and a higher moral and religious character than the rote exercises which have hitherto characterised the National schools of this country.' 'When in Dublin,' he continued, 'I said I was disposed to offer you the first appointment in my power.' Now, Irvine was told, the job of a reforming head was his for a salary of £200 per annum and lodgings at Greenwich for him and his family. Irvine would have three masters under him and some pupil-teachers to assist them. The school would be arranged according to practices recommended by the Committee of Council such as Irvine would understand from his knowledge of Aubin's school at Norwood which, as everyone knew, operated under the Committee of Council's watchful guidance. 'I recommend you to accept it at once and I shall then have you here under my eye and shall be better able to aid you than where you are.'[5] From the chief officer of the government's education department this was an irresistible offer. Irvine, like Graham, would have the authority, and the help of a politically powerful friend, to remodel a well-known institution according to his own reforming principles. Again, steered by the energetic Kay-Shuttleworth, Duncannon's committee had turned to an educational structure outside England to find a man most suited to its needs.

Everyone who knew Irvine, friend or otherwise, acknowledged him to be an outstanding teacher. He was also a great enthusiast for best educational practice and a believer in spreading its benefits as widely as possible. Within months of his arrival at Greenwich he requested permission to give evening classes in arithmetic twice a week for other schoolmasters so as to introduce them to the methods of Pestalozzi in teaching the subject. A letter of support from the Committee of Council ensured that the hospital Governor's consent was obtained. Irvine was strict and had high expectations from colleagues and pupils alike. But, unlike Graham, he was not outwardly imposing and, consistent with his character, sought to influence his charges through personal affection rather than the authority of his office. One colleague likened him to 'a father and a friend' in his dealings with his pupils.[6] Another spoke of the excellent example he set to all boys in his moral and religious character; if he had a failing, it was merely that 'his temper is a little warm and excitable.'[7]

Even an inspector of Tremenheere's experience was struck when

watching Irvine in his classroom. 'Your abilities and acquirements appear to me to be much above those which I usually find
in masters of elementary schools,' he congratulated Irvine in a
condescending tone. 'Your manner of examining the classes,' he
continued, 'combined in a greater degree than I have elsewhere
had an opportunity of observing, that judicious interchange of
seriousness and playfulness which is best calculated to keep alive
the attention, to impress the memory and to secure the confidence
and regard of those whom you are instructing.'[8] This reference
to a playful disposition was particularly gratifying. Irvine took
pride in his ability to convey knowledge efficiently and flattered
himself on possessing a highly personalised manner of instruction.
'Whenever the subject admits of it I endeavoured by anecdote
and cheerful remarks to keep up attention,' he reflected on his
years in the profession. Any flaws in his approach to teaching
could be born only of 'a too anxious and probably overstretched
desire to make my department the very first of its kind.'[9]

Spartan as conditions were in early nineteenth century schools,
the two new headmasters were not fully prepared for what
awaited them. Tremenheere's report of September 1840 had
mentioned overcrowding and limited facilities but he had not
ventured far into the rather squalid conditions with which children
as young as nine or ten were confronted daily. In fact, conditions
in most schools were sufficiently primitive that Tremenheere may
well have considered any description to be quite superfluous.
Rugby and Winchester both had epidemics in the 1840s.
Westminster's boarding houses were 'perfect pigstyes' until the
middle decades of the century.[10] At King's College school the
health of boys suffered much from cold stone floors until the late
1830s and the sanitation was so poor that in 1842 parents
complained until more lavatories and an urinal were provided.[11]
At Greenwich, in 1841, Graham and Irvine discovered only 12
privies for the 400 boys accommodated on one site and these were
constructed so that their occupants sat in full view of each other.
The lavatories and washrooms were constantly damp and in the
winter the floors never dried. One of the hospital doctors urged
that 'tepid instead of cold water be allowed in the depth of winter
for the boys to wash with.'[12] The naval authorities were wary of
such concessions to civilian luxury: tepid water was no training
for a life at sea. But even its hardest officers could not help but
notice that the health of the children was impaired by using
towels which for months could never dry and which at night
lined the walls of freezing and unventilated dormitories. The
Lieutenant Superintendent admitted in 1841 that although he did

not wish to 'coddle up these children' sickness was undoubtedly a problem.[13]

Diet, as elsewhere, was also deficient and the portions of food available were generally inadequate for boys of 14 and 15. There was an official allowance for bread, meat and potatoes and meagre breakfasts and suppers were provided. Every boy was also given a half pint of beer with his dinner. Quality was, predictably, dreadful. Pease soup was the dinner every Wednesday 'which however excellent, as the Governor has tested, is scarcely touched by one boy out of ten.'[14] But the greatest deprivation related to the playgrounds to which all boys were confined once school had ended for the day and when they were not in hall. In winter, for an hour or two after supper at 6:00pm, the boys simply huddled together under the arches and colonnades or behind the walls available to escape the wet and cold. 'I have known about 300 boys at the same time suffering severely from chilblains,' a hospital doctor reported.[15] It was essential for the boys' health that some recreation room be provided, perhaps by converting a coal cellar, so that shelter was available in bad weather. The playgrounds turned to mud in winter and the shoes and stockings given to the boys offered no protection. Was it surprising that so many boys tried to get over the walls and railings and escape into the town?

Again the naval authorities were not entirely unsympathetic though the cost of building works had always to be borne in mind. The Lieutenant Superintendent did press for a better playground surface since proper drills and parades could not otherwise be conducted. Money aside, the other problem was a chronic shortage of space on the site which, on investigation, made even the construction of a fives court impossible. Ball games, needless to say, were out of the question. An examination of facilities in 1839 explained that 'the boys are debarred from the manly and healthy exercise of cricket from the destruction it would occasion to the windows.'[16] That was why the boys were marched up to Blackheath for exercise on half holidays. Overall, the bad conditions in which the boys were kept had a demoralising effect upon them and, most naval officers acknowledged, made discipline more difficult to enforce. It also tended to reduce them all to the lowest standards of behaviour — an embarrassment considering that 100 or more of the pupils in the Upper school were sons of commissioned officers. The Lieutenant Superintendent wrote dejectedly early in 1841 that 'it is very painful to observe how soon these children after entering the school (with very few exceptions) lose the gentleman like manners and appearance many of them came with, and how soon they imbibe the manners of the vulgar.'[17] Progressive views were not necessary to believe that education was intended to have the opposite effect.

Graham and Irvine were advocates of comprehensive reform whose views were in line not only with those of Kay-Shuttleworth but with those of most other champions of effective popular education of their generation. One element in their philosophy was a rejection of physical punishment which they considered merely to brutalise the young and undermine the trust and affection necessary in the proper relationship between teacher and pupil. Irvine gave strict instructions to his staff that no boy was to be beaten without his permission and that in principle the Lower school would operate without corporal punishment. Under new regulations adopted by the Greenwich schools committee in May 1841, 'the discipline of the schools should as much as possible resemble that of a well-ordered family.'[18] Physical chastisement should be used, if at all, only for the most grave offences and even then the consent of both the headmaster and chaplain should be given. A record should also be kept and a report sent to the Governor. If such punishment occurred it should be witnessed by all the masters and done privately, rather than before the assembled school as had been the practice in the past. Good teachers, the theory ran, 'exercise their control with such intelligence and skill as would secure the willing obedience of the boys.'[19] Kay-Shuttleworth drew the logical conclusion that once the right masters were in place there would be little need for any punishments at all.

Given that so much would hinge on the quality of staff, not surprisingly both Graham and Irvine had firm opinions on what made a good teacher. Both believed in professional training, which, in practice, meant having attended a reputable normal school like those of Stow and Wood in Scotland. Again this gave them much in common with Kay-Shuttleworth and Eden whose commitment to raising teaching standards at Battersea was obvious. Irvine was in no doubt that a teacher should be judged by the results of his labour: a class of children examined for their knowledge on a prescribed syllabus would reveal all about the work of their instructor. But what made good teaching? 'Much depends upon the master knowing how to begin at the beginning and according to the abilities of his pupils,' he elaborated, 'proceeding by slow but steady steps, taking care always to keep up a knowledge of what was previously learned, and when one plan fails knowing how to adopt another.'[20] Irvine had a routine for boys entering the Lower school. On arrival, he would examine every boy and record the extent of the lamentable ignorance with which the school was challenged. He would then assign the pupil to the appropriate class and require the master responsible to report on progress after a period of between two and six months. This did not guarantee good results, but it did provide him with a mechanism for appraising the quality of junior colleagues and giving guidance for improvement where required.

Graham was even more specific about his criteria for a competent teacher. A 'liberal education' was one essential; the master must have an intellectual command over that which he was teaching. For a junior class, with children under 11, a teacher should be at least 24 and exhibit a clarity and accuracy in his reading skills such as would convey a good style of reading to his pupils. He was to have a thorough acquaintance with arithmetic: 'both in the *theory* and the practice,' Graham added. His knowledge of etymology should be sufficient to understand the derivation of most common words. But Graham looked for more than academic qualifications. A good teacher should have 'a *lively* and *energetic* manner.' He should keep order by a blend of firmness and mildness. He should believe in the system of education in which he was engaged, be devoted to the improvement of his pupils and desire, without reservation, to co-operate with his headmaster in promoting the interests of the school. On top of all this, Graham would look only to employ a man who had conducted classes in an establishment 'where a decidedly approved system of education is in successful operation.' Even then it would be necessary 'to exhibit evidence, *by trial*, of his skill in the employment of the *explanatory* and *interrogative* method, in teaching lessons on English grammar, history etc.'[21]

For children older and more difficult to manage, Graham's standards were higher still. A good master should be at least 30 and possess a higher and more varied attainment in scholarship. Experience, steadiness of decision and sound sense were all requisite at this level in a school; a master teaching older children should be of a stature and sufficiently able to co-operate closely with the headmaster in attending to the interests of the institution so that, when necessary, responsibility for administering it could be devolved upon him. Such a man should have an advanced understanding of English, its grammar and etymology. He should comprehend 44 theorems in geometry and be competent in simple algebraic equations. Some elementary scientific knowledge was also desirable. As to classroom skills, Graham recalled his days in Edinburgh where the directors of the academy required all candidates for teaching posts to conduct a class in their presence so as to judge in person how skills were applied. He considered this to be good practice. Teaching should be a respectable calling and should be placed, therefore, upon proper professional standards.

Consistent with this conviction was the need for effective teaching methods to replace the outdated monitorial system. Arriving from Dublin, though, Irvine was loath to condemn monitorial instruction out of hand as many HMIs were inclined to do. In Scotland and Ireland, he assured Kay-Shuttleworth in May 1841, monitorial teaching had been of great service in the spread of popular education; under proper supervision and when set targets for attainment, older children could convey knowledge to the others and achieve creditable results. Gibson, inspecting schools throughout Scotland in the 1840s, in fact confirmed this opinion: a system worked as well as those who operated it. In many elementary schools, of course, the mode of instruction was not so much one of choice but rather a function of the resources available. It was all very well to point out the shortcomings of monitors but, as HMI in south west England asked, 'without some such help, what can a teacher effect with one or two hundred children?'[22] At Greenwich, however, where proper masters could be employed, Irvine was certain that the monitorial system should be dispensed with.

Aside from his disposition to employ professional masters and to teach according to more intellectual methods, Irvine justified abandoning the monitorial system by reference to the academic standard of the boys which he discovered in the first class at the Lower school in April 1841. This was the only class in which any attainments of scholarship could be detected and of the 63 boys present Irvine considered that 40 could read well. He found a little understanding of English grammar and an ability to write clearly and to copy from exercises. But even in this, the best class, many boys did not know the meaning of words which they read and copied and they possessed no general knowledge — not even of basic geography. This was not the fault of the boys. 'Considering the system adopted in the school, that of Bell and Lancaster which insisted on mere rote exercises,' he notified Kay-Shuttleworth, 'I thought the boys of this class as well forward as might have been expected under the adverse circumstances in which they were placed.'[23] Without proper instruction, without maps and without books, save a few scripture extracts, what more could be expected?

Graham was equally committed to modern teaching methods as an essential part of the new educational system to be implemented in the Upper school. 'The mode of teaching proposed to be employed,' he advised Kay-Shuttleworth, 'is that known by the intellectual system, the characteristic of which is that whatever is lodged in the memory must previously find its way through the understanding.' There were, he conceded, different ways in which the comprehension of a topic, to replace the simple repetition of information from memory, could be conveyed to children but the most effective way was 'when the teacher combines the illustrative, interrogative and suggestive with or without simultaneous answering' or equally, he continued, 'when there is a combination of the explanatory and interrogative with the individual method of question and answer.'[24] This was a far cry from monitors holding up slates before uncomprehending pupils or writing exercises performed by children oblivious to the meaning of what they copied. For larger numbers of boys, for instruction about visible objects as in natural history, and sometimes for scriptural education Graham recommended Stow's gallery lesson — in practice a lecture from a raised position with occasional questions asked of the audience. In such areas as English literature, arithmetic, and the abstract sciences he favoured a closer mixture of explanation and examination by questioning throughout the lesson and with a smaller class.

The concept of the individual smaller class, each with its own teacher, was another fundamental aspect of the new teaching system which was to be employed in the Greenwich schools and which was wholeheartedly endorsed by the two new headmasters. It meant a certain amount of building work as the old open schoolroom of the Lower school, in which masters and monitors had formerly tried to keep the attention of their charges amid the noise of up to 400 children, had now to be divided into separate classrooms. The Greenwich schools committee recommended a specific plan for this in February 1841. The alterations were to cost £500 and would provide four rooms appropriate for the Lower school; building estimates for the whole restructuring eventually rose to £860. The plan was approved and the work authorised by Minto on 24 February. Kay-Shuttleworth applauded the progress which this internal reorganisation of the schools represented: they were 'extensive alterations' by which the schools 'are probably now rendered more convenient for the purposes of instruction than any other English schools of equal extent. These plans were suggested by an examination of many of the most approved schools in this and other countries.' Upper, Lower and Nautical schools would all now operate according to the principle of one master (sometimes with an assistant) per class, teaching within his own classroom. The average size of class in the Lower school was to be about 60; at any time roughly 150 boys from the school would be withdrawn from lessons to receive industrial training in the hospital workshops. In the Upper school each of the three classes should have class captains, chosen from the boys, Kay-Shuttleworth recommended. 'They might be trained as pupil-teachers, by being instructed in the evening, so as to aid the masters in the school.'[25]

Irvine's enthusiasm for individual classroom teaching by professional masters and qualified assistants reflected his commitment to the academic rather than the training aspects of school life. To his mind, Duncannon's committee and even Kay-Shuttleworth made too many concessions to the need to prepare boys from his school to be ordinary sailors. The two days every week which most Lower school boys were to spend in the workshops learning the skills of tailors, blacksmiths, sailmakers, carpenters, shoemakers, knotters and rope repairers were a 'decided loss in common school education.' Back in class the boys were less attentive because so much of their energy was diverted to industrial occupations. Nonetheless, it was a naval school and Irvine's plans had to conform to the nature of the institution. The four classes would have areas and levels of instruction which reflected a boy's progress by age and attainment. He and his assistant, James Hamilton, would take the most advanced first class which would then set the standard to which the other masters would work. Hamilton was a young but much trusted colleague. He had taught with Irvine in Dublin since 1838 and had now come to England to rejoin his old headmaster.

The first class would make boys proficient in the following: Bible study and a knowledge of the Anglican catechism, reading, spelling, etymology, writing from dictation, grammar, geography and arithmetic. Irvine's charges would understand the tenets of their Christian faith, the doctrines of their Church and the history of Israel and Roman Palestine. Their geography would include a knowledge of the oceans, tides and currents as befitted prospective mariners. They would also be taught some history, politics and natural history. Irvine prided himself on his attention to the improved study of arithmetic which he was anxious should receive an important place in the Lower school. 'The arithmetic of Pestalozzi, which forms a prominent feature in many of the schools of Switzerland, Germany and Holland, was introduced by me into the Lower school,' he later boasted. 'It is, as a system of mental arithmetic, admirably suited to develop the intellectual faculties.' In addition to their work with slates and written numbers, then, his pupils would be taught an understanding in the abstract and the skill of calculating in their heads.

The second class gave equal weight to scriptural and religious instruction. It also concentrated on reading, writing and etymology and it provided a basic competence in arithmetic and geography. An able boy would join the higher class for his final year or so at school but the top two classes were both designed to cater for children until the date of departure. Irvine was concerned, however, not only with the academic achievements of his ablest and oldest pupils but with the always less fashionable classes which contained both the younger and the intellectually feebler boys. These were always the classes which received the worst teachers, he mused, thereby naturally exacerbating the problems to the detriment of the school as a whole. 'It is a remarkable circumstance that the lowest class in every institution requires the highest qualifications in an educational point of view on the part of the teacher,' Irvine believed, 'while at the same time the smallness of the emolument prevents well-qualified teachers from accepting such a situation.' His insight indicated not only a concern in principle for education at the lower levels but also a realisation, based on experience, that the vitality and efficiency of a whole school was affected by its capacity to develop an interest among the very young and a sense of fulfilment among those whose academic horizons were perforce limited. 'While the third and fourth classes remain under the care of men who cannot, or do not exhibit even moderate advancement,' he concluded, 'the first and second classes must partake of their character to a certain amount.'[26]

Reform of discipline and material conditions in the schools, the employment of staff with professional skills, altering the buildings to provide individual classrooms and the introduction of advanced methods of teaching were all essential components of the new system of education which the Greenwich schools committee, inspired by Kay-Shuttleworth, intended that Graham and Irvine should bring to the institution. There were two further elements of such a system which inevitably would represent the greatest changes and hence would likely be the most controversial. First, implicit in many of the observations of shortcomings at Greenwich which the new headmasters made was a belief in a broadly based school curriculum such as was a growing feature of progressive educational thinking by the 1840s. Irvine's views on the range of his syllabus for the Lower school were made clear enough in his specifications for the different classes. Expectations here, though, remained somewhat limited since his school did not provide the higher training in mathematics required of ships' officers. The

Lower school neither contained specialist masters nor did its finished products interest the naval authorities to the same degree as those from the Upper and Nautical schools. Irvine's efforts to implement a general elementary education in his school were therefore never likely to be regarded with the scepticism and mistrust which greeted Graham on his arrival at the Upper school. In the view of the naval establishment at Greenwich, it was Graham's job to concentrate on raising the levels of mathematical knowledge in his three classes so that able boys might enter the hallowed precincts of Riddle's Nautical school. Graham himself did not see things in quite that way.

It was inconceivable to Graham, himself the product of a Scottish education and for years a master at a progressive academy there, that any school curriculum could be as narrow as that in the Upper school at Greenwich prior to his appointment. English schools were well-known for their restricted definition of what constituted learning. Even so, the mathematics and nautical sciences taught in the Upper school marginalised basic features of what was increasingly accepted in society as essential to schooling. Kay-Shuttleworth strongly agreed with Graham. 'The rudiments which compose the staple of an elementary education are not less necessary to the master of the ship than to the common sailor,' he professed with suitable imagery in 1841.[27] He wanted skills in English writing, grammar and etymology to be expanded, religious instruction to be given its proper priority, and geography, history, naval biography and basic sciences to be developed. Graham, then, had a ready ally for his plan to create a modern education for his boys, many of whom in reality would neither enter naval service nor display the aptitude for Riddle's training in the finer points of navigational techniques.

Graham took as his starting point in devising an educational plan for the Upper school the fact that the average attendance there was for three years before boys either joined the Nautical school or left the institution. The first year must therefore be devoted to basic education before any introduction to specialised study. This would require much the same coverage of skills and general knowledge as Irvine intended to implement in the Lower school. It was made all the more essential because of the low educational standards of boys when they were admitted to the Upper school, Graham emphasised. 'It is requisite that their attention should be exclusively confined to such a course as this for the first year of the curriculum,' he explained to Kay-Shuttleworth, 'that they may have an opportunity of acquiring, to a certain extent, an accurate and well grounded as well as a respectable acquaintance with the elementary branches of knowledge (so useful and necessary in every situation of life).' Only then could there be progression to 'the higher departments of science and literature.'[28] His experience in teaching had led him to conclude that once children entered the study of classics or mathematics they soon lost interest in learning about the proper use of English and other lesser branches of education.

Like Irvine, Graham believed that the worth of a school was to be judged as much by its lower as its higher classes. It would matter greatly, therefore, how his reforms were implemented in the second and third classes of the Upper school. Before 1841 there was 'no provision under the old system for instruction in the English branches.' 'It may easily be conceived' Graham reflected, 'how very defective the knowledge of the boys was in this department on leaving the institution.' He intended to make proficiency in the use and understanding of English the bedrock of education in the second and third classes — in particular the third, which was joined by most boys on entry to the school. The most junior class in any school, he noted, was of the greatest importance. 'It is the nursery from which the highest classes are to be supplied with pupils.' The ability of its master would clearly determine the speed with which children might advance in the school. 'If the management of the junior class is not characterised by vigour and efficiency, there will unavoidably be a *paucity* of pupils in the *higher* classes, or what is the other alternative, filled with pupils who have been transferred before being properly qualified, and hence an injurious reaction on the different classes.' Upon the results achieved in the lower classes depended 'the successful development of the new system.'[29]

The final element of this new system and the one which was always likely to provoke the most resistance at Greenwich was the increased responsibilities which were to be entrusted to the teachers, and consequently the diminished status of the naval authorities, in the daily supervision and discipline of boys. This would be an enactment of progressive thinking whereby the bond between teacher and pupil would be strengthened to the benefit of the latter's personal development and enthusiasm for academic study. Stow's school in Glasgow had pioneered this approach, especially for children under 11. Experiments in Aubin's school at Norwood in the late 1830s had also yielded impressive evidence of the benefits to be derived from constant supervision by the schoolmasters in class, at play and at every other stage of the daily routine. Irvine saw the teachers' role as providing, in every aspect of behaviour, the model to be emulated; by their work in class and the example of their lives they would convey moral and Christian values and instil in boys a respect for truth, civility and diligence. Boys should admire and not fear their masters. His boys would be nurtured and allowed to develop in 'a system of authority maintained as far as possible by moral means and founded on moral influences.'

By supervision at meals, in the playgrounds and in the dormitories Irvine was convinced that he was 'testing the soundness of this educational principle.'[30] As usual, there was support for reforming ideas from Kay-Shuttleworth who was ready with the arguments necessary to silence any doubters. 'Instruction conveyed within the *schoolroom* embraces only one, though an important, part of education,' he judged, 'and the formation of correct habits consequent on the inculcation of right principles is the most important object of education.' Because teachers were trained to comprehend and to regulate the habits of children, whereas naval officers and drill-serjeants were not, it was teachers who should have charge of the formation of character in the young, and this required the capacity to check and influence a child in all areas of activity. Hence the assistant masters would be directed to eat at the same table as the boys and to sleep in rooms adjoining the dormitories. Whereas naval discipline, as applied in the past, extinguished the individual will and reduced boys to 'military automata', the regulating hand of competent masters would permit the development of personality and afford the opportunity for boys to learn the priceless virtue of self discipline. Naval men would never appreciate 'the more gentle and persuasive methods by which a skilful schoolmaster succeeds in training the character of his pupils,' Kay-Shuttleworth lectured authoritatively to the Admiralty.[31] Who would dare challenge the tide of change and progress which in the spring of 1841 seemed to carry all before it?

4 • THE ADMIRALTY AND THE COMMITTEE OF PRIVY COUNCIL IN 1841

On arrival in April 1841 Irvine spent a week merely observing school routine and trying to discover just where most of his boys were. Some he found on sentinel duty at the gates: others were helping in the hospital. Eventually he managed to muster about 250 boys who could be identified as members of the four classes of the Lower school. Attendance at lessons, he concluded, was, to put it mildly, fluctuating. He sat in while the other masters tried to teach their pupils. What he saw in the top two classes, he wrote dismissively, 'was purely the old Bell or Lancasterian system without any of those modifications which the lapse of time and the growing experience of educational men in every country has superadded to the original.' There was no plan to anything that was done. 'A good portion of each day was spent writing on paper from copy pieces and occasionally from dictation,' he noted, 'and also at arithmetic on small slates.'

Irvine saw no books used other than Trimmer's abridgements of the Testaments. 'The lessons in these were gone over in a mechanical manner,' he added, 'without the attention of the children being pointed to anything beyond learning to read.' As he moved down the school things became worse. The third and fourth classes had no desks and many boys in the latter were totally illiterate and so lacking in every branch of knowledge as not even to know the meaning of the simplest words. The wretched state of ignorance left the boys depraved and almost inhuman, he insisted. In their appearance and habits they were ruffians: 'they were rude and exceedingly inattentive to even the most gentle and kind remonstrances.'[1] Nevertheless, Irvine was not despondent. By the beginning of June the building work to construct four separate classrooms had been completed and the Admiralty was appointing the assistant masters he required. Even before the summer holidays came he felt that he was making

53

some progress in reorganising his school 'and in introducing the improved system of instruction.'[2] This had produced a great change in the demeanour of the boys, especially the more able in the first class. They were now keen to learn, he assured Kay-Shuttleworth, and were applying themselves to a study of geography, etymology and Pestalozzian arithmetic. Most encouraging for Irvine, they asked permission to stay on with him at the institution so as to make amends for the neglect of their education in the past.

Anxious as reformers were to see the implementation of change, Kay-Shuttleworth at least was experienced enough to realise that difficulties were bound to arise. He was always careful to mollify the Admiralty by saying that the Greenwich schools were a naval institution and that educational ideas must always be tempered by an appreciation of the special function for which they were intended. In May 1841 he wrote on behalf of the Greenwich schools committee to acknowledge that the reorganisation which Tremenheere had suggested in 1840 'can only proceed gradually, and that the new arrangements must necessarily be progressive.'[3] This proved to be prophetic. By July there was an open rift on the schools committee over the question of how much out of school authority should be entrusted to the masters and Duncannon had given up hope that a unanimous recommendation to the Admiralty could ever be made. Gordon had recovered his health and was now a regular attender at committee meetings. As acting Governor of the hospital his views could neither be ignored nor easily overridden by his colleagues.

Gordon was a bluff and hearty sailor who held strong opinions but was frank in all his dealings and certainly bore no grudges. Even after heated argument he would happily sit with his adversaries recalling incidents from his career long ago and describing in particular the action in which he had lost a leg. This endeared him to Eden and Kay-Shuttleworth but did not reconcile them to his stubborn defence of naval discipline at the schools. On 28 June 1841 Eden and Kay-Shuttleworth sat up into the night 'revising the rules of the Greenwich hospital schools, making estimates for the future expenses of the establishment, and reading letters of remonstrance from the new master, whom we have sent there, complaining of the undue exercise of authority on the part of the naval officers of the establishment.'[4] Gordon, for his part, did not confine expressions of doubt to members of the schools committee. On 16 July he wrote to Minto to explain why he was so certain that a mistake was about to be made. First, authority within the institution would become too fragmented.

There would be three schools, each with its own headmaster and each exercising its own out of school authority. This would be particularly absurd at meal-times when the boys all ate together. How could any sensible lines be drawn which distinguished the authority of the headmasters either from each other or from the Lieutenant Superintendent and his drill-serjeants? It was a recipe for organisational chaos. He recommended that no change be made to the existing system whereby the masters' control was confined to their classrooms while the conduct of boys at meals, at play and in the dormitories was left with naval officers. The assistant masters could perhaps help in out of school duties, he conceded, particularly since these men 'will have little or nothing to do in the classrooms, as by the new system only one master can teach at a time.' They should not however be given responsibility. Discipline should remain in the hands of the military, as was the case at the army establishments at Woolwich, Sandhurst and Addiscombe.

The second reason Gordon gave for his defence of the *status quo* was simply that the alterations proposed by his colleagues on the Greenwich schools committee 'impose duties upon the headmasters which they cannot perform.' The burden of work would be too heavy. 'The headmasters and the subordinate masters who have the charge of classrooms, after exerting themselves in teaching from nine o'clock in the morning till noon will require some respite from their duty to take the meals,' he explained, 'and be ready to recommence their labours which begin again at two o'clock and continue until five.'[5] Very soon some of the out of school duties would devolve onto the inexperienced assistant masters and would not be conducted properly at all. It was a valid argument. The reformers, unfortunately, disagreed and Duncannon, in turning the matter over to the Board of Admiralty for a final decision, chose to ignore it.

By the beginning of July 1841 Kay-Shuttleworth was fairly sure of his ground despite the force of Gordon's arguments. On 29 June Eden had a meeting with the Lords of the Admiralty and reported back to his friend in jubilant mood. 'They are much pleased with the very beneficial changes in the management of the schools, with the character of the masters selected, and the evident improvement in the manners and instruction of the boys,' Kay-Shuttleworth noted. 'Much difficulty threatens to arise from the collision of the naval officers of the hospital with the headmasters in their respective departments,' he continued. However, 'Lord Minto promised to support us in improving the position of the headmasters.'[6] His other reason for confidence was Duncannon who, he sensed, had considerable influence with Minto. At a meeting of the Committee of Council on 1 July, 'Lord Duncannon promised his most earnest support in the discussions with the Admiralty on the Greenwich hospital schools,' Kay-Shuttleworth recorded. 'I expect to carry all our improvements in discipline by temperate firmness and perseverence.'[7]

Duncannon in fact posed two questions of principle for Minto to resolve. First, 'whether we as the committee appointed to reorganise the Greenwich schools are to be considered as confined to a strictly naval discipline, or whether we are at liberty to place the school upon the best system that we can suggest.'[8] It was fairly clear though what answer Duncannon wanted. Issues of practicality were not raised and the Admiralty was almost dared to challenge the maxim that out of school responsibility and the moral training of boys which should accompany it was a job for professionally qualified teachers. In fact, Duncannon assumed that Gordon's reservations would be overruled when he observed that a clear definition of the respective duties of the masters and the drill-serjeants would have to be devised. The second question related to the work which might be expected from the children in helping run the institution. If none, then the schools committee anticipated that for reasons of economy the establishment might have to become smaller. It might retain its present size if boys were employed in some of the daily tasks. Neither question was very tempting to answer. Minto confided that he was inclined to 'employ the assistant masters more and the mates less' and to allow the boys to 'perform some of the menial offices of the establishment.'[9] But he gave no answer to Duncannon for nearly a fortnight.

Minto's hesitation was not due only to Gordon's objections. He knew that Gordon spoke for the other naval officers at Greenwich and in particular for the strong-willed figure who had served as Lieutenant Superintendent since 1837, John Wood Rouse. Rouse was not a typical incumbent: traditionally the post was a sinecure for an infirm or disabled officer. One earlier occupant, indeed, had been an invalid who, despite the Admiralty's entreaties, refused to move from the accommodation available on the school site into the hospital where he belonged. Rouse came to Greenwich from the Royal Naval College at Portsmouth where since 1820 he had been in charge of the cadets. Rouse had been recommended for the post of Lieutenant Superintendent by an enthusiastic array of admirals and academics. He had been popular at the Royal Naval College with his blend of firm but kindly treatment of the young. The Admiralty had sent a senior officer to Portsmouth to make discreet enquiries which revealed nothing adverse in his character or temperament. Rouse had a 'steady, consistent discipline, even-handed sense of justice, amiability and gentlemanly deportment.'[10] Aged 52 in 1837, he was felt to be the right man to take charge of naval discipline in the schools.

Rouse certainly believed in discipline. Even Gordon had to admit that 'Lieutenant Rouse is rather hasty when he is contradicted or interfered with on points of service.'[11] He advocated drill and increased the amount required of boys soon after his arrival. As time passed he seemed to become increasingly frustrated by disorderly behaviour in the schools and began to see others as thwarting his attempts to restore proper naval order. He offended the long-serving Matron at the hospital by a lack of courtesy in correspondence and his temper grew ever worse by the account of most of his fellow officers. But there was never a suggestion that he ill-treated the boys. In 1841 Rouse jotted down much of his philosophy on education in response to the changes in the schools which had been proposed. He was not entirely convinced that corporal punishment was always an effective form of correction: for most offences he favoured parades, drills and long detentions. He believed that children needed amusement and recreation alongside their studies and other training. Music and rowing were his favourites; the principle was that it was important 'to keep the mind of youth constantly occupied.'[12] He was keen that boys should attend the hospital workshops and learn industrial skills both useful to a good mariner and capable of providing an honest livelihood. Making clothes and shoes would also save the schools money. It was a perception of education which the economy-minded Minto was unlikely to reject out of hand.

Whether Rouse was convinced of his own liberal credentials in the treatment of boys, Kay-Shuttleworth most certainly was not and prepared himself thoroughly for a meeting of the Greenwich schools committee on 7 July at which he knew there would be a great argument with Gordon. He knew that he would win on the issue of controlling the boys but wished nonetheless to avoid an open row which might make the naval officers at the schools unco-operative in the future. 'We are desirous not to disgust,' he confided. 'Our object is to get rid of the cat-o'nine-tails-discipline and to establish in its stead the harmony of a well regulated family.' This would mean removing from Rouse much of his former authority. 'I have hitherto been delaying the final decision out of respect for our opponents,' he added, 'and I perceive they mistake the delay for weakness.' Gordon had already denounced the Committee of Council and its reforming associates as 'sanguine theorists without any experience.' Kay-Shuttleworth told the admiral in response that 'his *experience* is that of the Quarter deck, and that a king's ship is as compared to a school, what a slave estate in Carolina is to an English park.'[13] It was, predictably, an awful meeting with two and a half hours of Gordon acting in characteristically stubborn and aggressive manner and then Kay-Shuttleworth, who fielded most of the admiral's invective with some assistance from Duncannon, losing his temper too. 'I have not been so animated on any subject for years,' Kay-Shuttleworth reflected afterwards. Nonetheless, he judged, 'we beat them in argument.'[14] Minto would now have to make his decision.

Minto confessed his dilemma to a senior officer at the Admiralty on 11 July 1841. 'I fear this double-headed monster of Greenwich school will not easily be licked into shape,' he predicted. 'The pedagogue and the first Lieutenant will not draw together in the same cart.' Left to himself, Minto pondered that he might have handed all control in the schools over to the headmasters. 'But this, considering Rouse's actual position, was impossible.'[15] There would have to be as clear a division of authority as possible between academic and naval personnel, such as Duncannon had requested. On 19 July Minto replied to the schools committee and made the point that Rouse was 'a fortunate exception' to the quality of man who normally held his position. 'It is not likely,' he emphasised, 'that another case should occur in which any of the Lieutenants of Greenwich hospital would be found to possess the qualities most essential for the government of schoolboys.' But there, he explained to Duncannon, 'I feel the difficulties of the question.' Admirable as Rouse had proved himself as Lieutenant Superintendent and persuasive as Gordon had been on his behalf, Minto conceded what the committee most wanted.

'I am of opinion with the majority of the committee on Greenwich schools that the moral training of the boys should be confided to the masters not to the Lieutenant,' Minto informed Duncannon. He based his judgment largely on a practical consideration. 'The masters are selected on account of their peculiar qualification for that duty, and if they should prove unfit for it they would immediately be dismissed.'[16] Four days later he justified this step in an Admiralty memorandum. There were really no grounds for rejecting the recommendations which Duncannon and his colleagues had made; indeed, he now regarded the masters' role in out of school authority as 'absolutely essential to the success of the schools.'[17] It was an important decision for the Greenwich schools. It was, however, one of the last which Minto made in office. After years in power, the reforming Whigs were decisively defeated in a general election and on 30 August 1841 Sir Robert Peel took office as head of a Tory government. It was a grave disappointment for Kay-Shuttleworth and many who had seen the Whigs as the party most sympathetic to the spread and state support of popular education. On 6 September the Earl of Haddington assumed office as the new First Lord of the Admiralty.

Kay-Shuttleworth had worried about a change of government as early as July 1841 when it seemed clear that the Whigs would lose. His only consolation, he wrote, was that 'the Tories on their accession to office would be constrained to do some popular acts in order to strengthen their party in popular opinion.' Kay-Shuttleworth and his friends thought it probable that the Tories would soon 'find it their interest to promote the progress of national education.'[18] Indeed, as the weeks passed his spirits revived. The new Lord President of the Council, Lord Wharncliffe, did not seem resentful of Kay-Shuttleworth despite the fact that in Tory circles, Wharncliffe reminded him, 'your former liaison with the Whigs is a notorious source of jealousy.'[19] Early in September Kay-Shuttleworth noted that his new political chief 'gives me hopes that my department may be somewhat developed. In this hope I remain, and I will not at present anticipate disappointment.'[20]

The Whigs had certainly hoped, before losing office, that the issue of state assistance for national education could be rescued from the arena of party politics and that a broad consensus in its favour would emerge. Kay-Shuttleworth's initial experience in Whitehall now made him optimistic that no reversal of government commitment to school provision was likely and that a good professional relationship between minister and senior civil servant at the Committee of Council would not be difficult to achieve. Political change in Whitehall in no way affected the momentum for reform at Greenwich where Graham, in particular, had already set about his task with much energy. Graham at once reached the conclusion that his Upper school could not be considered in isolation; given that many of his boys entered the Nautical school, it was logical to him that the character and procedures of the latter were proper areas for concern on his part. He was not impressed by what he saw. The 100 boys there were taught in four classes but the school had only two specialised masters — Edward Riddle and his son, John. Even in the Nautical school, Graham argued, the basic skills of education should not be ignored. Grammar and geography, for example, remained essential; indeed, he insisted, 'ignorance in these branches was attended with a retarding effect in the prosecution of the mathematical and nautical studies.'[21] Science teaching too might be broadened to include the study of steam engines, gunnery, practical surveying and building work.

Graham did not limit himself to suggestions for improvement. More significantly, he denounced the quality of what was already being done. Riddle passed his time with the boys explaining spherical trigonometry and how its principles might be applied to the solution of astronomical problems, Graham complained, and he introduced them to mathematical ideas about ratios and planes. It was, though, 'an amount of instruction compared with the time allotted for it extremely inconsiderable and which any good teacher with proper method could do in *one hour's* daily attendance.'[22] It was a savage indictment of Riddle by a man who had only recently joined the institution. To make matters more serious, these observations had all been made directly to Kay-Shuttleworth who immediately accepted them as true and who was determined to take up all Graham's criticisms of the Nautical school with the Admiralty.

Ignoring his own excellent advice that reform could only proceed gradually, Kay-Shuttleworth wrote scathingly to Sidney Herbert, the Secretary to the Board of Admiralty, on 16 October 1841. He elaborated on Graham's remarks about the narrow syllabus; boys knew nothing of globes or charts, Kay-Shuttleworth wrote indignantly, and nothing about tides, ocean currents, prevalent winds, meteorology and climate. All it appeared that they could do was to take a few lunar and solar observations. In the past this had been trumpeted as nautical science; it was, in reality, 'the most imperfect and extremely limited knowledge of the humblest elements of mathematics.'[23] Nor did it stop there. A few days later he wrote to Haddington who had previously indicated that he would permit a direct correspondence. Nautical science, 'to which everything else was sacrificed', was almost as poorly taught as was everything else at Greenwich. No disrespect to Riddle was intended and his long years of service were much appreciated, Kay-Shuttleworth insisted; nonetheless, the only conclusion which could be drawn was that 'the nautical instruction had failed as completely as every other department.' What further proof could be provided that, prior to the recent changes, the education system at the schools 'was effete and required a careful reorganisation.'?[24]

There was a reason why Graham and Kay-Shuttleworth were so eager to force the pace of change by October 1841 and why the latter felt it necessary to offer renewed justification to the First Lord of the Admiralty for the reforms already implemented.

Undoubtedly the changes made were not popular either among the academic or naval staff at the institution and those who promoted the new system were becoming worried by the development of an organised inertia which might yet frustrate their plans. Certainly Gordon on the Greenwich schools committee did not abandon all hope that he might still convince the Admiralty that Minto had made a mistake in sanctioning an out of school role for the masters. Both he and Rouse had tried loyally to operate the new disciplinary arrangements, he assured the Governor, Admiral Sir Robert Stopford, on 12 October 1841, 'but from the duties of the Lieutenant and the masters being so interwoven, I am now practically convinced that it is not possible this new and before untried experimental plan can be carried out.'

Gordon also resurrected the old issue of undue interference by the Committee of Council in running the schools and now suggested that the Admiralty was allowing too great a voice from this quarter. In 1840 Minto had requested an inspection and report from one of HMIs — but that was all. It was never intended that the result should be laid before the Privy Council or brought before Parliament. Gordon had been much alarmed at a remark by Duncannon on 1 August 1841 when the latter had spoken of his schools committee being under the surveillance of the Committee of Council. The alarm was further sounded when Duncannon subsequently accepted the suggestion, and then persuaded the Board of Admiralty to approve it, that the schools should be inspected twice annually by an HMI and that the reports should go both to the Admiralty and the Privy Council. Outside inspection was not objectionable in principle, Gordon was quick to point out; it simply should be done under the direction of the responsible department of government which alone should receive the findings. If not, then gradually the naval schools at Greenwich would pass under the control of the Committee of Council 'as all workhouse and district schools for pauper children are.'[25] Bound up with who controlled the schools was the sensitive issue of their educational and social status.

Gordon's reservations were, of course, well known and he had expressed them forcefully throughout the summer of 1841. Less apparent to Kay-Shuttleworth and the two headmasters were the views of the new hospital Governor who, so far, had not been involved in the process of reform. Stopford probably had no views, having only just returned to England from the Mediterranean. He had commanded at the capture of St. Jean D'Acre which had so preoccupied and impressed the Admiralty at the end of 1840 and he undoubtedly arrived at Greenwich as a naval hero.[26] Not all government ministers were happy with his appointment. The hospital governorship was a post of political patronage and Stopford was well known for his Tory sympathies. 'Strong doubts were urged from some quarters of the expediency of placing you in a situation where the political influence it afforded might be employed against the government,' Minto confessed in January 1841;[27] nonetheless, Stopford and Minto had enjoyed an excellent professional relationship and weighty confidential correspondence over many anxious months and Minto believed the admiral to be a man of such personal integrity that colleagues in Cabinet need not worry on account of his political affiliations.

Minto further anticipated that by the time Stopford took up his new position the changes at Greenwich would be completed and that the admiral's function, at the age of 73, would be largely ceremonial. In March, he wrote soothingly to Stopford that 'I hope by the time you come to take possession, we shall have got over some troublesome reforms and correction of abuses.'[28] Stopford duly arrived in the summer of 1841 only to find that Minto had been wildly optimistic. By October, indeed, Stopford was becoming uneasy about the way in which decisions were being made and the implication that the recent division of responsibilities had for his own authority over the conduct of the schools. 'This new scheme was directed to be tried under the apparent authority of the late Board of Admiralty,' he reflected. 'I say apparent because it is well known that a voluminous body of instructions from the Committee on Education was sent to the Admiralty on one day, and sent down the following day, not giving time, it is presumed, for their Lordships' examination.' Like Gordon, Stopford was quick to emphasise that he did not oppose all aspects of the educational plan adopted. He acknowledged that the boys would now receive a better general knowledge than before, even though he regretted that this might be at the expense of nautical training. 'But I do object to the constant interference of any member of the Committee of Education,' he informed Herbert. Once the Admiralty had decided what it wanted at Greenwich, the implementation of its policy should be a matter only for the naval authorities there.

Stopford wrote candidly of his own confusion now that so much out of school responsibility had been transferred to the headmasters: 'Since this new power has been introduced through the Committee of Council on Education I am at a loss to know where my authority as Governor begins and in what manner it is to be executed.' He also shared Gordon's doubts about the practicality of giving the masters so much out of school control: it seemed to him that the result would merely be a loosening of discipline as physical chastisement came to be replaced by less effective methods. 'What is called moral training of the boys, and the absence of all corporeal punishments except upon grave occasions, does not succeed,' he explained. 'When it is considered that at Eton and other public schools where a higher grade of boys still continue under wholesome discipline, it cannot be expected that 800 of a very different description of boys at the Greenwich schools can be kept in proper order without something similar.'[29] When the clerk of the works later wrote to the hospital Secretary reporting a considerable number of windows smashed by unruly boys he added caustically that 'the Governor wished me to state that this was the effect of moral training.'[30]

Faced with a growing resistance to educational reforms, then, Kay-Shuttleworth felt he had little alternative but to back as strongly as he could Graham's criticisms of the Nautical school. If the specialised instruction here could be discredited then, he calculated, defenders of the old patterns of teaching and naval discipline would be greatly weakened as the justification for all past practices was undermined. Kay-Shuttleworth wrote sternly to the Admiralty that before 1841 the majority of children at the institution were virtually uneducated 'and it was only about one fifth of the school concerning whom the *pretence* was set up that they were taught anything more.' 'Now it is the business of some interested persons at Greenwich to conceal these facts,' he warned, '— to pretend that the boys learned a great quantity of something called *nautical* science, and to urge a return to the previous arrangements.' Furthermore, these same opponents of the new system postulated that it was impossible to teach the syllabus now introduced. This was also untrue, Kay-Shuttleworth explained. '*Nothing* is proposed to be taught in the Upper school of Greenwich hospital which is not taught in the *secondary* schools in Scotland.'[31] Indeed, in Scotland the children also studied foreign languages which were not being introduced at Greenwich. There should be a proper outside inspection of standards in the Nautical school and Kay-Shuttleworth looked to the Admiralty to sanction this procedure. Once Graham's observations were upheld by an impartial academic authority the forces for progress would at last be fully in control.

Haddington could scarcely refuse an investigation. Resigned to a further condemnation of archaic practices in its schools, on 5 November the Board of Admiralty turned to the Astronomer Royal and two other leading scientists with a request for an examination of the Nautical school. Specifically they were to report on the arithmetic, algebra, mathematics and nautical science which was studied and on 'the results of the old system of management.' The Astronomer Royal was obliged to withdraw from the visit to Greenwich arranged for 10 November thereby leaving the matter to be resolved by Thomas Hall, professor of mathematics at King's College, London and his counterpart at University College, Augustus de Morgan, a widely respected mathematician of considerable personal and intellectual integrity. The task before them, they told Herbert, was not a pleasant one. De Morgan knew Riddle through the Royal Astronomical Society and even Hall, who had never met him, knew of the reputation which the old man had once enjoyed as a scholar and teacher of mathematics. The criticisms of his school by Graham and Kay-Shuttleworth were, however, so precise and detailed that the outcome seemed a mere formality. They were being sent to Greenwich effectively to put an end to Riddle's teaching career and hence to pave the way for more efficient methods of instruction.

The four classes of the Nautical school were examined in the two large rooms where they were taught for over four hours by the two professors. Riddle and Fisher were invited to be present. The ground rules were immediately established. Fisher was merely a witness; Riddle would be allowed to participate but only where he wished to press a boy beyond the questions posed by the two examiners. He was not permitted to offer help to boys in any way. The professors would choose which questions should be asked and they would select which boys should try to answer them. Graham was not invited to be present. The defects which he alleged were so simply and clearly expressed that Hall and de Morgan needed nothing further from him. Riddle did not seem much concerned as the examination started and as it proceeded the reason became increasingly clear. 'The state of the school is, in our opinion, altogether different from that which Mr. Graham has imagined it to be,' the investigators concluded. Incredibly, the outcome of the visit was a substantial vindication of Riddle's entire system of teaching.

In their report to the Admiralty Hall and de Morgan explained how scholars of such distinction had gone about testing mere children. 'The only mode in which a stranger can satisfactorily examine a class of young boys is, by beginning with very easy questions, showing a full belief that they cannot fail to answer all that is asked, giving approbation freely, treating a mistake as something which both examiner and pupil are to laugh at together, and feeling visible pleasure in their success.' Revelling in the opportunity to express such enlightened sentiments, the two men judged that 'if any of these things were wanting, and if the question, the look, or the manner bore the least intimation of wish to detect incapacity, there is no doubt that any class of boys in any school might be made to appear ignorant of the things they know best.' It was not clear how Graham had been able to form his opinions on the state of the Nautical school. On enquiry, it transpired that there had never been an occasion for him to examine the school and that, if he had done so, it could only have been very sporadically while some of the boys were in the Upper school on errands or other business. This, the professors declared, could be at the root of the problem; Graham, in short, had no real basis for his sweeping condemnation.

All that Hall and de Morgan witnessed led them to believe that Riddle ran the Nautical school according to an efficient system of instruction. The boys had answered all the questions with accuracy and enthusiasm and many, even from among the most ordinary, had the making of fine navigators. Riddle's reputation had been salvaged: 'a man who can produce the results which we saw and heard, on 100 boys, with only one assistant master, and in a schoolroom much too crowded for convenience, must be a person entitled to your Lordships' implicit confidence,' the Board of Admiralty was reassured. Algebra and spherical trigonometry were taught there, despite Graham's assertion to the contrary. Riddle also provided a good training in theoretical mathematics before he proceeded to its application to navigational techniques. The school was not perfect by any means: Riddle really required another assistant and he ought to consider increasing the algebraic component of his syllabus. Nonetheless, 'the intelligence and knowledge displayed by a *very* large majority of the boys would satisfy any competent examiner in one hour that Mr. Graham's allegations represent a school in a very different state from that in which we found the Nautical school.'[32]

Embarrassing as this outcome undoubtedly was for Graham and Kay-Shuttleworth, the former did not drop his criticism of the Nautical school. In mid December 1841 Stopford recorded that there was a growing tension between the different masters in the schools concerning both teaching standards and disagreement over disciplinary requirements. Rouse insisted that the boys were becoming generally disorderly and asked for a greater authority to intervene, but Stopford was now bound by Admiralty instructions to leave out of school control of the boys to the academic staff. Meanwhile all the papers relating to Hall and de Morgan's inspection arrived at the Admiralty where Haddington was quick to appreciate the irony of the outcome. 'It was, I think, Mr. Graham who called for the examination that took place,' he remarked dryly, 'and it is Mr. Graham who complains of the result. If on new enquiry it should be found desirable to have a new examination I shall not object to it — though I should doubt its expediency.' More worrying for Haddington were Stopford's comments on the decline in standards of behaviour in the schools which led him to question the wisdom of Minto's decision to sanction so much control for the masters such as Kay-Shuttleworth and Duncannon had wanted. 'I doubt whether order will ever be restored,' he minuted, 'while two different and discordant authorities are employed to maintain it.'[33]

Although Haddington and Stopford were clearly both beginning to worry about the benefits of reform in the schools, and although the reformers had received a setback from Hall and de Morgan's approval of teaching practices in the Nautical school, Riddle, of course, was greatly heartened by the outcome and now launched a counter-attack against the muddled thinking of the Greenwich schools committee. In November that committee had suggested the teaching of certain aspects of geometry which its members considered the most appropriate for education in the Nautical school. Riddle dismissed the idea as that of men who knew nothing of the subject and were not therefore competent to express opinions on the highly technical instruction of his pupils. The schools committee, by proposals contained in its minutes of a meeting on 3 November, he complained, effectively denied him the opportunity to instruct properly in trigonometry, instrument usage, mercator's sailing and the principles of intersecting planes. He was also required to explain lunar observations as they related to navigation with reference only to the celestial globe. 'Whoever thinks it possible to work out the results of a lunar observation on the celestial globe has a very erroneous idea of the nature of the problem,' he exclaimed triumphantly. It was indicative of 'the imperfect and superficial character of the course of scientific instruction which will be introduced into this institution if the spirit of that minute is to be carried out.'[34] Riddle stepped forward as an experienced teacher with his reputation much enhanced after November 1841 to defend the proven standards of mathematics teaching at Greenwich. Graham's attempt to discredit him having backfired, it was the proponents of reform who found themselves for the first time on the defensive.

Kay-Shuttleworth took it upon himself to defend the recommendations of the schools committee and in the process made it plain that he did not think that Hall and de Morgan had answered all the criticisms which Graham had made. The schools committee did not wish to enter a controversy with Riddle, he ungraciously remarked, but the opinions expressed after its November meeting had followed consultation with high academic authority. There were books, Kay-Shuttleworth continued, which explained mathematical concepts more clearly than Riddle's own textbook and which, if adopted, might save time in teaching and allow other areas of education to be brought into the syllabus. 'The committee have desired to rescue the boys from a ponderous course of mathematic instruction of which the greater part is unnecessary,' the Admiralty was abruptly informed. 'They desire to introduce in its stead a thoroughly efficient and comprehensive course of nautical and mathematical instruction which may not interfere with the acquisition of the elements of a useful general education.'[35] After months of debate there was clearly no compromise in sight on the issue of syllabus reform. Kay-Shuttleworth was not prepared to accept that a broader curriculum meant a lowering of academic standards.

On new year's eve Haddington surveyed his three-month experience of the Greenwich schools. 'Since my attention has been called to this subject I have had but one object,' he ruminated, '— namely to get all the good we could from the interference of the Committee of Education which on our accession to office we found in full operation.' Like Minto before him, he was wary of the growing voice of another department of government in what he believed was the Admiralty's preserve. He was happy to work with Kay-Shuttleworth but 'without the least wish to devolve on the Privy Council or any body appointed by them the control and management of the Greenwich schools.' He had inherited 'a system of experimental education' and although he was not enthusiastic about this he had judged it best not to interfere with procedures already set in motion. 'I thought at the same time,' he confided, 'that the period was approaching at which we might hope, with the aid of those experiments, to come to a final and satisfactory conclusion with respect to the future management of the schools.' In no sense was the new First Lord's approach dogmatic. As with his predecessor, the main consideration was what would produce the desired results.

Haddington was happy to concede that changes in the schools had been necessary and that the outside advice taken had proved worthwhile. 'Great benefit will be derived from the adoption of much that has been introduced under the sanction of the Committee,' he concluded. 'I believe that a great improvement in the general education of the boys will be the result of the changes made by them.' Having read the papers relating to the examination by Hall and de Morgan in November he was also persuaded that the reforms introduced in the schools did not in themselves compromise the essential responsibility which the institution had for nautical training and preparing boys for maritime careers. Indeed, he reflected, 'I cannot comprehend why these changes should injuriously affect the training of the scholars in the Nautical school.' But what disturbed him was the suggestion from the Governor that the boys were becoming more difficult to control and that frictions between the masters and the naval authorities made the daily management of the schools ever less effective. It had been hoped that, with time, satisfactory procedures for practical administration would have emerged and that a working compromise between the champions of change and the sceptics who resisted it might be found. By the end of 1841 these hopes were far from fulfilment.

'The time has arrived at which it is our duty to interfere,' Haddington informed the Board of Admiralty. He was not committed to any specific course and ideally would have wished more time to allow the educational experiment at Greenwich to run. But the existing state of the schools and in particular the growing rift between the masters and the naval officers meant that matters simply could not be left as they were. There was the added complication of 'the differences that prevail between the authorities of the hospital and the majority of the committee.'[36] Duncannon could no longer get agreement from his colleagues on the Greenwich schools committee and even when recommendations were made they were being questioned and sometimes rejected by those required to implement them. It was unlikely, however, that Haddington really knew the full extent of the problems which had surfaced at Greenwich. Personal bitterness and rivalries were, by the beginning of 1842, the most conspicuous element in the life of the schools. Irvine and Graham, who nine months earlier had begun their reforming work with such enthusiasm, were on the point of losing control. Graham, in particular, found himself confronted with established masters in his Upper school who both resented him and hated everything he stood for.

5 • GRAHAM AND HIS STAFF, APRIL 1841 TO MAY 1842

It was not, of course, unknown for headmasters to be at odds with their colleagues and assistants. Personality, religious principles and teaching methods were always fertile sources of dispute — not to mention pay and the stipulation of oppressive duties. In many schools in the late eighteenth and early nineteenth centuries junior masters were paid and treated more like servants than fledgling members of a defined profession. In the public schools, where these like other matters were best recorded, internal clashes created tensions which could span a generation. It was rare for staff on leaving any school for a better position to have cause to thank an old headmaster for help or advice in career development.

Although conditions of service, arbitrary dismissals and animosities were often at their worst at the small private and preparatory schools, even in more respectable establishments antagonisms found their way into correspondence destined improbably for survival or into the reports of frustrated school inspectors. At the King's College school in the 1840s there were unquestionably divisions both among the staff and with the headmaster. One young teacher complained pointedly to the head that 'no-one's efforts can be of the slightest avail if they are thwarted by a colleague.'[1] The College imposed a rigid control on all its staff and refused to create any senior positions in the school to which enterprising masters could aspire. At Sedbergh an inspector found that the two masters of the school had not been on speaking terms for 15 years. The head blamed the abysmal academic standard of the higher classes on the stupid teaching methods used in the forms below. The master of the lower classes responded that it was a waste of time preparing boys for progression in the school on account of the absurd and useless courses taught in the forms above.[2] Admissions to schools and the discipline of children could also be contentious issues. So too was the area of staff appointment and promotion. Coming to Greenwich, Graham encountered this difficulty right from the start. He had not been a popular choice for the headship of the Upper school in 1841. One of his colleagues in particular, John Hartnoll, considered that he possessed a better claim.

Hartnoll had been appointed second master to teach mathematics in the Upper school in 1821. He was a man of very modest scientific and literary attainments, giving public lectures on what he described as philosophical subjects. In 1827 he wrote a *Practical Treatise on Navigation* for the Society for the Diffusion of Useful Knowledge. He had earlier composed poetry for a list of subscribers headed by George IV and was the author of accounts of the lives of eminent scientists which appeared in a four-volume biographical work entitled *The Georgian Era*. He turned his attention to journalism, being for several years in the 1820s editor of a London monthly magazine and subsequently editor of the *Greenwich Gazette*. Hartnoll tried his hand at publishing too. He became proprietor and manager of the *Gravesend Journal* and *Chatham Telegraph* and was founder of two other political periodicals. He also had aspirations as a linguist and produced a pamphlet relating to efficient systems of language teaching. This clearly showed that 'I have not been indifferent to the various modes of instruction recommended and adopted by theorists and experimentalists,' he proclaimed. A man of such accomplishments and with excellent character references to match might have expected to progress in his calling.

When the Upper and Nautical schools were separated in March 1841 and Edward Riddle retained his headship of the latter, Hartnoll's expectations were aroused. He wrote to the schools committee pointing out his length of service, his accomplishments and his considerable personal skill in imposing a rigid discipline while 'securing the affections of those I instruct.' In fact, Hartnoll considered that he had been passed over twice before: in 1821 and again in 1831, when the headship of the Lower school was vacant, he had not been approached — a disappointment, to be sure, but confirmation in his eyes that the Admiralty saw his future in the Upper school when the opportunity arose. 'To place me in a subordinate or inferior position to a new master would affix, undeservedly, a spot upon my forehead,' he urged on 20 March 1841.[3] Nonetheless, the appointment went to Graham. Hartnoll observed bitterly that 'there is little room left for a *hereafter*, in this life, to a man who has exhausted twenty of the best years of his existence in the public service.'[4] Graham would receive £135 per annum more than Hartnoll and without any claim to such consideration. Hartnoll railed that he had 'always maintained the feelings, habits and associations of a gentleman.' 'A large measure of disgrace,' he concluded, 'has been unmeritedly inflicted.'[5] 'I have been passed over without any alleged complaint against me.'[6]

This was not a good omen for Graham's leadership of the Upper school. In May Hartnoll tried unsuccessfully for a transfer as a second mathematical master into the Nautical school. What he really wanted was to be transferred to a clerical branch of the Admiralty's operations or else retired on a pension of £300 per annum, but neither of these options was on offer. The tensions between Graham and Hartnoll grew as the months passed, to the extent that in December 1841 Graham recorded that 'Mr Hartnoll threatened to strike and bullied me in the presence of his class.'[7] Nor was Hartnoll the only problem. By the end of 1841 Graham was also at loggerheads with his third master, James Sharp.

Sharp was appointed to the Upper school in 1828 to teach mathematics and its application to the principles of navigation and nautical astronomy. Colleagues respected his abilities as a teacher and vouched for his commitment and efficiency in all that he did. He was also steady and circumspect in his personal conduct; he appeared to fit well into the little world of the Greenwich schools and aspired to the headship of the Nautical school in the event of Riddle's retirement. Like Hartnoll he had some literary attainments. He also read Latin and French with facility. Graham's dispute with Sharp arose in November 1841 over the supervision duties required at meal times; the latter produced a surgeon's note advising that on grounds of health he should be exempted from this task. Graham wrote despairingly to the Governor asking how he was supposed to discharge his out of school duties when his colleagues claimed illness as an excuse for absence. Stopford's reply was not overly helpful: 'you must manage as well as you can without them.'[8]

But even before then Hartnoll had expanded the clash with Graham way beyond the performance of duties. On 11 October 1841 he wrote a vitriolic letter to the Governor stating that he considered the new teaching procedures in the Upper and Nautical schools impractical and that the effect of broadening the syllabus, at the expense of nautical instruction, would be prejudicial to the nation's maritime interest. He knew better than Graham what the Greenwich schools needed and he knew best how to provide the education required for a lower cost. 'If, in reward of my long service, the management of the Upper school had been entrusted to my hands,' he chided Stopford, 'I feel confident its particular objects would have been better sustained than they can be under the new arrangements.' His bitterness at being passed over had in no way diminished. He was, he inveighed, 'deprived of promotion by a gentleman who is my junior in age and who is not my superior in any one quality which can give force and effect to the discharge of the duties of his office.'[9] He faced the prospect of ending his career in an establishment which was deviating from its purpose under the guise of educational experimentation.

By January 1842 news of Graham's difficulties with his senior staff had filtered back to the Committee of Council where Kay-Shuttleworth, as usual, decided to give his support to an educational reformer in conflict with outdated practice. Writing as a member of the Greenwich schools committee, he expressed to the Admiralty full confidence in Graham's literary and mathematical attainments and his competence as headmaster. Perhaps, as head, he was not accustomed to maintaining order in such a large establishment, Kay-Shuttleworth conceded; all the greater reason, though, for expecting prompt and efficient support from his subordinates. The committee was sorry to hear that this had not been forthcoming. Kay-Shuttleworth knew that the Admiralty was unhappy about deteriorating discipline in the Upper school and that it was considering a reorganisation requiring Graham's dismissal. He therefore introduced an alternative: 'removing the second and third masters.'[10] This put the navy in a difficult position. Did it back up the authority of the man in charge or did it countenance mutiny among those placed under him?

Stopford had no confidence in Graham but he was a stickler for naval discipline. On 17 January he wrote sharply to Hartnoll informing him that the headmaster had complained of a lack of punctuality in attending classes and, on occasions, an absence from school without prior permission. This would have to stop. Hartnoll then much simplified the problem by continuing his disobedience even in the face of the Governor's warning. On 11 April Graham wrote to Stopford again to complain of insubordination, this time by both Hartnoll and Sharp. Neither would perform their out of school supervision duties. Hartnoll simply disappeared on one occasion while Sharp, notwithstanding previous reproaches from the headmaster, ignored instructions as he pleased. 'I am reduced to the alternative of allowing the school to fall into disorganisation or take upon myself Mr Sharp's duty,' he wrote gloomily; 'I have chosen the latter.' On the previous day both Hartnoll and Sharp had missed their morning classes for religious instruction and neither had even troubled to send an explanation. 'The conduct of these gentlemen has placed me in a very painful as well as trying position,' Graham observed; they were 'neglectful of their duty, inattentive to the regulations, give an example of gross insubordination, and set at defiance not only my authority but that of the Governor himself.'[11]

The complaints were all passed on to Herbert. Stopford added that he hoped the Admiralty would now do something about the 'negligence and disobedience' of the second and third masters.[12] He assured Herbert that he had already demanded explanations of conduct from Hartnoll and Sharp. But the Governor was intriguing on his own account and was, in fact, using the bad behaviour of the two masters to manoeuvre Graham out of the school. On 19 March Sharp had tendered his resignation because of the onerous out of school duties. He wrote openly to Stopford that he could no longer continue in the Upper school in such a manner as would befit the institution and that he did not wish to become an obstacle to the implementation of change in the educational regime. Stopford sat on the letter, hoping that the out of school duties to which Sharp referred would soon be removed from the masters and returned to the drill-serjeants; Sharp would then change his mind 'provided Mr Graham leaves the school.' On 28 March Stopford informed the Admiralty that 'the Upper Greenwich school is in a disorganised state and I should recommend the Rev. Mr Fisher, the chaplain, to be placed at its head,'[13] As late as 16 April, and despite Hartnoll's persistent challenge to his own authority, Stopford still kept the option in play of retaining Hartnoll and dismissing Graham. Although he did not condone Hartnoll's insubordination or the language of recrimination which the latter had used against Graham, Stopford went no further, when writing to the Admiralty, than explaining that 'it was impossible for these two persons to act together with any benefit to the school.'[14] Hartnoll did not lack influential allies in the struggle at Greenwich. His difficulties arose too often from his own impulsive and impertinent manner which made it increasingly hard to help him.

Hartnoll had direct access even to Herbert. He had an interview in which Herbert took pains to spell out the changes which were taking place at Greenwich. These changes were 'allied with some system of education that had been tried with success elsewhere, and which it was expected would produce corresponding results in these schools.' Hartnoll was not happy with this account of why he had been passed over for promotion and later wrote sarcastically: 'I could hardly place my length of service in opposition to the benefit which it was presumed would arise from the extreme measure of conferring the mastership of the Upper school upon a stranger.'[15] His criticism of Graham went beyond frustrated ambition, however, and he returned to the argument of falling academic standards which he had used in October 1841. He would prove that the new teaching methods did not work. In April 1841 150 boys of equal ability had been divided between the two classes of Graham and Hartnoll and taught exactly the same branches of science and mathematics. Weeks later they were examined for promotion to the Nautical school. Twenty six boys passed the test, of which 19 were from Hartnoll's class and only 7 from that of Graham. What further evidence did the Admiralty require? Graham had later stated that Hartnoll's teaching was not satisfactory. Hartnoll retorted angrily: 'I shewed that Mr Graham did not possess sufficient scientific knowledge to examine my class.'

So acrimonious was the relationship between Graham and his colleagues that by mid-April 1842 every aspect of school business was an issue for disagreement. Graham accused Hartnoll of punishing the boys in a physical manner contrary to regulations; Hartnoll threw back a charge of hypocrisy, saying that such criticism ill became a headmaster who had himself recently smashed several two-foot scales when beating boys while thundering that it mattered not since the institution could afford the breakages. Graham had also sunk into a frame of mind where every petty offence by boys merited equally petty punishments, even to the extent of depriving them of corresponding portions of their food at mealtimes. 'My experience as a teacher enables me to state with confidence that the best mode of preserving discipline among boys is not by frequent and worrying penalties,' Hartnoll advised, 'but by decisive punishment in obstinate cases.'

Absence from class was another topic for exchanging accusations. Graham had already made his complaints against Sharp and Hartnoll known to the Governor; they, in turn, pointed to the headmaster's own failing in not having attended a single lesson in his evening class for over two months. Sharp denied that he had missed any class other than through illness and had provided proper medical evidence. Not only that, but Graham had known that he was ill and should have made the necessary arrangements to cover for him. The head was simply out of his depth, Hartnoll concluded: 'I have been a painful observer of the evils brought upon this school by Mr Graham's inexperience in the nature of its requirements.'[16] Graham had tried to cover his own shortcomings by laying injudicious charges against his colleagues and had thereby destroyed any chance of harmony within the school.

Undoubtedly one element in all this recrimination was physical fatigue. The strains of conducting such extensive duties were taking their toll on all concerned, and especially, it seemed, on Graham. On 17 March 1842 he outlined what had been for some weeks a typical working day. He mustered the boys before breakfast at 7:45 a.m. and superintended the meal between 8:00 and 8:30. He taught in class between 9:00 a.m. and noon. He mustered boys again at 12:45 p.m., supervised their luncheon until 1:30, and then taught again between 2:00 and 5:00 p.m. The boys were gathered again at 5:45 and attended in hall until 6:30. Dormitory supervision was between 7:00 and 8:00 p.m. Besides this routine, he sighed, there was a variety of daily problems always needing his attention. 'I have suffered much in my general health,' he informed Stopford: 'more especially I beg to mention that after 5 o'clock I feel myself much exhausted.'[17]

The message from Hartnoll was, of course, much the same: the pressure on all the masters made the schools dysfunctional and there was no way in which early morning, evening and week-end out of class duties could be satisfactorily divided between them. The different supervision duties, if undertaken as Graham insisted, would leave him only one evening per week to be with his family, Hartnoll observed. 'No man can labour harder than I do for 6 hours in the day, during the greater portion of which time I am standing and talking,' he continued, 'and at 5 o'clock I should be glad of repose, to recruit my energies for the succeeding day's duties in the classroom.'[18] By 5:00 p.m. he was invariably drained from the 'tropical atmosphere' of his schoolroom and his terms of employment should require nothing further from him. He argued too that the authority of masters was diminished by the performance of any non-academic duties. The control of children in halls and dormitories called for 'a robust command incompatible with the quiet influence which a teacher exercises in his classroom.' Teachers were in schools to teach an academic syllabus and not to attend to the daily problems of, and discipline over, those receiving the benefits of a proper education. It was a rejection, in effect, of all that Graham, Irvine and Kay-Shuttleworth were proposing with the new system of schooling at Greenwich.

Hartnoll never hid his distaste for all the changes introduced at Greenwich nor the fact that he had repeatedly asked to be excused out of school duties. Nonetheless he denied that he ignored Graham's directives and insisted that, when absent, he always arranged a proper replacement. Hartnoll wrote to Stopford on 14 April explaining that in his weariness and desperation to operate an unworkable system Graham sometimes saw disorder where there was none and he made out his colleagues to be less co-operative than was in reality the case. Answering a recent charge by his headmaster that he had absented himself from dining hall duties one Saturday evening, Hartnoll had the immense satisfaction to point out that the headmaster of the Lower school, no less, had obliged him by standing in on that occasion and that his assistant had covered for him afterwards in the dormitories. There had been no trouble at all that evening. Graham, nonetheless, had tried to prevail upon one of his young assistant masters, James Bryan, to say that the boys had been boisterous in Hartnoll's absence; to his credit, Bryan had assured Graham that that was not so. In fact, Hartnoll raged, he was the only one who did keep order among the boys during out of school hours and in suggesting otherwise 'Mr Graham has certainly made an ungenerous return for my exertions to repair his authority.' The accusation that he had missed a Sunday class for religious instruction was also a gross exaggeration by Graham; Hartnoll had arrived ten minutes late on one occasion but then extended the lesson by 15 minutes at the end.

Hartnoll went on to alert the Governor to Graham's obvious ploy to rid the Upper school of those who did not share his opinions by presenting them as in a conspiracy against him. By condemning all his subordinates for the same failings, and for the same want of co-operation, Graham could spread the idea that he represented a force for progress while others intrigued behind his back to defend vested interests and old-fashioned methods. 'In coupling my name with Mr Sharp's there is evident intention to produce in your mind an impression that we are acting in some kind of concert,' he warned Stopford. Far from it, Hartnoll protested: 'I requested Mr Sharp to be particularly careful not to introduce to my notice any correspondence whatever that might pass between himself and the headmaster.'[19] All trust between the head of the Upper school and his staff had visibly collapsed. Graham was also in conflict with Bryan whom he rebuked for persistently flogging boys even when ordered not to do so. The fault lay with Bryan, Graham insisted. Bryan was well qualified to teach but he was hopeless at keeping order. Graham regarded Sharp as little more than a liar. Sharp had been 'absent from duty these *three weeks* on the plea of delicate health,' he recorded, 'though, to all appearance, he is going about enjoying the fine weather, while his *unfortunate* class, already much too behind, has lapsed into a state of disorder.'[20] It was hard to see where there was any opportunity for recreating an atmosphere in which these men could work together.

By the end of April 1842 Graham's problems had gone beyond disagreements with his own staff. He also criticised the Rev. Fisher's procedures for selecting boys to enter the Nautical school, alleging that Fisher was, like others, determined to discredit educational reform. The reason for separating the Nautical from the Upper school had been to enable boys in the latter to receive a good elementary education before going on to the specialised mathematics necessary for the study of navigation. Previously the old Upper school had taught almost nothing else but navigational techniques. Fisher now was rejecting many of Graham's pupils as insufficiently qualified while giving preference to those from Hartnoll's class whose knowledge and attainments, Graham insisted, were inferior to those from his own. Fisher argued that Hartnoll's boys had a better grasp of mathematics, which was all that concerned the Nautical school. Writing to the Governor on 21 April, he was unrepentant and savage in his criticism of the Upper school which tried to teach too many subjects and which evinced 'a *total* want of proper organisation in the system of instruction.' In passing even a few boys from Graham's class, Fisher declared, 'I regret to say that I have been obliged to reduce somewhat the standard of qualification.'[21]

On 26 April Graham pressed Stopford for an investigation of Fisher's fitness to examine the boys and scorned the chaplain's assertion that accepting his pupils would lower standards in the Nautical school. His boys were well versed in reading, grammar, geography, algebra and geometry, as well as mathematics; they were therefore better qualified than any others to progress to the specialisation of the Nautical school. Graham showed his utter distrust of all around him by requesting that any investigation should be 'by those who are divested of local prejudice.' He wanted it publicly shown that not only had Fisher acted unfairly by delaying the transfer of excellent boys into the Nautical school but also that Fisher had 'acted as *injurious* to my *character* as *a teacher.*'

Graham took this opportunity of the request for an enquiry into selection procedures to raise again with Stopford the urgent problem of staff insubordination and how it threatened to frustrate the Admiralty's wishes to see a more modern system of education introduced at Greenwich. 'I set out with two masters whose cordial co-operation was essential to the success of the new system,' he reflected: unfortunately both Hartnoll and Sharp held 'a strong prejudice against myself and a hostility to the new arrangements.'

'I have stated frequently,' he continued, 'that while these gentlemen remained there was no hope of a favourable development of the principles of the improved system of education.' Their behaviour towards the headmaster had gone beyond simple disrespect and equivocation; they had proved themselves insolent, vulgar and untruthful to such an extent as to have 'deeply wounded my feelings and injured my peace of mind.' In such circumstances the Admiralty would surely understand that shortcomings in the management of the Upper school could not be blamed on him. 'I have done my duty,' Graham wearily concluded, 'as far as the circumstances in which I was placed would permit.'[22]

Realistically, Graham knew he would receive little support from Stopford. His only hope of finding help lay with Herbert at the Admiralty whom he knew to be personally interested in the quality of education which the Greenwich schools provided. On 2 May Graham wrote, almost in desperation, to describe the woeful standards of instruction now prevailing in the classes of his second and third masters. This had a knock-on effect throughout the Upper school since boys coming up to his class were inadequately grounded in essential branches of their education. The problem lay primarily, of course, with Hartnoll and Sharp, but extended also to H. James, Hartnoll's assistant in the second class, who, much to Graham's surprise, had recently applied for the position of third master. Intellectually, James was inferior to most of the boys in the first class, Graham considered, and lacked any capacity either to teach or examine children. He tried hard but had proved himself quite incapable of managing boys in the Upper school. It was a further illustration of how the difficulties of Graham's position far exceeded anything which the Admiralty had anticipated at the time of his appointment.

As if to prove the point, on the following day the headmaster was called to James' class where he discovered the assistant greatly agitated with one of the boys. James was 'guided by a furious passion' and, in front of the class, insisted that Graham should administer a public beating. Graham declined and begged James to compose himself, whereupon the latter 'threw down his cane and left the room' while protesting the lack of support which he had received from the headmaster. James then sulked and whined that he would not return until the boy in question was properly punished. Graham admitted to Stopford that he had lost control in the Upper school on account of the inadequacy and uncooperativeness of those with whom he had to work. In disciplinary failures, he noted, the fault lay more often with the teachers than their pupils. 'When my masters through *their own inexperience* and *mismanagement* find a boy misbehaving, they *dun me* with leave to have him punished.' When Graham advised that a rebuke would be sufficient, the masters then blamed him for the poor order prevailing in the school. In open defiance of the headmaster's instructions, and in his absence, the other masters had 'made a trial of their own views of discipline by indulging in severity.' 'The consequence of the experiment,' Graham was in no doubt, 'was a complete loss of their influence over the boys, till I had in my own way interposed to restore it.' Even in the face of this failure his colleagues still wielded the rod oblivious of the fact that 'the misconduct of the boys arises entirely from the masters not possessing the gift of managing.'[23]

Stopford's response to the long-running bickering among the masters of the Upper school, and the disorder there among the boys, was to recommend a complete change of personnel. Writing to the Admiralty on 5 May 1842 he surmised that there was no hope of improvement while Graham remained headmaster and he recommended the latter's immediate removal before even a replacement could be named. Fisher and Riddle should be given control of the school in the meantime to put in place whatever arrangements for education they thought necessary. Hartnoll had been so insubordinate that he too should be dismissed; James likewise should not be allowed to continue. Stopford had warned that out of school discipline could not be operated by schoolmasters and was quick to point out to Herbert that he was now proved correct. However, running alongside the conflicts in the Upper school was another protracted dispute at Greenwich which also came to a head in May 1842. In the Lower school there were also serious tensions, not so much between the headmaster and his staff but, more spectacularly for all observers, between Irvine and the naval authorities. Irvine and Lieutenant Rouse, like Graham and Hartnoll, had suffered a deteriorating relationship even to the point that their personal hatred could not be disguised. This clash too undermined all attempts to maintain discipline and therefore became another grievous problem for the Governor and for the Admiralty in London. Its origins also lay in the attempt to introduce the new educational procedures recommended by the Committee of Council into the schools and the appointment of a reforming headmaster.

6 • IRVINE, ROUSE AND THE RETURN OF NAVAL DISCIPLINE

When Irvine joined the schools he established a good rapport with Rouse. The two men seemed friends and Rouse entertained the headmaster at his house on several occasions. In July 1841 Irvine wrote to thank Rouse for the help and kindness shown since his arrival. According to both Rouse and Gordon, Irvine's attitude changed when he learnt that the schools committee intended to do away with naval routine and entrust the headmasters with all aspects of discipline. He began to express a growing contempt for all things naval and later in July he astonished Rouse with the off-hand and unprovoked comment that 'I had a respect for naval officers until I knew Sir James Gordon and Lieutenant Rouse.'[1] Rouse ignored this insolence and did not report it, claiming later that he had no wish to fall out with Irvine or do anything which might work against the new system of control in the schools which the Admiralty had adopted. Irvine made a similar remark to Gordon who was equally bemused. 'Had I not had the interests of the schools much at heart, and considered him to be an excellent teacher,' he reflected, 'I should have suspended him from his duty and recommended the Admiralty to discharge him.'[2] From these reports, Irvine appeared unable to cope with his new-found authority.

Irvine later complained of 'the difficulties, which from the first day I encountered at every step' and described Rouse as a man with whom co-operation was impossible. 'Before I was three months in Greenwich Hospital he treated me so badly in the presence of Sir James Gordon that I had no alternative but to ask the Admiralty for an investigation of his conduct.' That much was true, though Gordon knew what had happened to bring about such a state of affairs. On the occasion of a visit by the acting Governor to the Lower school Irvine had grumbled that his room had not been swept out before the morning class. When

80

Rouse joined them Gordon passed on Irvine's displeasure. Rouse stated that he was sure the pensioners under his authority had swept the room which 'lead Mr. Irvine to consider that he had received the lie direct.'[3] Irvine insisted that they had not and 'in a manner that I considered was not fair,' Gordon observed. 'Mr. Rouse, having a complaint made against him to his superior officer naturally felt hurt, and treated Mr. Irvine roughly.'[4] To head off a formal request for an investigation to the Admiralty, Gordon prevailed upon Rouse to offer an apology. The matter went no further but neither man ever forgot or forgave. As Captain Thomas Huskisson, Rouse's immediate predecessor, recalled nearly two years later: 'that was the origin of the whole split.'[5]

As the weeks passed Irvine ceased to communicate first with Rouse and then with Gordon. By September 1841 he would write only to the Governor, for which he was reproached by Stopford. Early in November another dispute arose between Rouse and Irvine over granting leave to boys. In the past this had been the headmasters' prerogative and had been perceived as a mechanism for reward or punishment. On 1 November, however, Stopford restricted the right of the masters to give leave and transferred it to the Lieutenant Superintendent. Irvine at once complained that Rouse was granting passes into the town for some of the worst-behaved pupils, thereby effectively encouraging them to be disruptive in class. Rouse retorted that the boys to whom he had given leave were the same ones similarly favoured by Irvine himself only a few weeks earlier. On 20 November there was another altercation when, Rouse asserted, Irvine inveighed against him using provocative language in front of one of the nurses. Long before the end of 1841 the hatred between the two men was common knowledge throughout the institution.

The new year merely saw things worsen. On 28 February Rouse wrote Irvine a stiff note informing him that Stopford wished six boys to be birched across their hands for out of school offences. The time and place being fixed, Rouse, as required by regulations, requested the presence of the headmaster or a deputy. Irvine attended and said formally once the birchings were over: 'May I ask, Mr. Rouse, by whose authority you sent for me?' Rouse spat out his reply: 'By the Governor's, I have written it on my note. Look if I have not — if I have not I will, but you will see I have.' Rouse recalled that 'not a word more was spoken.'[6] It was only a matter of days, though, before they were at each other again. This time the issue was not that of the physical control and punishment of boys but, even more serious Irvine considered, that of their moral welfare. Recriminations here were sparked off by the occasion of a theatrical production.

On the evening of 7 March 1842 several of the Upper school boys put on a play *Jack Junk* for the entertainment of their friends and the staff of the institution. Rouse had approved it and attended; he was accompanied by two of his naval cronies, Commander Sulivan and Lieutenant Malone. Hamilton asked Irvine if the Lower school masters might attend, to which the headmaster replied that he did not approve of theatrical performances himself but would not stop others from watching if they wished. Irvine had, in fact, given permission for some of the Lower school boys to be present for fear that he would otherwise be accused by Rouse of obstructing harmless out of school entertainment. Hamilton was aghast at what he saw and heard. One boy was dressed as a loose woman, with looks and gestures to match. Others used language which shocked the young assistant master: 'Oaths, imprecations and asseverations (such as I am happy to inform you I have never before heard uttered by the boys) pervade the whole,' he later complained to Irvine. 'Some of the expressions were all but *lewd*; others quite adequate (without broad assertion) to create in the mind gross and unchaste ideas.' The evening was 'a catalogue of all that was low and loathsome.'

Hamilton recorded the most offensive details of the play. At various times boys exclaimed 'My God', 'Eh Damn me', 'Oh! God', and then progressed to an irreligious ditty whereby the *dramatis personae* ridiculed the Tract Society. Worst of all, Rouse and his friends sat through all this laughing and applauding. Some of the boys in the audience had looked confused and apprehensive, Hamilton considered — and no wonder. In years to come, he lamented, some would doubtless fall in battles honourably fought for their young Queen or else be lost to the perils of the deep and they might *in extremis* recall this evening as having 'blunted their moral sense and led them from the paths of rectitude.'[7] As headmaster, Irvine would know how best to take up the matter with the proper authorities.

Irvine was reluctant to make a fuss to Stopford following the latter's reproach six months before. Hamilton had put him in an awkward position, though, for he could scarcely do nothing in the face of a report from his young friend of such a corrupting influence among the boys. 'I contend against evils which militate against the well-being of the institution,' he alerted the Governor when passing on Hamilton's letter the following day.'[8] Stopford sent the letter on to Rouse for an explanation. Rouse, predictably, refuted all Hamilton's charges. There was nothing in the performance which could possibly be construed as indecent, Rouse reassured the Governor; that was the opinion of Sulivan and Malone too, both of whom were fathers and serious-minded naval officers. Other masters from the schools were also there, he continued: James and Bryan, the assistants from the Upper school, and Willes, from the Lower. None of them had protested. By way of gaining support, Rouse persuaded Sulivan to put his views in writing which the latter did on 11 March. Satisfied that he could demonstrate Hamilton's allegations to be groundless, Rouse confidently explained to Stopford that the only motive Irvine could have in pressing them was 'with a view to my injury.'[9]

Forced, as before, to choose between the headmaster and the Lieutenant Superintendent, Stopford had little hesitation. It was clear that there had been some bad language but Sulivan's assurance that Rouse had cautioned a leading boy in the performance at an early stage against excessive use rather seemed to turn the matter to Rouse's advantage. As for the comic song about the Tract Society, Sulivan offered independent judgment that nothing offensively irreligious had been done. The reference 'might perhaps have been omitted, and being a very old subscriber to that Society myself, I thought so at the time,' he reflected.[10] Nonetheless, Hamilton's disgust was grossly exaggerated. Stopford replied dismissively to Irvine. He had now read the play and could discover nothing of a depraved tendency. 'I must confess that I should be very sorry to possess a mind or disposition which could extract so much imaginary evil from passages in themselves harmless and void of offence,' he concluded.[11] Hamilton was fastidious in the extreme and impertinent in his judgment of Rouse's behaviour. Irvine and Hamilton were both to understand that Stopford would receive no further correspondence on this subject.

By March 1842 tensions among the school authorities were also affecting the behaviour of the boys who had soon spotted the estrangement between Irvine and Rouse and worked out the opportunities for mischief afforded by the change of disciplinary regulations. Escorting a column of boys marching from the workshops back to class, drill-serjeant Aylmer was frustrated by his inability to stop them talking and to make them keep their places. One lad cheekily responded by giving a false name and announcing that he would talk if he pleased. 'This is almost the complaint of every person now who has anything to do with the Lower school boys,' Rouse recorded on 1 April. The boys were in the habit of proclaiming that 'Mr. Rouse has nothing to do with them. Mr. Irvine is their master.' When Rouse sent for the boy who had been impertinent to Aylmer nothing happened, Rouse noted with astonishment; the boy refused to come 'without orders from Mr. Irvine.' Rouse was not having that. 'I sent the serjeant to enforce my orders which he did, and the boy was punished with twelve cuts of the birch over the palm of the hand.' But it had not been easy to bring the culprit for punishment. Seeing Aylmer approach, the boy had run up to Irvine for protection and it was some time before the latter consented to allow Aylmer to lead him away. 'It is clearly evident that the boys have been told by Mr. Irvine that they are not to come to me when sent for without first obtaining his leave,' Rouse fumed. Irvine's annoying interference with naval discipline tended only 'to create mutiny and dissatisfaction.'[12]

Unsuccessful as Irvine's remonstrances to Stopford had proved in the past, he felt the need to write again on 1 April 1842. His pretext was to request a week's leave from his duties. But his reasons for the request were nothing more than a string of accusations against Rouse. Specifically, Rouse had recently inflicted corporal punishment on five unoffending boys from the Lower school. This had been much resented and a great deal of care by the masters had been required to prevent a 'ferment of insubordination.' Rouse seemed determined to return to 'the tyranny exercised by him' when Irvine had joined the school and when, Irvine recalled, 'the birch was in daily requisition.' Freed from such a regime, his school now in class, in the dormitories, in hall and in the playgrounds was an orderly and happy place and he wished to keep it that way. So severe had Rouse's punishments been in 1840 and early 1841 that 'all lament that power should be given into his hands.' He reminded Stopford that in 1841 authority to punish had been given to the chaplain and headmasters 'as a safeguard to the ungovernable temper of Lieutenant Rouse.'[13] The charges, needless to say, were indignantly denied. Stopford replied to Irvine that he had personally ordered a recent birching for insubordination to a naval officer and that the headmaster's request for leave was rejected.

Taunts and accusations about cruelty to the children and the effectiveness or otherwise of the different disciplinary regimes were not just matters for the personal rivalry of Rouse and Irvine. It was obvious to all observers with a willingness to accept reality that by the beginning of 1842 order in the schools had collapsed. Whatever Irvine's claims, the dormitories were almost out of control with boys jumping naked at the windows shouting to passers-by in the road and playgrounds below. The subordinate masters were ill-treated when they tried to intervene and the headmasters were regularly defied. A witness reported the scene late one night with boys 'under the gas light playing at dominoes, others moving about the dormitories lifting up their shirts and shewing their private parts.'[14] On another occasion, in January, Bryan was pelted with shoes when he entered one of the dormitories. This followed a fight he had had with one of the boys during the day after which 73 pairs of shoes had been thrown through the windows. Graham was eventually summoned but was met by insulting songs and hissing until he left the room. In the mornings the boys would not wash and were not only dirty but increasingly ridden with lice.

The dining hall was no better. Early in 1842 Irvine was called to restore order when his assistants had failed to do so. He was forced to withdraw to the playground where he asked drill-serjeant Howcroft for assistance. Howcroft refused on the grounds that his instructions did not permit it. 'The dining hall was entirely under the Upper and Lower school masters and wholly out of the jurisdiction of the naval department,' Rouse stated to justify this indifference to the chaos taking place inside. 'Any interference on our part would have been clashing with the masters.'[15] In desperation, Irvine approached John Lethbridge, the Secretary of the Greenwich hospital, who was passing on his way home. 'Mr. Irvine came up to me in a state of great agitation,' Lethbridge remembered, 'and requested I would go into the dining hall, for the boys would not obey the masters, nor quit the hall.' He found the hall 'in a complete state of uproar, many of the boys on the tables and forms.'[16] After an angry address in which he castigated the boys for disregarding their teachers Lethbridge formed them up and marched them out.

The boys of the Upper school rebelled at dinner again in May. 'The whole Upper school was in a state of riot,' Irvine recorded on 13 May, '— boys running about shouting and bawling etc.'[17] The junior masters demonstrably could not keep order. When Bryan had been on duty a few nights before 'he was assailed on all sides by potato peelings and the refuse of the boys' plates,' James observed. 'On the boys leaving the hall, Mr. Bryan was assailed with the boys' wooden spoons to the imminent danger of his body.' He also had his food stolen from his plate. The following evening it was James' turn to receive abuse. He too was attacked with spoons 'one of which struck me on the head but luckily did not hurt me.' It was often impossible to say grace decently amid the noise and disorder and even some of the boys themselves had grown disgusted by the prevailing confusion.

The breakdown of authority soon spilled into the classrooms.

When, on 13 May, James refused permission to a boy who for no good reason had wished to leave his class he watched with dismay how the boy simply opened a window and climbed out, ignoring James' insistence that he return. Bryan meanwhile was wilfully struck in class with a piece of rope tied in a well-practiced turks head. James later noticed that his hat had been deliberately crushed and was then abused by some boys when he enquired of the culprit. Towards the end of the day James confessed that his patience had finally snapped. When an inattentive pupil was insolent during a geometry class he grew so furious that 'losing almost instantly command over myself, I have no doubt that I have bruised him as I was both violent and agitated.' The boy had been struck with the fist on the sides of his head and also on the lip as he had tried to avoid further blows. 'I have not since attended the classroom,' James recorded soon after the incident, 'as I have not felt myself equal to the task of teaching boys so manifestly insubordinate.' 'I trace its source to the dining hall, where the boys, who know that we have no legal command over them except in the classroom, first learnt to disregard us and to treat us with contempt.'[18]

A concomitant vandalism was evident in the schools by early 1842. By April many of the hammocks in the dormitories had been cut down and much of the bedding was strewn all over the floors. Rouse noted also the amount of glass visible nearly everywhere: 'The breakages is now become enormous: it is only a few weeks (I believe within a month) that every square was replaced, and now there are 57 broken on the Upper school side.' The boys were quite beyond the control of any of the masters, he lamented. 'The wanton destruction of property is becoming truly serious, not only as regards the cost, but the effect it must have upon the morals of the children in the schools.'[19]

None of this was lost on Stopford who wrote to Rouse and the headmasters on 10 February about the deplorable state into which the Greenwich schools had sunk and informed them all that he was taking matters into his own hands. 'The insubordinate and disorderly conduct in the boys of the Upper school having reached a pitch requiring immediate restriction; their constant practice of throwing heavy stones and brick-bats in every direction, endangering the persons passing in the neighbourhood,' he decreed, 'and as the masters and their assistants will not, cannot, and certainly do not check these outrages, I feel myself called upon to exercise my authority as Governor in maintaining good order.'[20] He directed Rouse and the drill-serjeants to report to him any boy guilty of disorderly behaviour so that he might be publicly punished. But offenders were not just from the Upper school; Stopford informed Irvine on the following day that some of the Lower school boys had attacked and injured a group from the Upper school and that he should do whatever he could to suppress such disgraceful violence.

Stopford knew that by restoring some authority to Rouse and his drill-serjeants he was contravening Admiralty orders. He explained to Herbert that his directive of 10 February was an emergency measure 'for the purpose of maintaining some degree of order within the school grounds.'[21] But he stressed that more was needed. Proper control of 800 boys required more serjeants and more nurses; until now too much of the general supervision, along with the cleaning work, had been left to pensioner-labourers drawn from the hospital. As the masters had now proved that, as a body, they were incapable of taking responsibility for overall charge of the boys this was the opportunity for the Admiralty to re-order staffing in the institution. Writing to Haddington on 13 February, Stopford recommended dismissing the three assistant masters in the Upper school and the four in the Lower and replacing them with new drill-serjeants. The schools would thereby have just three Upper and four Lower school masters (one for each class in the schools) and, more usefully, a total of eight serjeants so as to provide a realistic proportion of one for every 100 boys. 'A more efficient control over the boys when out of school is absolutely necessary,' he insisted.[22] His scheme would also cost less money. To Haddington and Herbert these seemed impressive arguments for changing the rules.

On 5 April 1842 Stopford pressed Herbert again. He forwarded papers to the Admiralty to show 'how wholly inefficient the assistant masters have proved themselves either to regulate the conduct of the boys in the dormitories or to prevent the wanton destruction of property.'[23] The Admiralty, however, had already been arranging changes after consultation with the Committee of Council. Herbert jotted down what he thought the outcome might be as far as staff at Greenwich were concerned. 'I understand that Mr. Graham is to be advised to resign. That Mr. Hartnoll retires. That Mr. Irvine continues. That Mr. Riddle continues,' he speculated. 'That Lieutenant Rouse will retire and Captain Huskisson be named. I avoid putting these personal matters on record. Dr. Kay has expressed his readiness to recommend a headmaster.'[24] Stopford's instructions, sent out on 11 April, in fact made no specific reference to personnel. The Admiralty instead decided to reconstitute the management of education in the schools.

Herbert confirmed the Admiralty's commitment to 'the improved system of education' and to the measures to implement it which had been adopted in the past 'under the superintendence of the Committee on Education.'[25] In future, though, the Greenwich schools would be run under the inspection of a visiting committee appointed by the Admiralty to consist of two Lords of the Admiralty, the Secretary, the Commissioner of the Office of Woods and Forests, the Paymaster General, the hospital Governor and two others whom the Admiralty judged expert in the inspection of large schools and academies. The schools would be inspected every six months and reports presented to Parliament. Within the schools the duties of staff would be redefined so that the masters retained authority within the classrooms and the dining halls but out of doors and in the playgrounds the Lieutenant Superintendent would take responsibility. In the evenings the masters would conduct prayers but thereafter the drill-serjeants would attend to all matters in the dormitories. The Admiralty partially adopted the Governor's re-staffing proposal: four of the assistant masters would be dispensed with and replaced by extra drill-serjeants. These changes were to be effected as soon as possible.

The revised regulations became operational on 1 May 1842. In practice, however, they were unworkable since they did not adequately allow for the chaos into which the schools had lapsed. On 2 May six of the masters wrote to the Governor explaining why the modifications made were insufficient. Edward and John Riddle from the Nautical school, Hartnoll and Sharp from the Upper, and Edward Hughes, the second master in the Lower school, all attested that their health had failed on account of the onerous burden of supervising boys in hall as well as in the classrooms and in support they provided a letter of endorsement from three of the hospital's medical officers. Dining hall duties, they urged, should, like other out of school activities, be returned to military supervision. 'The wearing, the harassing nature of this attendance materially impairs the energy with which the masters ought to enter on the duties of the schoolroom,' they petitioned. 'They have not a moment for rest or recreation; no time for their own meals, and coming from the heat and effluvium of the hall, they cannot be supposed to have an appetite for enjoying their food.'[26] Interestingly, Irvine also signed the letter though, as he made plain, he was not prepared to concede, even implicitly, that out of school duties were not the proper function of teachers. 'I altogether objected to the different reasons stated in that document for asking to be relieved from the duty,' he pointed out to Gordon, but he had been obliged to recognise that the present arrangements were not working and, with current colleagues, could not be made to work either.[27] On 2 May Stopford wrote to the Admiralty urging the most serious consideration of the masters' letter.

The final straw came with the riots in the dining hall early in May. Bryan's experience of food and cutlery being showered upon him was merely illustrative of the ill-treatment suffered by junior masters in the past eight or nine months, Stopford wrote to Herbert. Complaints to the headmasters had achieved nothing and in desperation Bryan had appealed to the Governor for help. On 13 May Stopford demanded that his letter of 2 May be acted upon and that control of the dining halls too should at once be restored to Rouse. The Admiralty consented and Rouse, his triumph over Irvine complete, resumed authority of the boys there later that month. But Irvine, despite signing the letter with the other masters on 2 May, could not reconcile himself to this and addressed the boys at dinner just before the drill-serjeants began their duties. 'Mr. Irvine told the boys that the drill-masters had no right to lay a hand upon them or in any way to ill-use them, and that he would not suffer it', William Willes, fourth master of the Lower school, later recalled. 'If any of the boys were touched or laid hands on by the drill-serjeants, the boys were to tell them they had no right to do so, and to say that they would tell Mr. Irvine about it.'[28]

Rouse, naturally, was livid and regarded Irvine's remarks as inflammatory and intended to undermine the drill-serjeants. He afterwards approached Irvine when the latter was in conversation with Joseph Kay, the hospital architect, and an engineer visiting the schools, Captain Denison. It was an 'unpleasant collision', as Kay remembered. 'Mr. Irvine was attacked in a very base and needless manner.'[29] Denison later recounted how Rouse had remonstrated with Irvine not to interfere with boys now placed under his control. 'Lieutenant Rouse's manner was overbearing,' he considered. 'I felt for Mr. Irvine at the time. I would not have adopted such a manner myself. I thought it was natural that Mr. Irvine should feel hurt.'[30] Both Kay and Denison observed that Irvine did not reply to Rouse with intemperate or disrespectful language. Rouse might have had grounds for his initial complaint but, as so often, he had weakened his case by his 'infirmity of temper.'[31]

7 · CONTINUING CONFLICTS, MAY TO DECEMBER 1842

Stopford's measures of May 1842 effectively brought an end to one aspect of the new educational system which had been introduced into the Greenwich schools in 1841. The return of disciplinary authority to Rouse and the drill-serjeants did not affect the changes to the syllabus which had been made at the instigation of Graham and Irvine but it did mark the failure of the experiment to place masters in control of all aspects of the boys' individual development. Of course, the naval authorities at the schools had never accepted the Pestalozzian assumption that pastoral responsibilities were the proper function of a teacher in the first place; rather, naval training, as befitted the likely careers of so many of the boys, was far better suited to form the habits of an ordered mind and a due respect for command among the young. That the Lower school took boys from the dregs of society and through its charity raised them from their origins was itself a cause for satisfaction and a justifiable limit on what was necessary. The job of a teacher was to convey basic knowledge and to examine in the classroom.

By reinstating Rouse's authority over out of school activities Stopford hoped for more than simply the restoration of good order in the schools. Behind much of the animosity between Rouse and Irvine in 1841 and early 1842 had lain a mutual resentment of the other's duties; settling so many of those duties now on Rouse would hardly repair the relationship between them but it might reasonably be expected to remove areas of overlapping responsibility and thus some of the opportunities for discord. Irvine's intemperate address to the boys in hall as Rouse took charge was not a good omen for harmony but the hope was that both he and Rouse would tire of their perpetual quarrel and might in future work together, at a distance, for the sake of the institution as a whole. Stopford also hoped that a warning issued to Irvine by Haddington in April 1842 would have some impact. Haddington had visited the schools in the company of Herbert and other members of the Board of Admiralty and had been dismayed to discover the allegations which had been made by Irvine against Rouse. The Board did not accept that Irvine had cause for constant complaints such as he made against Rouse and the naval authorities and Haddington reprimanded him, in front of Stopford, for his uncooperative attitude. Haddington's effect proved short lived. Before the month was out Irvine was lambasting one of the junior officers for beating a boy with a rope — an accusation which on investigation proved to be quite unfounded.

Irvine, not unexpectedly, absolved himself from all blame. He had heeded 'the kind advice of Lord Haddington' and done everything possible to avoid reopening the dispute with Rouse. It was Rouse's language to him in the presence of Kay and Denison early in May 1842 which had made this impossible, however; on 18 May he wrote to Stopford to observe that 'still I find myself subjected to his insults. I have therefore to ask that you will protect me from a recurrence of any such attempts on the part of Lieutenant Rouse to renew hostilities.'[1] Stopford did not reply. Three weeks later Irvine wrote again, this time to protest that Rouse was having the classroom doors of the Lower school watched for several days at a time in order to record irregularities in the hours when pupils were discharged from lessons. Lessons which overran, it was claimed, caused problems for the drill-serjeants when mustering the boys for their recreation breaks. Spying on the teachers in this manner was outrageous, Irvine asserted, and was typical of Rouse's high-handed attitude towards the academic staff. The drill-serjeants could not keep proper control of the boys out of class and so Rouse sought excuses by blaming others. This reopened the whole argument about who was best qualified to understand and deal with children. 'A more wanton or direct untruth was never stated nor framed,' Irvine fumed, than that the masters had failed to control the boys whereas naval authority had now succeeded.

To support this, Irvine forwarded to the Governor a petition signed by all colleagues from the Lower school: Hughes, Gillespie, Willes, and his assistant Hamilton. Breaktimes were meticulously observed, they insisted; it was the drill-serjeants who were always late returning pupils for the next lesson and then returning them in such a state of noise and disorder that much teaching time was wasted in merely settling them down. Since Rouse took charge in May, Irvine confirmed, 'a system of uproar and disorder has been allowed every day.' This naturally increased the difficulties which the masters faced in class and undid 'that order and discipline which were so remarkable while I had the superintendence out of school.' Given the chaos into which all observers agreed the schools had lapsed before May 1842, Irvine's interpretation was extraordinary and might well have been dismissed by Stopford as the outpourings of a man who had lost touch with reality but for the support which his colleagues had uniformly provided. Was it possible that having taken out of school discipline away from the masters and returned it to naval officers the problem was getting worse?

So unruly were boys in the Lower school in early June 1842 that on two occasions Irvine called at Gordon's house to register his concern. Gordon refused to deal with the matter and referred him to the Governor. Irvine knew that he had no credibility with Stopford and that his constant harping on Rouse's failures only lowered his standing in Stopford's eyes. Nonetheless, unsolicited as his comments were, it was his duty to notify the hospital authorities that order in the institution was worse now than ever before and to warn the Governor of 'this other renewed attempt of Lieutenant Rouse (one I fear among too many) *to prejudice you and the committee against me.*' This was not paranoia, Irvine continued. 'I am too rigid a disciplinarian, and too well acquainted with his feelings towards me personally, to leave any duty undone which would afford him the most remote ground of complaint.'[2] Distasteful as it was, Stopford found himself once more caught between the personal feuding of Rouse and Irvine and again required to arbitrate for the sake of maintaining the semblance of a functioning institution.

The revelation that Rouse had been watching and recording class times was embarrassing since it laid the naval authorities open to the charge of intimidating the masters and would be certain to bring censure from Kay-Shuttleworth and the schools committee. Stopford felt he had to offer the Admiralty some sort of explanation, which he did by reference to small differences in accuracy between the hospital clock, by which the drill-serjeants were guided, and those inside the schoolrooms which the masters used. This was why co-ordination of breaks and lessons had grown so difficult. It was not very convincing but it gave Stopford the occasion to vent his frustration upon Herbert. Timekeeping was a petty problem and on the road to a simple settlement, he wrote angrily, 'if Mr. Irvine's incessant exaggeration of every circumstance, all tending to lower and disparage the military authorities, had not interfered'.[3] There were no problems between

Rouse and Graham in the Upper school, he pointed out; all disputes stemmed from Irvine's fertile imagination, the latter having effectively ignored Haddington's warning in April and gone on creating difficulties from the most trifling causes in the hope of discrediting all the naval officers in charge of the schools. Contrary to Irvine's statements, he had found on enquiry that the behaviour of the boys had improved markedly in recent weeks. The Admiralty should feel at ease, therefore, that his decisive action taken in May was producing the desired effect.

Irvine was not deterred by Stopford's dismissive attitude. At the end of August 1842 he took up the cause of boys who had informed him of ill-treatment by Rouse. Since May Rouse had tried to restore discipline by the introduction of ever more draconian punishments; these included the frequent use of iron chains, padlocks and strait-waistcoats for offenders. Irvine cautioned the Governor that if this went on then there would be a mass absconding from the schools such as had occurred in September 1840 when between 60 and 80 boys ran away in one day to escape the regime which Rouse had imposed. This remark reopened an old contention with Rouse who branded it a lie by Irvine which had long since been exposed. Irvine had been spreading the story of a large break-out from the schools in 1840 for over a year: his purpose had always been to damage naval authority and to boost his own case for professional teachers being the proper guardians of children. In fact only 39 boys had climbed over the wall in September 1840, of whom 19 returned voluntarily later the same day. The gross distortion of this incident was one of the failings for which Haddington had specifically reprimanded Irvine in April 1842 and Rouse now called upon the Governor to prevent Irvine renewing this insinuation.

Rouse was also incensed by Irvine's latest accusations of ill-treating boys. In fact, he assured Stopford, none of the boys mentioned by the headmaster had been disciplined at all. Irvine had suggested that one boy had complained of excessive punishment in a letter home, yet Rouse had a letter from the boy's father denying that any letter from his son was ever sent. To Stopford's mind, the evidence was conclusive and he replied to Irvine accordingly on 1 September. By restating his falsehoods about events in September 1840 Irvine displayed 'evil prejudices towards the military authorities' such as the Governor would not countenance. Furthermore, the state of disorder in the Lower school was so marked in contrast to that in the Upper that clearly any discontent among the boys must be a reflection on the teaching staff. 'Instead of supporting the military authorities out of school, you lose no opportunity of deprecating that authority in the minds of the boys,' Stopford castigated Irvine. 'Finding that you maintain and inculcate those opinions of insubordination in spite of the admonitions given you by Lord Haddington and the committee, I shall represent to his Lordship that I consider you a very unfit person to continue at the head of the Lower school.'[4]

Stopford's uncompromising defence of Rouse was born in part from a need to justify his own judgment to revert to naval discipline in May 1842. But there was another underlying factor which inclined the Governor to believe that order at Greenwich was improving as time passed and that niggling complaints by the masters reflected nothing more than a bitter disappointment that expectations aroused by the experimental regime introduced in 1841 had not been fulfilled. Stopford had long been wary of outside interference in the schools. Irvine's behaviour, and the constant trouble which Graham had experienced in controlling the Upper school, merely made him more intransigent and ever more suspicious that the two headmasters were the willing proponents of an educational philosophy expounded by reformers who meant to use his institution to test their theories without any concern for the navy's requirements. He had first expressed these worries in February 1842 when trying to convince the Admiralty that what the schools really needed were fewer assistant masters and more drill-serjeants. His suggestion was, he conceded, 'in the teeth of all theoretical opinions to the contrary'; nonetheless it was by closer supervision and tighter discipline that 'the boys will be more comfortable and better trained for every useful occupation.' As for the recently appointed assistant masters, he had cautioned Haddington, 'I have very good reasons for supposing that they have been introduced into these schools more for the purpose of training them for other schools at the expense of this institution than for the actual benefit of the Greenwich schools.'[5]

Haddington, like Stopford and Rouse, was alert to this danger. Kay-Shuttleworth and the schools committee undoubtedly had their own agenda, a significant element of which was to further the influence of the Committee of Council. The Admiralty came under pressure in March 1842 when Duncannon complained to Haddington that progress at Greenwich was not satisfactory. The schools were overhauled in 1841 because they 'had been suffered for many years to be under a system of education established by Dr. Bell,' Duncannon recorded. Changes had been recommended, yet the manner in which the Admiralty was implementing them 'appears in many respects to be diametrically opposed to the

system on which the late improvements were founded.' Specifically, the schools committee was not satisfied with the method
of inspection which the Admiralty had adopted; in 1841, under
Whig administration, the principle of inspection by one of HMIs
had been granted whereas now Haddington, a Tory minister, was
guided by an inspector appointed by and reporting only to him.
The schools committee was also dismayed to learn in the spring
of 1842 that naval officers at Greenwich wanted a return to naval
discipline.

Duncannon reminded Haddington of what his predecessor had
agreed. In essence, that the system of education adopted in the
schools 'much depends on the supervision of the masters and the
influence they may thereby obtain over the boys.'[6] Returning
discipline to the drill-serjeants was not consistent with this
approach. Duncannon gave three reasons for adhering to the 1841
arrangements for inspection and supporting the authority of
teachers — all of which echoed the views of the Committee of
Council. First, the basis for educational practice in the naval
schools should be the same as the Privy Council had approved
and promulgated for the guidance of other publicly funded schools
in the country where clearly teachers had to be entrusted with a
wider care than classroom duties alone. Secondly, and politically
the most sensitive, the Admiralty should show confidence in the
judgment of the Committee of Council as the department of
government charged with responsibility for elementary education.
Thirdly, given that the annual cost to the tax-payer of the Greenwich
schools was two-thirds the sum of the annual parliamentary vote
for the provision of national elementary education, it was only
right that independent reports of those schools should be laid
before the Commons alongside all the others from HM Inspectorate.
Haddington was indelicately reminded too of the mournful state
into which the schools had sunk under Admiralty inspection
before Tremenheere's visit in September 1840. Clearly, it would
not be easy for the Admiralty to return to conducting affairs at
Greenwich free from outside scrutiny.

Damage limitation was the policy for both Stopford and
Haddington and the latter's response to the schools committee
on 18 March was a model of political tact. 'Let me say, as I have
said before,' the First Lord assured Duncannon, 'how much we
have benefited from the assistance of the Privy Council Committee.'
The Admiralty had no intention of evading the reforms recommended in 1841. Changes would be implemented: 'that will be
so as long as I occupy my present position. Also, I see no reason
why future Admiralty Boards should not wish to do the same.'

Haddington affirmed that professional inspectors were needed to safeguard standards in the schools and that the old system of an annual visit by members of the Board of Admiralty had amounted to little more than a nominal supervision. But the schools did now have a specific committee of management such as could make arrangements for a proper inspector to be appointed; that committee was not controlled by the Admiralty and the inspector appointed would be experienced in the administration of schools and not an officer on the Admiralty's payroll. Inspectors should be independent professional men with reputations within the world of education to protect. This would give their findings great weight with the schools committee and hence with the Board of Admiralty.

These worthy principles exclaimed, Haddington went on to illustrate his particular difficulty with respect to the Committee of Council. The Admiralty had wanted an arrangement with Kay-Shuttleworth whereby an HMI could be engaged for the Greenwich schools but the scheme had foundered on disagreement as to where reports would be presented. This was an important point, Haddington considered. Kay-Shuttleworth had told him that an HMI could only be used if the report was made to the Committee of Council, 'and it was admitted to me,' Haddington emphasised, 'that the object of his reporting to the Privy Council was to give the control of the naval school to the Committee of that body.' Kay-Shuttleworth had overstepped the mark and had given Haddington the opportunity to explain that the Greenwich schools were peculiar and served an important national interest. 'We are convinced at this Board,' Haddington firmly explained to Duncannon, 'that it would be most inexpedient that the boys hereafter to enter the navy and the merchant service should be withdrawn altogether from naval control and discipline.' The navy had no objection to reports on its schools being laid before Parliament. The proper channel for so doing, however, must remain the Admiralty and not any other department of government.

To stave off the Committee of Council further, Haddington made sweeping and largely sympathetic allusions to the enormous progress taking place in the provision of education in Britain in the 1840s. 'Great experiments are now in the course of being made in the education of youth,' he observed. Furthermore, 'it is not for me to dispute the wisdom of the rules laid down by the Committee of Education for the discipline and management of schools.' His only reservation was that insufficient time had yet passed to judge what was best amid emerging educational practice. The great experiments which he so much applauded 'have not yet assumed the form of a regular system having the sanction of long experience to recommend it for universal adoption in all schools of every kind.' He approved the scheme of wider responsibility for teachers which Irvine and Graham had tried to operate at Greenwich. But by March 1842 it was clearly not working well and some authority would have to be returned to naval officers. 'I cannot persuade myself that subjecting the boys to the control of the officers and serjeants in the playground and dormitories can be fairly decried so vital a departure from the system recommended by the committee,' Haddington concluded. 'It will always be in the power of the masters to ascertain what passes in the playgrounds and in the dormitories,' he reassured Duncannon; the Governor would always be there to listen to every reasonable suggestion from the headmasters for the improvement of the institution. After all, the Greenwich hospital was 'a great public establishment and the public have an interest in the prosperity and efficiency of its schools.'[7]

* * *

Staunch as his defence of the naval regime at Greenwich was, Haddington's case continued to be undermined by the problem of enforcement. At the start of a new term in September 1842 the second and third masters from the Upper school had stones thrown at them by boys in the school grounds. On a separate occasion Graham and his third master, Alexander Davidson, were stoned when they went to investigate a disturbance behind the classrooms. Davidson was hit, the culprit identified and Graham demanded the boy's expulsion. Rouse, now firmly back in charge of discipline, refused this on the grounds that the boy's mother was caring for her seven other children while his father served with the squadron recently in action at Canton. In the end both masters had to make do with a formal public apology.

More serious was the disorder which erupted in the Lower school on 17 November 1842 and which again became an issue of contention between the masters and the naval authorities. For staff who had served for over two years at Greenwich this seemed on a par with the organised absconding in September 1840 and more recent rioting in December 1841 when, during two or three days, many windows had been broken on receipt of the news that Christmas leave was to be suspended. Much to Irvine's satisfaction, in December 1841 he had been given the credit for restoring order — initially by the Committee of Council and later, though less willingly, by Stopford. In November 1842, however,

Irvine was on the receiving end of an outbreak which followed the beating of four boys in his class. The incident had been audible in the adjacent classroom where boys, even while singing a verse during prayers, heard Irvine's raised voice and the impact of his rod. At the end of the afternoon on 17 November boys from all four Lower school classrooms gathered outside Irvine's door to hoot and shout out their protest. As usual, glass was broken and the drill-serjeants insisted that they were pressed to keep their unruly charges back from mobbing the headmaster.

Explaining this rebellious response from the boys, William Willes, the fourth master, described the way in which Irvine had been obliged to set aside his own principles in order to keep control in the Lower school. Prior to November 1842, 'the birch was not used, by Mr. Irvine's advice, for some time.' 'This system was persevered in by Mr. Irvine for five or six months until it was found absolutely necessary to resort to corporal punishment to maintain common order,' Willes continued.[8] The boys had become increasingly rebellious because they thought that corporal punishment had been forbidden in the schools. It was difficult to know just how intent on violence the boys were on 17 November. For over 20 minutes they cried out: 'Paddy, will you box; Paddy, will you fight.'?[9] Stones were hurled at the classroom door behind which Irvine and his assistant were kept prisoners for half an hour. Irvine later insisted that he knew 11 of the ringleaders in this riot, but Rouse did nothing since the drill-serjeants swore that so many boys were involved that identifying individuals was impossible.

Irvine's assertion that he received inadequate protection by the drill-serjeants on this occasion inevitably reinforced his endless dispute with Rouse. Bitterness had already resurfaced two weeks earlier when events at the hospital's Festival dinner illustrated more plainly than anything preceding it the contempt which Rouse felt for Irvine. Stopford presided at the formal dinner, the headmasters were invited and, to entertain the naval officers present, 20 of the band boys were brought to play some appropriate music in the library. Irvine was pleased with the boys' performance and, after coffee had been served, walked over to speak with them and to respond to their anxious enquiries as to how their efforts had been received. Seeing Rouse approaching, and wishing to avoid him, Irvine left the boys and moved to one side of the library ante-room. Rouse nonetheless loudly ordered both Harris, the bandmaster, and the Warden of the hospital to clear the room of all persons save the boys. It was obvious to the boys and to all others present that a slight was aimed at Irvine; the latter, though, made no response. Rouse then confronted Irvine directly and called upon him to leave the room. Irvine replied: 'I stand here, Sir, as an independent officer and a gentleman. I am not interfering with anyone, and you have no right nor authority to address me in this manner.' Rouse then shouted out: 'You are beneath my notice!', and ordered the Warden to bring the guard to 'remove this person.' Much ashamed for Rouse's behaviour, the Warden did nothing. Rouse then threatened Irvine that the boys would get no food that evening and, turning to them, declared: 'boys, you can have no supper while this person remains. You will get it some other time.'[10] The boys were then marched off. Irvine returned to the dining room where he spoke to some of the officers who had noticed the fuss and of whom he enquired whether he had appeared to be at fault. Rouse, meanwhile, walked backwards and forwards behind him as if intending to elbow his back. The evening ended with Irvine still in polite conversation with naval officers while Rouse was enquiring if others present thought him to be 'tipsy.'[11]

On 5 November Irvine complained to Stopford about Rouse's 'wanton and rude attack', adding that it was 'but one of a series to which I have been subjected from this individual.' 'As a public servant, as the head of an important department of this great national institution,' he concluded, 'I ask you as the Governor to institute an investigation and to render me that redress and protection from insult which the service entitles me to expect.'[12] Given the witnesses present, Stopford could not deny the incident and grudgingly conceded that Rouse's words had been 'harsh and hasty', meriting a severe reprimand. But he still reproached Irvine for allowing himself to be drawn into a public quarrel. For the Governor, keeping out of the disputes among his senior staff was becoming an important part of his job and he informed Irvine frankly that he did not consider himself called upon to attend to 'the private altercations between two parties who are perpetually at variance.'[13] Irvine had to console himself that his enemy had made a spectacle of himself in public and that even the Governor acknowledged it.

Stopford had a more pressing problem by the autumn of 1842: the Committee of Council and the Admiralty had agreed that the schools should be inspected again. The Lower school was to be visited once more by Tremenheere while the Upper and Nautical schools would be reported upon by the Rev. Henry Moseley. Stopford was not pleased to be facing outside inspections at a time of such low morale and turbulence in the schools and his attitude to Tremenheere in particular was far from welcoming.

The latter arrived a few days before the Christmas break and informed Stopford on 23 December that he would return to complete his work in the new year. Stopford forwarded this letter to Herbert as a pretext for conveying his own views to the Admiralty well in advance of any critical report from Tremenheere. He had every reason to be satisfied with the disciplinary arrangements introduced in the summer and he believed that Rouse exercised his duties in a responsible manner. The Admiralty should bear in mind, whatever Tremenheere concluded, that controlling 800 boys from every description of social background was no easy matter. Stopford therefore trusted that the Board of Admiralty 'will not authorise any fanciful theoretical changes to be introduced which do not tend to improvement.'[14] But, as Stopford was well aware, inspectors from the Committee of Council would investigate not only the effectiveness of discipline. The danger was that they would reopen the wider debate on academic standards and syllabus content at Greenwich which had lain dormant since the masters' authority had been diminished in May 1842.

8 · DISORDER AND RIOT, 1842–43

Stopford was right to be worried about the effect which new inspections might have. Even if he had convinced himself that the division of out of school responsibilities had been put on a more practical basis in May 1842 there was still discord, both among the masters and with the naval authorities, about modes of teaching and examination and about the correct curriculum. Graham and Irvine had undoubtedly suffered a setback in their efforts to reform the Greenwich schools when Rouse resumed control of discipline. Arguments about educational practice, however, were far from over in the summer of 1842 — as Graham reminded Herbert on 14 June.

'I am not actuated by a controversial or intermeddling spirit,' the headmaster confided. 'My sole object is to promote the grand object for which I came here — to establish on a firm and successful footing a sound, intellectual system of education, in accordance with the most enlightened views and recent improvements.' It remained the case, though, that 'my notions regarding education cannot be otherwise than North and South Pole to the views entertained by the teachers who have been long in this establishment, which views appear to me altogether antiquated and obsolete.' His chief complaint was still against the system of examination whereby boys were judged for their suitability for promotion in the schools by those who had neither taught them nor understood the methods of instruction. This called into question a basic principle, Graham insisted, such as he had discussed with eminent teachers in the past. 'No man, however great his learning, or extensive his information,' he had concluded, 'is competent to teach or examine a class unless he has been for several years a *practical, operative teacher.'*

Graham had already identified the problem in his school back in April 1842: it was that the quarterly testing of boys for transfer

101

to the Nautical school was done by Fisher. When last conducting the examination, the latter had again incensed Graham by an offhand remark that academic standards had to be maintained. 'The educational routine of the Upper school is impractical and comprehends too many branches of knowledge,' Fisher then explained condescendingly, 'the attention to which is inconsistent with suitable progress in mathematics and navigation.' This was nothing less than an endorsement of the outdated educational attitudes which Graham had done so much to try to change. It was also contrary to the judgment given by Hall and de Morgan after their visit in November 1841. On that occasion, of course, Graham had not got the support he had hoped for from the two professors, but they had considered nonetheless that there was a 'melancholy ignorance' of the essentials of an English education within the Nautical school — something which Graham was determined to put right by proper provision in the Upper school. Graham again asserted that his boys had a perfectly good knowledge of mathematics and geometry — and a lot more besides. Fisher's assessments, however, pointedly took no account of accomplishments in reading or a command of English grammar; in effect, the chaplain was still strangling reform by persistently refusing to give credit for anything that had not been a part of the old curriculum.

Even the way in which Fisher examined mathematical attainment prejudiced the performance of Graham's pupils. He did not put questions verbally — as had been Riddle's method of eliciting knowledge from boys when he had been responsible for examination procedure. Fisher's method was to dictate a series of exercises in the rules of arithmetic, algebra, geometry and plane trigonometry which he had devised. These exercises, when taken down in the boys' copybooks, had then to be solved on paper in his presence. 'No explanation, not the slightest help is allowed, nor any idea afforded of the manner in which any question, however difficult, is to be solved,' Graham complained. After a certain time, the question, if uncompleted, had simply to be abandoned. 'I submit this is conducting the examination with undue rigor,' the headmaster appealed to Herbert, 'and the impression which such a mode of examining leaves upon my mind is that there is a marked disposition in the examinator to find fault.'

The effect of this, Graham was convinced, was a serious under-performance by boys whom he had taught — doubtless as Fisher intended. 'Everyone the least acquainted with such matters knows the great difference it makes to a class when they are examined by a *stranger* and their *own master*,' Graham stressed. 'How well they may do, when examined in the way they are familiar with — and, when the mode of examination is different from what they have been used to, how perplexed and defective they may appear.'[1] A few simple words of explanation from Fisher would often have been sufficient to clarify what he expected boys to do, but even this was not permitted them. The system of selection for the Nautical school thus, in practice, Graham reiterated, did all it could to undermine his credibility as a teacher. To counter this, Graham invited the Lords of the Admiralty to stay longer in his classroom when next they visited the schools and to see for themselves how his question and answer techniques proved far superior in discovering the real understanding that children had of what they were being taught. He looked to Herbert to persuade his naval superiors that they should make the time required available.

From Graham's behaviour in the summer of 1842 it was plain that the pressures on him were beginning to tell. On 14 July he took the extraordinary step of writing an anonymous letter to Herbert — an almost pointless exercise given that it was written in his own undisguised hand. His anonymous observations also added little to his other criticisms of the academic regime at Greenwich: they did serve, though, as the record of a meeting which Graham had held with Herbert at the Admiralty during the preceding week when he had specifically asked for the opportunity to explain in person the insuperable obstacles which he encountered in the Upper school. His problems with Hartnoll, Sharp and other subordinates had, of course, been understandable at the Admiralty in the familiar context of rank and discipline. Fisher's case, as a senior clergyman, was somewhat different. Between 1821 and 1823 Fisher had also been chaplain and astronomer on polar voyages of discovery before taking up his position at the schools in 1834. As moral guardian of the young, his authority in the schools was considerable even if less clearly defined than that of the masters. The navy was unlikely to feel confident about challenging Fisher's competence to judge education such as Graham wished it to do.

Fisher was, Graham explained, 'most unsuitable' for the task of assessing educational attainment and the fact that he was a clergyman was no justification for him being entrusted with such important work. In an age when authority of the clergy in all aspects of education was seldom publicly questioned perhaps this was why Graham had been reluctant to put his signature to such an assertion. Graham cited two reasons why Fisher's position should be challenged. First, the latter was deeply prejudiced against the change which the headmaster had introduced to the Upper school. 'He openly avows this,' Graham exclaimed. 'He never speaks of it but in terms of contempt; he remarked to me in my classroom that it was all absurdity and that the person who drew it out knew not what kind of education was suitable for this place.' Secondly, Fisher was ignorant about what he was required fairly to examine. He was 'totally unacquainted with the principles of the new system and the recent improvements in education,' Graham continued; 'he is therefore perfectly incompetent to judge of the merits of the scholars who have been instructed on this system — as much so, as an old schoolmaster is incapable of teaching it.' This was unequivocal language and a damning judgment not only of a respected colleague but also of the methods still employed at the schools whereby such a capacity for the obstruction of progress was vested in the hands of any individual. Graham however realised that to be credible he must give some reason why the Admiralty should accept his opinions as more authoritative than those of Fisher.

Graham was not moved by anti-clerical sentiment nor was there any indication that his frustration spilt over into a questioning of the role of the Church or of religious principles as guiding forces in education. Nonetheless, Graham believed that changes were needed everywhere and that a reformed curriculum and a greater professionalisation of teachers were the cornerstones on which improvements must be built. His experience of this in Scotland, he believed, justified his overthrow of the old order at Greenwich. 'It is well known throughout Scotland that the most respectable clergymen resorted to my classroom to observe and acquire the knowledge of my mode of instructing,' he proclaimed, 'that they might be capable of superintending and directing the schools in their own parishes.' Fisher, therefore, needed to be persuaded that what he considered important was but part of a broader educational requirement.

The best hope of support, as the headmaster realised, lay with an appeal to the Board of Admiralty to back up its own decisions: Graham was the man appointed in 1841 to implement the change to a wider curriculum which the Admiralty had wanted whereas Fisher, though a long servant of the schools, was impeding the progress desired. Fisher's refusal to ask boys to demonstrate any knowledge of a general education and his obsession with solving problems in abstract science should thus be interpreted as a challenge to naval authority. Fisher's examinations, both in their difficulty and narrow range, resembled more 'the competition of students for the first honour of the university than of a number of boys whose average age is 13 and a half.' Not only that, but in many cases these same boys on entering the Upper school merely a year earlier had little education beyond a modest capability in reading, writing and the most basic arithmetic. For this last reason alone Graham's systematic approach to all-round educational competence was much in need at Greenwich, whatever opposition it provoked. Fisher examined the boys in such a manner that they were bound to fail, Graham concluded, and then wrote to the Governor regretting how academic standards were falling. To create such a widespread belief, Graham warned, was 'the very object anxiously wished by the enemies of the recent educational arrangements.'[2]

The summer holidays gave Graham temporary relief from his mounting problems in the Upper school. By late September, though, he felt obliged to press again for redress. This time he wrote to Stopford and requested an official inspection to be made of his school. He was grateful that in one important area the Admiralty had complied with his wishes: Hartnoll and Sharp had been dismissed and two new masters were now in place who were expected to work in harmony with the headmaster. There would undoubtedly be significant improvement in the months and years ahead, Graham confidently predicted; he wanted an outside inspection now when the state of his school was at its worst so that the extent of that improvement might be properly measured in the future. Perhaps more urgently, he also wanted an inspection to deal with Fisher who was placing Graham in an intolerable position. Fisher's selections for the Nautical school were 'so much at variance with my own judgment as to excite my surprise and disappointment,' Graham revealed to the Governor. Not infrequently the weakest boys were taken simply because they fulfilled Fisher's myopic criterion. The effect was that some of Graham's ablest pupils were forced to repeat work in the Upper school which had long since been mastered. 'They are only going over the same ground as before,' the headmaster lamented. The final year or more at school was thus in many cases being largely wasted.

To justify his stance against Fisher, Graham expanded on his own educational values and their relevance to the children in his charge. The object of schooling and examination was not to quibble over children's imperfections in narrow areas of accomplishment but to take a perspective of overall competence. He knew his boys were not perfect. 'Several are slightly defective in writing, for instance,' he admitted, 'who, however otherwise talented, never can be taught to excel.' But that was not the real point and Fisher had no justification for his blinkered concern with minutae, under the guise of preserving standards. Graham's pupils were instructed in 'the *essential departments* of education'; they should have the advantage of navigational exposition 'as soon as is consistent with a suitable progress in their preliminary studies.'

Outside inspection and an independent examination of pupils would serve a final function for Graham: it would correct any false notion of low academic standards in the Upper school. Given his past problems with subordinates and his continuing dispute with Fisher, Graham was understandably sensitive on this account and eager to demonstrate that his teaching was effective. Specifically, the problem for the headmaster was that whereas the school was inspected every six months, the examination for entry to the Nautical school occurred every quarter. Many of the best boys were thus always removed from his school before the inspector visited and their accomplishments were always credited to the Nautical school after transfer. This had a demoralising effect on the Greenwich schools as a whole, for any inspector would be 'necessarily led to form an estimate of the standard of education in the institution much below what it really is.' 'Though the elite of a school are not to be taken as a criterion of its general merits,' Graham impressed upon Stopford, 'it is well known and acknowledged that it is only through such, can be shown the full development of the system employed in the school.'[3] All levels of the educational structure at Greenwich deserved their share of acknowledgement for the successes of its ablest pupils.

It was against this background that Henry Moseley arrived at the Upper school to begin his inspection early in December 1842. As both clergyman and scientist, Moseley certainly had impressive credentials for the task. Since 1831 he had been professor of natural philosophy and astronomy at King's College, London and was an authority in those areas of mathematics which much interested the navy as was revealed by the publication of his *Treatise on Hydrostatics and Hydrodynamics* in 1830. In his youth he had briefly attended a naval school in Portsmouth before going on to Cambridge in 1821. At King's, he was a colleague of Thomas Hall and John Allen. Moseley had developed an interest of his own in popular education and was quite willing to address Mechanics Institutes where his explanations of the laws of natural science were always well received. This interest was extended to schools, both from a genuine concern for the improvement of the indigent young and from his own experience with the older boys at King's who were occasionally allowed to attend his lectures.

Moseley was a restless scholar at King's where he found himself increasingly frustrated by a lack of enthusiastic students, low emolument and the inefficiency of college administration. As early as 1832 he rued that 'the result of my connexion with the college has been perfectly ruinous to me.'[4] Six years later he struggled to persuade the college Secretary to compensate him for the cost of equipment broken in the course of experimental work and in 1839 he complained that, despite verbal promises, the college authorities failed to provide the support he needed for the engineering department. In the same year he and Hall became involved in planning the conduct of courses in mathematics, mechanics and chemistry at the new mining school at Truro. More significantly in 1839, he was drawn into the orbit of Kay-Shuttleworth when one of the masters at the Battersea training college consulted first Allen and then Moseley about devising a science syllabus appropriate for the training of elementary teachers. In the summer of 1841 Moseley was asked, albeit unofficially, about science teaching at the Greenwich schools in response to which he advocated specific lessons in mechanics. Although Hall and de Morgan in November 1841 had felt this to be unnecessary, Moseley already had credibility as a man of impartial judgment and important expertise with both the Admiralty and the Committee of Council.

The Admiralty regarded Moseley not only as a very fit authority to report on teaching in the Nautical school but also as just the person needed to arbitrate in the dispute about standards between Graham and Fisher. Moseley, for his part, soon developed a greater interest in the way in which Riddle taught mathematics and the attempt being made to persuade this old and trusted servant of the schools that some concessions to modernity were required. On 13 December Moseley wrote Riddle the most complimentary of private letters extolling the virtues of his class: indeed, he concluded, 'I do not think that the boys of your own class could possibly be better taught on the system you have adopted.' Any observations made were 'with no other than a feeling of respect for your attainments as a mathematician and your zeal and ability as a teacher. I have been much pleased with the geometrical knowledge shewn by some of your pupils. They supply undoubted evidence of the general rigor and efficiency of your mode of geometrical instruction.'

In truth, Moseley stumbled across that which Graham had long suspected: ancient teaching methods and a curriculum in the Nautical school so restricted as to reinforce Fisher's draconian method of selection. Moseley tactfully sent Riddle the authoritative text used for trigonometrical teaching at Cambridge and at King's, and proffered other works, one by his friend Hall, which together could reduce by half the time taken to convey the principles of Riddle's current courses. Riddle was urged to produce himself a short and definitive text in mathematical instruction incorporating the latest ideas with his own — a task for which Moseley deferentially offered his assistance. Diplomatically delivered, the message was discernible enough: Moseley recommended that Riddle should adopt simpler and newer methods of instruction such as had already been introduced in other parts of the Greenwich schools.

Looking at the present state of the Nautical school, Moseley reflected, most of its 368 boys, however good their mathematics, would leave without a full understanding of the principles involved in nautical astronomy or indeed without even acquiring a mere practical knowledge of the subject. In those circumstances, he concluded, 'we are not justified in neglecting to avail ourselves of the most approved methods of instruction and adhering to a system by which the labor of the course is so much increased.' The figures were more damning than any verbal judgment: out of 368, only 17 boys, the top sub-division of Riddle's own class, had a competent command of nautical astronomy. 'I confess that I am not myself astonished at it,' Moseley continued. 'A system by which the same stage of mathematical knowledge might be reached with less than half the geometry and by far easier and fewer steps of trigonometry would yield very different results.' There was more than a suggestion of support for Graham in Moseley's analysis. Any further time devoted to nautical astronomy such as to raise the general level of comprehension would be impossible 'without an improper neglect of other branches of education.'[5]

For all his tact, Moseley failed to persuade Riddle to reconsider his methods. Riddle's response to the suggestion of change was merely an offer to republish his own substantial, though moribund, work on the teaching of navigational techniques; after consulting with Fisher he declined Moseley's invitation to introduce new teaching methods into his school. On 27 December Moseley made plain that he regretted this and urged Riddle to consider the pressing need for improvements which could not be produced by clinging to the old ways. As for nautical astronomy, Moseley explained 'the urgent necessity which exists at the Greenwich school of reducing and simplifying the theoretical part of the course.'[6] For Graham it was a disappointing end to the year. Even pressure from an official inspector seemed unable to break down the entrenched attitudes which prevailed in the Nautical school.

On completing his inspection Moseley submitted a long and detailed report on the Upper and Nautical schools to the Admiralty which reinforced the remarks he had already made privately to Riddle. 'I lament that the masters have not been persuaded to introduce that simplification in the mathematical course. . .which the advancement of scientific knowledge has placed in their power,' he remarked, 'and which the extension of the general system of education adopted in the school seems to require.' Nonetheless, Moseley acknowledged that an immediate change in practice was unlikely. 'However desirable such a change might be in every other respect,' he concluded with an air of resignation, 'it would not in my judgment be expedient to introduce it in opposition to the views of the masters who are to carry it into effect.' During the last year, it could not be denied, difficulties and obstacles to successful teaching had arisen such as were 'common to every change in a long established order of things.'

Moseley also reported that some of the classes were too large. Two of them, each under the care of one master, had over 100 pupils; 'great facilities are afforded to indolent boys to fall behind the rest of the class,' he warned. The solution was more specific attainment criteria for every class, failure to meet which would be punished by three months of attendance at a remedial class to be conducted on the Wednesday half-holiday afternoon. The master in charge of this remedial instruction should be one of the more able and should receive additional remuneration for the work. Circulation within the Upper and Nautical schools was also felt to be insufficient: too many boys spent too long without transfer to a higher class. The expectations of masters were sometimes unreasonable when transfers were considered and there was, in any case, no standard procedure. Moseley suggested an examination of each boy after six months of attendance in a class, success at which would merit a promotion. Although he did not mention names, this was an implicit reservation about how entry into the Nautical school had been restricted by Fisher in the past.

The inspector proceeded to give an opinion on the way in which religion, lunar observations, navigation, geometry, algebra, chart-drawing, writing, reading, spelling, grammar, history and geography were all taught in the Upper and Nautical schools. He was critical that insufficient time was allowed for religious instruction in the latter although he conceded that the Nautical school required another assistant master if all Riddle's duties were to be properly discharged. In the Upper school, Campbell was singled out as an excellent teacher of geometry and Graham praised as an inspiring geography master. Both men were commended for their attention to religious instruction. There was a need for library books to be provided for the masters, Moseley decided, which would not only extend their knowledge but also make available the latest innovations in teaching practice. Recent changes at Greenwich had brought novel methods and new subjects requiring instruction which had sometimes placed masters 'in positions of no little difficulty and embarrassment.' In these trying circumstances most had done well and deserved sympathetic consideration by the Admiralty.[7]

The navy was impressed with Moseley's thoroughness and with his open-minded approach to the disputes between Graham, Fisher and Riddle. Admiral Sir George Seymour, on the Board of Admiralty, concluded that 'there seems *no prejudice* on his part which would sway him for or against the present masters.' But respect for long service was strong and there was no real will to press the inspector's recommendations on the Nautical school. On 15 January 1843 Seymour informed Herbert that 'old Riddle is and has been so good a master that although his method is rusty it will not do to *make him* alter it.' Riddle 'might be coaxed into shortening his road,' Seymour felt, but nothing further would be appropriate. As for another recommendation by Moseley that some measure of advanced navigation and lunar observation might be extended to the whole school, Seymour again accepted the judgment but was sceptical about implementation. 'I hope Moseley is right in thinking it is possible,' he wrote wearily, 'but considering what they are at 11, I doubt if it can be acquired in all cases by 15, but it is right to try.'[8]

*   *   *

By the end of 1842 Graham's persistent representations that he was obstructed in bringing improvements to the Upper school by the innate conservatism of men who were unfit to judge his methods, seemed to have produced little reward. The Admiralty felt unable, even when his views were supported by outside inspection, to interfere in matters of teaching and examination practice. Momentum for reform in the schools was maintained, nonetheless, when, on 30 December, Irvine recorded a serious indictment of moral behaviour among the boys and of the inadequate supervision of their welfare in a report submitted to the chaplain. Irvine had seen boys in the town who, having plainly escaped over the school wall, mixed with young women of questionable character. This was possibly the result of girls loitering unchecked at the school gates where they could communicate easily with boys in the playgrounds. On 29 December three or four Lower school pupils were detected in Nelson Street in Greenwich, one of whom 'took hold of a girl in a libertine way.'[9] Irvine was horrified and beseeched Fisher to use his authority as chaplain to persuade Stopford to tighten up on absenteeism and thus to protect his pupils from such dangers.

Irvine's alarm at what he had seen on the streets of the town, and indeed the nature of his allegations, ensured that the matter would be taken further. Fisher was obliged to pay attention to anything concerning the boys' moral welfare: indeed, he had himself complained to Stopford as far back as March that too many boys were roaming the town and associating with 'idle and worthless people.'[10] He showed Irvine's letter to Rouse and then passed it on to the Governor. Irvine commented sarcastically that he was 'comparatively lately acquainted with the state of morals in England.' After years in Dublin, however, he could safely say that 'the streets of Greenwich present on every night of the week scenes of drunkenness and immorality to be found almost no-where else.' Fisher replied that although he knew absenteeism had been a problem in the past he believed Irvine now to be exaggerating. Rouse, as always, responded angrily to any criticism of his ability to keep order and assured Stopford that this was but another attempt to discredit the drill-serjeants and naval authority in general.

Writing openly to Fisher, Irvine explained that poor discipline exercised over the boys out of school had repercussions for the masters even though their duties had now largely been confined to the classroom. He had noticed of late that the attention of many boys in class was suffering due to increasingly disorderly habits and that the birch was being frequently used to keep order. When Tremenheere had begun his inspection of the Lower school two weeks before, disorder broke out in one of the junior classes: so tired and irritable were the boys that the master could not keep control even with the inspector and Lieutenant Governor in the room. This naturally gave a very bad impression of teaching quality in the Lower school. Tremenheere would soon be back to complete his work, Irvine remarked, 'and I am very desirous for my own character's sake that all should go on well.'[11] Discipline and education, as Irvine and Graham had always argued, could not readily be separated. External inspection of the schools now made all concerned vulnerable to the shortcomings which attended this artificial division of authority.

By January 1843 the Admiralty was thoroughly confused about

the schools at Greenwich. Both headmasters were claiming that proper teaching was nigh impossible, for which they blamed flaws in the structure of in-school authority and out of school discipline. In the course of 1842 the Admiralty had brought in inspectors to try to tackle the former and had changed the regulations, on Stopford's recommendation, concerning the latter but the problems persisted and seemed insoluble. In desperation, it was decided to switch inspectors. Tremenheere was abruptly pulled out of his inspection of the Lower school even before he had a chance to examine the efficiency of the workshops, the value of special instruction provided and the propriety of out of school supervision during gymnastic drills and leisure time. 'Such being the case,' Tremenheere informed the Admiralty indignantly on 7 January, 'I feel that I have been unable to do more than state generally to your Lordships that I found the two junior divisions of the Lower school in a very unsatisfactory condition.' The other two classes of the Lower school, he wrote dismissively, were 'as well advanced as could be expected under the present circumstances of the school.'[12]

Tremenheere's incomplete inspection exposed once again the practical difficulties surrounding Fisher's authority as chaplain and the almost illogical separation of teaching from examination. Graham's problem with Fisher was confined to mathematics and the criterion for transfer from the Upper to the Nautical school. In the Lower school, however, Tremenheere found Fisher insufficiently attentive to religious instruction and moral guidance. There was no record of any spiritual teaching by Fisher predating September 1842. Furthermore, Tremenheere found boys, even after confirmation in the Church of England, who could give no explanation of the meaning of the catechism which they recited. Fisher was furious at this implicit criticism, claimed that he did have records which went back to 1841, and was adamant that it was not his job to teach moral values or religious knowledge but to examine the boys in those areas and thus to ensure that the masters had performed their duties. As for confirmation, the headmasters helped select those boys to be presented to the bishop when the time was right and the fact that they may subsequently have forgotten what once they knew did not mean that they had been improperly examined beforehand. It had to be remembered, Fisher added, that many boys once at sea might never return to a routine of life conducive to entering the Church and that some latitude towards confirmation standards at the schools was understandable.

Fisher was doubtless delighted when Tremenheere's inspection ended prematurely though there is no evidence that he had a hand in bringing it about. The Admiralty's decision to replace Tremenheere was the result of finding Moseley and, following the latter's meticulous report on the Upper and Nautical schools in December 1842, its growing conviction that he was the only man with sufficient academic standing to reorder the schools. On 15 January 1843 Seymour informed Herbert that Moseley had clearly taken great pains to acquaint himself with the work of the schools on which he reported: 'I do not think we shall get anyone more competent for the same job in the Lower school, and much of the information he has acquired will be advantageous to him in executing it.' Fisher gained nothing by Moseley's appointment to inspect the Lower school. The latter was critical of the chaplain's spiritual neglect of boys in the Upper and Nautical schools and had suggested a restructuring of religious teaching throughout the institution whereby boys learnt different aspects of the subject at different times and with this continuous course of instruction being completed in the higher classes. Because this would disadvantage boys who left the schools before reaching the higher classes the Admiralty did not implement Moseley's original plan, but it rejected out of hand Fisher's alternative for an epitome providing elementary material for the junior classes and it adopted instead a modified version of what Moseley had proposed. Fisher's credibility with the Admiralty was certainly lowered as a consequence of outside inspection and the suggestion that he had been slack in performing duties over the years was succinctly conveyed by Seymour in his letter to Herbert. 'The sooner someone has to give religious instruction to the Nautical school the better,' he remarked. With characteristic irony Seymour then asked: 'Is Mr. Fisher too much employed to do it himself?'

Handling the awkward Fisher, particularly on the delicate subject of religious education, increased Moseley's stature further. 'I think considering it was a polemical dispute that the two reverends have come to a right conclusion,' Seymour noted dryly.[13] It was another reason for entrusting Moseley with the inspection of all three schools. There seemed a good chance that recommendations from him would be acceptable to the Admiralty while at the same time the academic establishment at Greenwich could be brought to implement them by the persuasive manner in which he went about his business. Moseley inspected the Lower school early in February 1843 and commented on all aspects of the curriculum which he listed as religion, reading, writing, spelling, arithmetic, grammar, geography, history and singing. He regretted that religious instruction and writing were poorly taught in the

third and fourth classes, the overall academic levels of which were
'very discreditable to the institution.' The standard in the two
higher classes was satisfactory and they compared favourably
with their counterparts in similar schools. 'The masters (Mr. Irvine
and Mr. Hughes) are obviously men of ability, perseverance and
zeal in their profession,' Moseley concluded, 'and the method of
instruction adopted by them appears to be well suited to the
circumstances under which it is applied.' In arithmetic, Pestalozzian
techniques had been adopted with remarkable success: indeed,
he considered, 'the method of Pestalozzi gives to it the character
of a science of demonstration and renders it an easy and an
admirable expedient for developing and for training the reasoning
faculties.' Spelling was taught by writing from dictation and in
the higher classes the writing itself was neat and carefully done.
Etymology and grammar were taught in Irvine's class, though in
their conversation many of the boys displayed little benefit. In
reading lessons the books produced by the Commissioners of
National Education in Ireland were in common use, 'and great
pains are taken to induce the boys to attend to what is read and
to make them understand and recollect it.' 'In these respects,'
Moseley judged, 'the method of instruction adopted in the
Greenwich schools appears to me to present a marked improvement
on that heretofore in use.'[14] The Admiralty recognised that time
would be required for these improvements to be consolidated;
detailed inspection and reporting, even by a man committed to
the task, was a lengthy process and rapid results were not
attainable. Events took a dramatic and unexpected turn, however,
with the outbreak of a riot at Greenwich on 19 January 1843.

* * *

Early nineteenth-century schools were, by and large, rough and
disorderly places where the ethos prevailed that boys governed
and amused themselves when not in class, free from the control
of adult authority. This was not, of course, the thinking of the
naval officers and drill-serjeants at Greenwich but even they could
not entirely isolate the institution from the cult of independence
which pervaded the nation's larger public and residential schools.
Most schools turned a blind eye to the high-spirited excesses of
their boys unless either local residents or parents felt that matters
were sufficiently out of hand that life and property were put in
danger. Fighting, bullying and annoying nearby residents were
intrinsic parts of school culture, as if extensions of the aristocratic
licence such as existed at Eton and Winchester. Even the day boys

at King's College school regularly entertained themselves by throwing stones through any windows within range on Strand Lane and Surrey Street. Since the house on the corner of Strand Lane was a brothel whose occupants spent much time calling and waving to the boys, the headmaster in 1838 despaired of doing much to raise standards of behaviour. By 1840 the school owed £14 in damages to the inhabitants of Strand Lane alone and it was school practice to have all classroom windows wired outside. Another solution to indiscipline, the head implored, was to relocate the lavatories to a more prominent position on the site which would 'place the youths under control and observation from which they are now exempt.'[15] Vigilance, at all times, was the price of a functioning school. Meanwhile, in the school corridors older boys linked arms and ran along flooring any smaller children too slow to make an escape. 'The school was very rough,' an old boy recalled, 'and boys were badly knocked about at times.'[16] The new headmaster at the Merchant Taylor's school in 1838 found to his dismay that at breaks and in the lunch period his boys mostly roamed the streets of central London often from one public house to the next.

In the absence of organised school games before the 1860s and 1870s most energy was expended in bullying the weak and fighting. At Christ's Hospital this was an ordeal for every boy, a former pupil recollected. At Marlborough after 1843 the same was true and when unruly boys were not in conflict with each other they were loose in the surrounding countryside killing squirrels, rats and rabbits or raiding the poultry yards of irate farmers. Stone throwing at passers-by and public drunkenness were qualities displayed by Harrow boys in the 1830s and early 1840s. At Eton, window smashing seemed to be preferred. Arnold had tried to stamp out the worst abuses of rowdiness and intimidation at Rugby in the 1830s with his system of sixth-form praeposters but with only limited success. Organised rioting in defiance of unpopular authority or in protest at the restriction of a traditional privilege was, in many schools, but a small step beyond the normal run of lawlessness.

Eton experienced rebellions in 1768 and again for several days in 1818. In 1832 its head flogged over 80 boys to prevent a further outbreak of trouble. Winchester saw violent disorders in 1793, 1818 and again in 1828. In 1818 the boys had to be suppressed by two companies of soldiers with fixed bayonets. The Riot Act was read at Rugby in 1797 when fires were started and soldiers had to be called. Shrewsbury also saw disturbances in 1818. There was more trouble at Winchester in 1848 and disorder at King's school in London in the same year when restrictions on leaving the premises were introduced. Marlborough produced one of the last such insurrections in November 1851 when several hundred boys smashed windows and refused all discipline for several days. The headmaster resigned at the beginning of 1852.

The riot at Greenwich began early on the morning of 19 January. Amid dense fog the head drill-serjeant, Howcroft, rushed to Rouse's house in the town to report the most frightful behaviour among boys of the Upper school. All windows at the back of the building had already been broken. To limit the damage, Rouse ordered that the boys should be kept in the dining hall when they came in for their breakfast. Rouse arrived as the fog began to lift, lectured the Upper school on its disgraceful conduct and had the boys marched round to the scene of the outrage. Strewn across the ground were the remains of 272 panes of glass. Again Rouse admonished the boys and, when he thought he saw some signs of contrition, ordered the bugle to be sounded for the march into school.

However, when the drill-serjeants returned to duty to supervise the mid-morning break Rouse learnt that the rioting had continued inside the classrooms. Most of the windows in the rooms of Graham and Campbell had been smashed from the inside with marbles or by the boys breaking up writing slates into convenient sizes for throwing through the glass. Gordon arrived in the afternoon and decided to inspect the schoolrooms in the company of Rouse and two of the drill-serjeants. Graham, by then, 'was under such a state of excitement as not to know what he was about.' His response to Gordon's enquiries 'was so extremely violent and implacable that it was impossible to come to any satisfactory conclusion.'[17] Surrounded by the wreckage of the morning, Graham, to the dismay of those listening, insisted that no glass had been broken. In fact, the breakages continued sporadically until supper time when the last stone thrown went through the window of Rouse's office. The bill, of course, would be considerable — as the hospital commissioners complained to the Admiralty. Much money had been spent on the Greenwich schools in the past two years, they pointed out, yet nothing seemed possible to protect property against wanton destruction by the boys. On 11 February the hospital commissioners revealed that in the last few weeks 'we have been called upon for a considerable outlay to repair the consequences arising therefrom.'[18]

The riot brought the ills of the school to public attention in the most unwelcome manner. The report in *The Times* made sensational reading and confronted the tax-payer with an account of naval indiscipline at an institution funded by the state. The pressure for a full investigation of events was irresistible and the Admiralty was quick to appoint a commission of three men for the task. Admiral Sir Thomas Hastings, the Superintendent of the Royal Naval College at Portsmouth, would protect the navy's interest as a senior officer. The Rev. William Webster, the principal mathematics master at Christ's Hospital, was invited to serve and obviously brought to the enquiry experience of conducting a large school and of teaching a syllabus comparable to that which existed in the Nautical school at Greenwich. The Commission would be led by Moseley who had the confidence of both the Admiralty and the Committee of Council and who by now was already familiar with the schools and most of their problems. He was expected to be the dominant figure in the tribunal. In accepting the responsibility, Moseley, at the age of 42, was changing the course of his career.

In the Admiralty's instructions issued to the commissioners on 18 February 1843 Herbert surveyed the background to the predicament which the schools faced. Fleming's report and Tremenheere's inspection in 1840 and the special committee set up to reorder the schools in 1841 were all explained — as was the decision to bring in new headmasters and to place the discipline of the boys under their control. 'All the improved methods of instruction were introduced,' Moseley, Webster and Hastings were assured; equally, 'the headmasters were selected by the committee with great care and upon excellent testimonials.' But, Herbert made plain, this was not to imply any shortcomings in the naval regime at Greenwich. Rouse was also commended to the three commissioners as 'an officer of very high character.' The problem, as the Admiralty saw it, was a lack of harmony and a general ill-discipline within the institution which required thorough investigation. The Commission was to look into all the allegations about excessive corporal punishments, the boys' association with loose women in the town and the reasons for the 'riotous and mutinous conduct' on 19 January. It was to recommend a proper and workable division of authority between the masters and naval officers and to report upon the accusations made by Irvine in his letter to Fisher of 30 December 1842. In concluding the instructions, Herbert felt it right to stress that the welfare of the boys should remain throughout the uppermost consideration. Those in the Lower school merited a special concern. They came from poor and uneducated families, or were orphans, and were frequently disturbed by the depravity of their earlier surroundings. Such boys 'have especial claims on the sympathy and care of those to whom the task of their reclamation is entrusted.'[19] When in doubt, Moseley and his colleagues should be guided by common humanity.

9 • THE COMMISSION OF ENQUIRY, 1843

Moseley arrived at Greenwich to begin the enquiry on 20 February 1843. The first witness called was Irvine who gave a graphic account of the breakdown of control at the schools and the consequences which had followed from it. He had seen young women at the gates and communicating with boys from the adjacent park. In the course of last summer, and since, he had seen and heard boys leaning over the walls while calling and gesturing indecently. In the autumn of 1842 he had seen as many as 20 boys at a time pass through unfastened railings to enter the park, sometimes in broad daylight. He had reported this and other incidents to Howcroft and Graham. Boys also left chapel, as nature required, but did not always return. Even when they were at divine service they often slept, talked, laughed and read irreligious literature. After morning service and in breach of the sabbath, they played at whipping tops and marbles or slid on ice in winter while the drill-serjeants did nothing to restrain them. A tree on the lawn had been torn down by a group of boys, Irvine recalled. He enquired as to the culprits but wholly in vain, for 'the boys who gave the information were beaten by the others.'

Worse still, on Wednesday and Saturday afternoons when the boys were marched to Blackheath for recreation the supervision of the drill-serjeants was quite inadequate. The boys roamed freely until they mustered for supper in the evening. It was at these times that they drifted into the town, entering public houses and, as Irvine harped on, before his own eyes on one occasion taking 'an indecent liberty with one of the girls of the town.'[1] Boys used obscene language in the schools — sometimes to Fisher's female servants. In May 1842 Fisher had complained to Irvine that he did not wish his daughters to grow up resident in the institution. Things had not been this bad when the masters had out of school control of the boys, Irvine bragged. It was Rouse's laxity and omission of duty which lay behind all the problems of recent months.

Irvine was strongly supported by the next witness, Hamilton, who confirmed the high levels of absconding and who had himself encountered groups of boys on the streets of Greenwich and Deptford without any authorisation. Hamilton had not dared confront these boys 'for fear of being ill-treated by them.' He also informed the Commission of beatings and canings by the drill-serjeants. One took place beneath his own window in January 1843 when the cries from a boy were almost drowned out by the sounds of blows being landed and Aylmer's frenzied threat that 'By God, I will give you what you will never forget for snowballing me.' Most disquieting were Hamilton's accounts of unspeakable 'evil' in the dormitories. On his first visit to the dormitories at the end of 1841 he had found several boys together in the same hammocks. He reported this to Irvine and the offending boys were punished by being made to stand out undressed after bed time. Whether the practice had since been stamped out by the drill-serjeants he could not say. On this point, Moseley recorded: 'Mr. Hamilton has not questioned boys because he was in personal fear of them.'[2]

On the following day the commissioners questioned Graham. As head of the Upper school where most of the rioting took place on 19 January and having since had a month in which to speak with his boys about it, Graham was expected to know the explanation. Graham gave the reason for the trouble as an interference with parcels sent to the boys from their families or friends. Indeed, since the boys were not displeased with their masters they had confided to him the following version of events. A pupil in the Nautical school had become drunk on spirits acquired on an illicit trip into the town. Rouse however had suspected that alcohol was being sent into the schools through the post and had decided to search all deliveries. Disturbances began before breakfast on 19 January but then got out of hand and continued throughout the morning, in and out of school, with the drill-serjeants either unable or unwilling to restore order. Graham added pointedly that since the Governor had previously reproached him for interfering in Rouse's disciplinary responsibilities it clearly had not been his duty to try to restrain the boys. After these accounts from the masters Moseley decided that it was time to hear from those charged with the task of controlling the boys' behaviour.

Before interrogating Rouse, the Commission asked for testimony from the drill-serjeants. Most came from Howcroft who had served at the schools since 1841 and who cut an imposing figure as a former Royal Artilleryman. Before the commissioners, Howcroft naturally spoke gently about the boys and insisted that the cane which he carried was a badge of office for them to see rather than an instrument of physical punishment. Boys did go off the heath on recreation afternoons, he willingly conceded, but so long as they joined the march back to the schools they were not deemed to be missing. Relations with the boys were satisfactory, he reported; boys were generally respectful and a touch of his cane now and then was all that was required to keep them up to the mark. He had charge of a dormitory and could state categorically that no perversions took place under his watchful eye. Before his time, though, it was common for boys to transfer their bedding to the floors and for five or six to lie together. Moseley did not wish to pursue this but instead pressed Howcroft on the punishments employed, especially the use of strait-waistcoats and padlocking. Waistcoats were a punishment for stone throwing, Howcroft explained; padlocking boys to furniture in the dormitories for six hours or so was reserved for bed-wetting and misconduct in the dining hall or chapel. Howcroft evinced some sympathy for the young when describing the ill-drained playground and the absence of proper shelter from the elements; indeed on the worst days of winter, he added, boys were probably grateful for any form of punishment which kept them indoors. Howcroft agreed that some boys escaped from the premises in the evenings though he had not heard of any absconding during chapel services. On the sabbath he tried to check the playgrounds since he believed it was 'a bad habit for boys to acquire to treat Sunday as other days.'[3] But, no doubt, they played with tops and marbles when he was not looking. He prevented any form of cricket or football but realistically could do little more.

Rouse gave his evidence on 22 and 25 February. He rebuffed any suggestion that boys could or did mix with women outside the schools though he did confirm that boys sometimes wandered off the heath on recreation afternoons. Doubtless boys occasionally left and entered the premises illicitly, but the rules required that passes be given and he had no reason to believe that they were commonly flouted. Rouse stressed that he played no part in classroom discipline and would not expect the drill-serjeants to enter classrooms even if requested by a master. His duties were entirely out of school, where there had been a marked improvement in behaviour in recent months. Boys were not beaten by the drill-serjeants. He had birched boys caught sleeping in the same hammock but, in general, the dormitories were much better ordered since his drill-serjeants had resumed authority there. He permitted no games or amusements on the sabbath and had received no reports of marbles or tops being used in the playgrounds. Whatever the deficiencies of the schools, Rouse impressed upon the commissioners that no blame could be attributed to him or to those under his command.

After three days of enquiry it was plain to Moseley that he had reached a deadlock between the evidence of the masters and that given by the naval authorities. Each side, predictably, blamed the other for whatever was wrong. When Gordon answered questions he merely galvanised the broad division of opinion. The boys were much better behaved under Rouse than when the masters had control, he insisted: 'it could not be expected that those young and inexperienced men who were appointed as assistant masters could form the boys in order and keep them silent.'[4] Too much had been expected from the masters from the start — as he had warned in 1841. When they had had complete charge their day had commenced at 6:00 a.m. to awake the boys and had not ended until bedtime in the evening. It was only thanks to Rouse's fine qualities that order in the schools had been restored so quickly after 1 May 1842. The recent riot was but an aberration. Rouse had been right to check all parcels entering the schools for alcohol and there was no excuse for the boys reacting as they did.

The Commission continued until the middle of March listening to expressions of entrenched opinion. Graham was recalled and complained of Rouse's habit of questioning boys in his office about the nature of punishments inflicted by the headmasters in school. The effect which this had was 'to diminish the respect of the boys due to their masters,' Graham asserted, 'and to subvert the interior discipline of the schools.'[5] John Campbell, his new second master, then informed the Commission that in practice the drill-serjeants had little control of the boys. He had had stones and insults thrown at him while the drill-serjeants stood idly by and his rooms in school had been broken into several times without Rouse or the drill-serjeants taking any notice. When he first came to the Upper school in August 1842 he had felt wretched on account of harassment by the boys. Things were better now, he explained, because of his own growing authority and the personal support which Graham had provided. 'I don't attribute anything to the Lieutenant or the drill masters,' he added disparagingly. 'The drill masters rather tend to diminish the authority of the masters.'[6] Davidson, the third master, agreed with Campbell while Hughes, from the Lower school, reported the drill-serjeants as largely indifferent to whether the teachers had any authority over their pupils.

The masters' allegations were refuted by the Governor who supported his fellow naval officers. Stopford recalled that when, before May 1842, the masters had been given the opportunity to take full responsibility for the boys they had demonstrably failed and that he had been obliged to recommend that the Admiralty restore the authority of the Lieutenant Superintendent. Looking back, it could scarcely have been otherwise. The burden of work had been too great; in any case, he added, 'the word Master did not convey that authority to the persons having that name, as if they had been of a better class and of a different age.' Stopford was outspoken in his criticism of Irvine who had systematically opposed all military-style discipline in the schools. Irvine was a good teacher but he was unable to work with others. He brooded on petty grievances and then lashed out, usually at Rouse, with exaggerated and libellous accusations. Admittedly Rouse himself could be irritable: after all, Stopford jested, 'no man is perfect.' But he was convinced that Rouse acted in the best interest of running the schools efficiently. 'I am sorry to say,' the Governor advised the three commissioners, 'I think Mr. Irvine is the great and sole cause which has given you gentlemen the trouble to come here.' 'The schools never can go on in tranquillity and due subordination as long as Mr. Irvine continues here.'[7]

Stopford was an impressive speaker and, as Governor, his testimony was bound to weigh with Moseley and his colleagues. Beyond that, however, there were two serious issues which had come to light by early March 1843 which also tended to undermine the evidence given by the masters in their criticism of naval personnel. The first of these were accusations, thrown back at the teachers by the hospital authorities, of cruel and excessive punishments meted out to boys. This dispute had arisen before the Commission was even appointed; on 7 January Rouse wrote officially to the Governor informing him that in December 1842 one boy had received 48 stripes on the belly and 'bare posteriors' from Graham who had subsequently frightened the boy into keeping silent. This beating was much talked about among the other boys who informed the drill-serjeants that Graham had then obscured the entry in the punishment book so as to cover his tracks. Rouse inspected the book and believed this to be so. Initially Graham had not specified the number of stripes inflicted. More recently, the number 12 had been marked in the book 'thus tending to corroborate the story of the boys that there had been a false return.' 'This must, I fear,' Rouse continued, 'have the very pernicious effect of so lowering the headmaster in the eyes of his pupils as to subvert all proper and becoming respect towards him.'[8]

At the hearing, three of the drill-serjeants elaborated on the sufferings of some boys at the hands of their masters. Howcroft had seen cut hands and bruised legs and thighs and had taken some of the worst cases to medical officers in the hospital. Aylmer recalled seeing Joseph Andrews, an assistant master in the Lower school, kicking and beating a boy for no apparent reason. 'I saw him kick the boy twice with a strong kick,' Aylmer reported, 'having previously knocked him down.'[9] Serjeant Sherlock remembered how Bryan had beaten boys using a walking stick with nails driven into its point and how James had administered a thrashing early in 1842 by first knocking a boy into a corner before repeated strikings about the face and head. Equally bad was the punishment of 'mast-heading' whereby an offender was sent up to the crow's foot on the gymnastic pole. Sherlock recalled how on the coldest day of the winter in December 1841 one of the masters had left a boy up there for two hours, after which time the lad was visibly suffering from exposure and could barely get down unaided.

All the masters protested their innocence. Graham dismissed any suggestion that he had inflicted hasty punishments or ever lost self control. He and Irvine both wrote to Hastings assuring him that the numbers of corporal punishments in school in recent months, and while they had been responsible for out of school discipline too, had been low and were all for either six or 12 lashings as in the book. Campbell and Davidson likewise wrote to the Commission to support their headmaster's assertion that no boy had ever been struck on the belly or received 48 blows. But this evidence was not convincing. Three surgeons from the hospital all testified to seeing cuts and bruises well beyond that which any ordinary birching could produce. Notwithstanding their reforming credentials and expressions of humane sentiment, on the issue of cruelty the masters came away from the enquiry with their reputations for protecting boys from an overly severe naval regime seriously damaged.

The second issue which came to light in the course of the enquiry was even more embarrassing, particularly for Irvine, and involved the use of obscene language in class. Complaints had been made by some of Irvine's pupils and had been given credence by the school authorities. Moseley and his colleagues now had the impossible job of discerning fact from schoolboy fiction, knowing, as he certainly did, that a highly respected teacher's career was at once placed in jeopardy. Rouse, when asked if he had known of such utterances, took the high ground by informing the Commission that although he had heard rumours of sexually explicit language used in class he had taken no notice since he could not believe a headmaster capable of such things. Perhaps he should have done something when verbal reports first reached him? 'I find that at the very least there is cause for enquiry,' he continued. After all, he teased Moseley mischievously, 'the headmaster, like myself, would rather meet such a matter boldly than have his character whispered away.'[10]

Accounts of Irvine's language to his class were inevitably based in part on hearsay. Bandmaster Harris reported stories told him by some of the boys and serjeant Wainwright recalled a conversation he had overheard between others. There were variations and inconsistencies in the evidence but, in essence, the allegation was that on three or four occasions in recent months Irvine had addressed his boys in the following ways. When lecturing on the properties of microscopes, Irvine had added that in Ireland there were lenses which could turn a girl upside down so as to reveal every particular. On another occasion, while talking about natural history, he had asked if boys had seen their mothers' 'diddle'. Moseley noted discreetly that the term was a vulgarism for their mothers' pap. In a lesson on etymology Irvine had explained the derivation of aqueduct from its Latin stem, and then gone on to announce, by way of example, that 'our cocks were aqueducts.' Irvine denied all this and stated that he had no objection to the boys in question being called to give evidence against him.

Moseley called 15 boys before the Commission — the boys 'being selected for their good character.' Some had no recollection of improper language while others reiterated the asides made during the natural history and etymology lessons. Other incidents of impropriety came to light too: Irvine had asked boys with hands in pockets whether they were holding their 'cocks'. Most boys remembered one incident especially which had taken place during a lesson on the properties of the compass. Irvine had asked: 'if we were to go out into the ground and turn to the North Pole to make water, which way our little cocks would turn?'[11] But the really damning testimony came from Willes who, as a master, recollected that in a spelling lesson on 17 January 1843 the word belly had arisen, at which point Irvine, in Willes' presence, had asked one of the feebler intellects in the class what was at the bottom of his belly. Everyone was silent for a few moments until Irvine roared out: 'it's a cock to be sure, not a doubt of it.' Willes added apologetically that the boys had all laughed heartily and that 'Mr. Irvine is in the habit of saying things to amuse the boys: he is very facetious as part of his mode of instruction.'[12] Nonetheless, Willes had ensured that all the allegations of boys and drill-serjeants could not now be dismissed as gossip. Irvine realised that he was in serious trouble.

Irvine stuck to his denial of all obscenities save that to which Willes had referred. He decided that, alongside Hamilton, it was best to give his own version of the incident. Hamilton had also been present during the class on the magnetic compass and was specifically asked by the commissioners for his recollection. Hamilton described a dreary lesson in which the boys were particularly inattentive in their answers to Irvine's questions. In desperation, Irvine had brought the class to life with his joke about the North Pole and joined in the good-natured response. 'This excitement seemed to answer the purpose, he, I am sure, intended,' Hamilton pressed upon the commissioners, 'viz. to rouse them from their stupor. This was all that passed.'[13] He had never heard Irvine make any remarks of a licentious nature; Irvine was a model teacher who cared greatly for the moral welfare of all his pupils.

Immediately after Hamilton had given his support, Irvine was asked to account for his behaviour. Willes had placed quite the wrong meaning on his harmless attempts to awaken his class, he insisted, and went on to state that the commissioners should pay no heed to the evidence presented earlier. 'Mr. Willes is dissatisfied with me because I have reported him not to be a competent teacher,' he explained, 'and he is only a master on probation.'[14] In public, Irvine left the matter there and said nothing more beyond dismissing all other accounts of inappropriate language as falsehoods. Afterwards he wrote at great length describing Willes' unsatisfactory service to date and how Tremenheere, after the inspection in December 1842, had reported him to the Admiralty as unfit to teach. 'This, and my having frequently to check him for want of progress in his class, has created a feeling against me which I believe influenced him to make his statement founded on an expression of mine wholly perverted by him,' Irvine concluded.[15] In a further letter on 4 March Irvine again stressed the innocence of his remarks in the spelling and compass lessons, both of which he could now remember after further conversations with Hamilton. Looking back, his words had been injudicious and he regretted their use.

Irvine's real intention in writing, though, was to convince Moseley that there was a conspiracy afoot against him and thereby to salvage his own career. Willes was in league with Harris who had sufficient influence over his band boys as to induce some of them to give false evidence. Willes and Harris well knew of Irvine's bad relations with Rouse and Gordon and that, on production of this evidence, efforts would be made to remove him. From the day the Commission had arrived in Greenwich Irvine's enemies had schemed to discredit him publicly. This had been done, Irvine was sure, 'under the sanction and approval of Lieutenant Rouse who planned and concocted, I verily believe, the whole plot.' Irvine thus placed his future in the hands of the three commissioners who, he trusted, could see how well his duties to elevate the moral and religious tone of the Lower school had been discharged and would wish justice now to be done. 'I cannot but feel deep and intense anxiety relative to the consequences should my character be placed in jeopardy on the evidence of boys well trained as I much fear for the occasion,' he confided. 'As a teacher I would be utterly and irremediably ruined — left without a home, without character, without means, with a small helpless family to support thrown upon the world.'[16]

According to Hamilton, who wrote to encourage his headmaster on 5 March, many of Irvine's suspicions were correct. Hamilton took aside four of the boys to try to discover what pressures had been brought to bear on them. 'I thought it prudent for once to try the weapons used by the originators and sustainers of this foul conspiracy,' he confessed. One of the boys had behaved strangely in class in recent days and this Hamilton believed was because 'he was being trained with the others.' Hughes had helped in this surreptitious investigation and had discovered that another boy had, during the hearing, been kept in the constant company of serjeant Aylmer. When alone with Hamilton, some of those who had given evidence admitted that Irvine's language in class was humorous and incapable of any sinister interpretation. Nonetheless, Hamilton reported gloomily, 'the majority of the boys of Greenwich hospital schools have somewhere or somehow contracted habits of lying such as I have never met elsewhere.'[17] They had been easily led by Harris into believing and saying anything — a point supported by Hughes in testimony at the end of the enquiry on 15 March. Boys might well be induced to tell lies in return for the favours of Harris and thus to secure the privileges which went with membership of the band, he told the commissioners. 'My opinion about the system, which I have understood is going on, is that it would make the very best boys first guilty of exaggeration, and then liars and defamers.'[18]

Huskisson also had reservations about the testimony of boys. 'I think they might be influenced against their masters (particularly the band boys) by Lieutenant Rouse,' he judged. 'The band is kept together by a system of favouritism, and could not otherwise be kept together, and I think its existence has a bad tendency for the schools.'[19]

In a touching reflection on all that Irvine had tried to achieve at Greenwich, Hamilton reported to him the baleful effect which the Commission's enquiry, and the inevitable rumour and speculation which accompanied it, was having in the schools. The banter was that Irvine and Graham would both be dismissed: the former for immorality and the latter for an excessive beating fraudulently entered in the punishment book. The boys were consequently difficult to control in class and disrespectful to all the masters in and out of school. 'I could not but lament that we had accomplished so little after the time we have spent among them, as that they would thus rejoice at what they believe would give others pain,' Hamilton wrote. 'Yet, they are but boys, and the moral guilt of such a feeling rests with those especially who have excited it.' The damage would be lasting, however, if those responsible could not be exposed. 'Any good the masters of the Institution have accomplished will be blighted by these counter influences, and a barrier raised that will effectually prevent their usefulness in future.'[20] Irvine naturally forwarded his assistant's helpful correspondence to the commissioners.

Even with all the depositions before him it was impossible for Moseley to know exactly what Irvine had said and, as important, how he had said it. He had received a good deal of impressive testimony in support of Irvine's character and abilities, though, and had had the chance to see how the conflicting evidence was presented to him. Irvine was helped here not merely by the demeanour of Hughes, Hamilton and his third master, James Gillespie, whose support was so emphatic, but by the scene which Harris had created when questioned by the commissioners on 25 February. Harris had led people to believe that he had heard Irvine's obscenities; when pressed, he admitted that his knowledge was merely hearsay. At this point, Moseley noted, 'he was reproved by the Commission for the loose way in which his evidence was given.' Harris brought the session to an end 'by his intemperate and disrespectful conduct,' Moseley continued, threatening to 'report the Commission to the world.'[21] He then stormed out of the room. When recalled on 4 March, Harris apologised for his unruly conduct. His credibility as a witness though could only have been tarnished.

From the array of witnesses called it was clear that most were interested parties to one of the many disputes and clashes of authority within the schools, or else, like Stopford, had to account for the proper discharge of responsibilities. The commissioners felt that only two men stood aloof from the appalling state of ill-discipline and acrimony which they had uncovered and whose evidence, therefore, was sufficiently disinterested to merit special scrutiny. One was Fisher who, despite his disagreement with Graham, spoke as a former headmaster. He considered that discipline out of school had improved since Rouse regained control in May 1842. The dormitories were chaotic when the masters had been in charge whereas the dormitories and the dining hall were now kept in proper order. He had never seen boys playing with tops and marbles on Sundays and would certainly have complained had he done so. He had seen girls and young women around the gates and walls making signs to boys and had even called the police to remove them. Yet a sense of perspective was needed here, Fisher implied. On the occasion when the police came the girls had started crying and pointing to their brothers inside the school. Investigation of another incident had revealed that a boy claiming to be chatting to his female cousin through the railings had in fact been telling the truth.

Fisher also commented disapprovingly on the behaviour of both Rouse and Irvine. Irvine's temper was 'exceedingly violent', he remarked. When asked if Rouse's conduct was best calculated to produce harmony, he answered at once: 'no, certainly not.'[22] Temper aside though, he found Irvine a man of irreproachable character and a first-rate teacher who would never have used licentious language. He also believed Hamilton to be a young man of great integrity who would not lie to screen his headmaster. Like Huskisson, he was critical of the band and of the poor moral and educational effect it had upon its 18 members.

The other impartial witness was Huskisson who, from retirement, agreed to state his opinions frankly to the Commission. Having been in charge of discipline in the schools during the 1830s, he now stated bluntly that the whole experiment to give complete control of boys to schoolmasters in 1841 and to abolish corporal punishment had been an enormous mistake. Equally, though, he had not seen much improvement in discipline since May 1842. Boys mischievously rang his doorbell and made unruly noises outside his house. Servants and tradesmen from the town did not enter the playgrounds when the boys were there for fear of abusive language and stone throwing; a hail of stones had even greeted his vintner recently, breaking two bottles during a delivery.

He did not think that Graham was a good teacher and, like Fisher, he judged Irvine to have a hasty temper. The same was true of Rouse whose harsh manner made him an awkward man to work with and whose removal from the schools he had actually recommended before he left. Rouse confused drill with discipline, Huskisson explained, and seemed to believe that the more time a boy spent on the parade ground the better his moral character would be. He concluded by stating his belief that the drill-serjeants did their best for the boys, 'but they don't appear to me to have much knowledge of the management of children.'[23]

March 24 was the final day on which the three commissioners met. Hastings wrote wearily to a friend that they had worked for six or seven hours on every day, save Sundays, and that beyond the many sessions at Greenwich they had also met at King's College and at Christ's Hospital to read over all the evidence and to draft a report. Their findings touched on the six allegations made by Irvine as indicating grave deficiencies in the running of the schools. First, they agreed that it had been possible for some boys to communicate with improper persons in the adjacent park and on the public road and they recommended that iron railings should be erected inside the school grounds so as to keep boys further back from the perimeter. Secondly, they concurred that too many boys had been able to frequent the town and that there were insufficient checks at the gates for boys leaving or returning to school after hours. In particular, the band boys had enjoyed excessive freedom to be out of school. It was also apparent that boys could and did climb over the walls and that, in the past, even heightening them had failed to prevent the practice. Thirdly, the Commission regretted that some drill-serjeants had, by their own admission, turned a blind eye to games played on Sundays. Such disrespect for the sabbath could not be condoned, though given that the boys had nowhere to read or even shelter when not in chapel or at meals it was perhaps explicable.

Considering order in the schools, the commissioners rejected Irvine's fourth charge that standards had declined since Rouse had resumed responsibility. In fact, the opposite appeared to be the case. In the dormitories and dining hall the boys were better behaved than when the masters had out of school control. Nor was there any reason to uphold Irvine's related complaint that by passing discipline back to the naval authorities respect for masters in the schools was automatically corroded. The Commission also dismissed his last allegation, that under Rouse corporal punishments had increased in severity. They were more frequent, it was true, but not excessive. The contradictory behaviour of the masters in this matter before May 1842 had also clearly been exposed in the course of the enquiry. On one hand Irvine had tried to abolish corporal punishment: on the other, his own staff had administered it.

The commissioners put as charitable a gloss on this as was possible. Part of the problem, they ruled, was that there was no alternative method of correction for minor offences and so the cane and rod were often resorted to by default. No boy should ordinarily receive more than six strokes of a cane or more than 12 of a rod, and the imposition of such punishments should be restricted to headmasters at the end of a school session. There was no reason why the drill-serjeants should carry canes at all; all were respectable men, the commissioners acknowledged, but were ill-qualified to punish children with the necessary discretion. Moseley and his colleagues were likewise critical of the other punishments which were available. Strait-waistcoats and chaining to dormitory furniture had 'a tendency to degrade rather than reform.' Such measures 'must go far to blunt the moral feelings and brutalize the characters of the boys.' Written impositions, restrictions on leave and detentions would be more appropriate for minor offences, the Commission urged, 'thus diminishing the necessity for corporal correction of any kind.' Even these, however, should only be ordered by the headmasters.

Finally, the reason for the January riot was addressed though in the course of the enquiry this had not proved to be a controversial issue. The trigger undoubtedly had been Rouse's quite justified attempt to counter drunkenness by inspecting parcels entering the schools; the boys had also believed, wrongly, that they would be denied visits from friends. 'Artful ringleaders who have not been discovered worked on the discontented minds of the other boys and led them into rebellion,' the commissioners reported, but they went on to remark that the recent disturbance was not an isolated event. Previous outbreaks of violence in August 1840 and December 1841 could also be explained away, yet 'the Commission cannot but intimate its belief that the true source of the evil is more deeply seated.' The boys were subjected, in general, to too much military drill at the expense of time for natural play and relaxation. Above all, though, were 'the unhappy divisions which have existed so long and so unfortunately for the welfare of the schools between the Lieutenant Superintendent and the headmasters.' 'It is impossible,' the report concluded, 'that these schools should be well conducted whilst the present jealous heats and personal animosities exist between persons whose duties are so interwoven.' Masters ignored misdemeanours committed out of school and Rouse's drill-serjeants refused any assistance to a teacher in the classroom or when otherwise ill-treated by unruly pupils. Bitter divisions within the schools were at the root of all the ill-behaviour in recent years.

This said, the principle of divided responsibility was accepted. The burden of out of school control had proved too great for the masters alone and this had eventually been acknowledged by almost all of them. Rouse and his drill-serjeants thus had a prominent role 'notwithstanding the wretched and baneful spirit of disunion which exists.' The Commission pronounced that the character of the schools was and should remain essentially naval: the origin of the children was naval and most required an early exposure to naval discipline such as would best serve them in their later careers. Pleasing to the Admiralty, too, was the specific recommendation that the schools should remain under the control of senior officers at the Greenwich hospital. This gave firm protection against any attempt by the Committee of Council to wrest control. But at the same time the Admiralty had to put its house in order. It must make plain to any Lieutenant Superintendent that it was his duty to uphold the masters in the esteem of the boys and to suppress at once any signs of disrespect. Any drill-serjeant indifferent to this task should be instantly dismissed. Equally the masters must be told 'that any attempt to overturn the present system by intrigue or to impede its working by a systematic course of provocation' would also lead to their removal.[24]

Not everything was fit for an official report. In addition to their formal conclusions the commissioners wrote privately to Herbert on 24 March. Herbert had asked them verbally to recommend a solution to the personal animosities rampant in the schools — in particular the enmity between Rouse and Irvine. The commissioners were scathing of both. Rouse was zealous in his work but his temper and deportment made him unfit for the duties entrusted to him. Irvine was an able teacher but had been so captious and insubordinate to senior naval officers that he too was ill-suited to serve at Greenwich. The Commission cleared Irvine of charges of obscenity. 'but it cannot acquit him of having used expressions of an unjustifiably coarse nature.' His credibility had been saved by excellent testimonials, in particular one from Kay-Shuttleworth. Rouse was likewise spared further censure by personal support from Hastings. In the end Moseley hedged his bets. If the high personal esteem in which both were held by their respective supporters was to be taken into consideration by the

Board of Admiralty then 'the same lenity which is extended to one of these parties should be equally extended to the other.'[25] There was also no recommendation for the dismissal of Graham since it had been impossible to prove that any boy had been beaten repeatedly on his belly or the punishment book subsequently falsified. For the time being, it appeared that Rouse and the two headmasters would have to continue working together.

10 · MOSELEY TAKES CONTROL, 1843–45

The Admiralty asked Moseley to report separately on the business of discipline at Greenwich. He did so on 31 March 1843. Inevitably his observations overlapped with much of what he and his fellow commissioners had said in their report seven days previously and most of his additional information did little more than list individual punishments of boys in recent months according to the register. Despite all the accusations which had been aired in the course of the enquiry, Moseley felt able to reassure the Admiralty that excesses were not commonplace. Indeed, he judged, the discipline of the institution was administered on the whole with 'much lenity and forbearance.' More than two months after the riot, he believed that decorum now prevailed in the classrooms with masters receiving due respect from pupils and with proper attentiveness shown during lessons. After such a traumatic period stretching back to the summer of 1840, the naval authorities received with great relief an explicit assurance that the schools were at last in working order and capable of delivering an education in keeping with modern standards. 'The Greenwich schools may claim a favourable comparison with other public institutions,' Moseley added, 'where the boys, taken from a different class of society, have had the early advantage of a more gentle nurture and a more careful training.' The Admiralty should bear in mind that most of the boys in all three schools were the sons of sailors and, in the case of the Lower school, 'they have not unfrequently passed their previous lives among the lowest haunts of a sea-faring population.' For such children, moral and religious restraint, and good manners, could not quickly be acquired even under the most progressive system of education.

Moseley used his report on discipline to revisit one issue covered in the findings of 24 March — the status of teachers. While conceding the peculiar character of the institution and the role

133

of drill-serjeants out of school, he did not think it right that a master's authority over boys should be strictly confined to the classroom. Authority 'cannot be placed at one time in abeyance without being impaired in its proper and legitimate influence at every other,' he decreed.[1] The teachers' role as moral mentor and as an exemplary figure required that breaches of good conduct by their charges were always a matter of concern. Moseley disapproved the fact that all too often masters passed through the playgrounds without boys giving any sign of respectful recognition. In August 1843 he was requested to visit the schools again and to report specifically on disciplinary procedures. There had undoubtedly been a further improvement, most noticeably in the Lower school, Moseley commented, though the total number of recorded punishments remained high. He offered no explanation for this. Stopford, however, was quick to apportion blame to petty-minded teachers constantly reporting trifling cases of misconduct. 'In some cases I have found the complainants more in fault than the persons complained of,' Stopford confided to Herbert. 'This must inevitably occur unless the masters practice that tact and occasional forbearance which ensure respect from the boys more effectually than perpetual harassing complaints.'[2]

In July 1843 Moseley conducted his half-yearly inspection at Greenwich during which he gave renewed impetus to the process of reform in the schools. 'The naval service of the country requires not less than any other the union, with scientific attainments, of those general and varied forms of knowledge,' he reminded the Admiralty. In the Upper school it was still the case that too low a level of general instruction was provided relative to the competence expected in mathematics and navigational training. Restricting admission to boys who already possessed a reasonable elementary education was one way of raising academic standards, Moseley argued, even at the risk of a smaller school. The rate of progression from the Upper to the Nautical school was more satisfactory than six months previously, but he implicitly supported Graham's criticism of the manner of selection when he urged that the chaplain might relax the examination still further. The teaching of geography and religion in the Upper school remained exceptionally good, while lessons in algebra, geometry and arithmetic were well conducted in the higher classes. Elsewhere, progress was harder to find. Reading in the third class of the Upper school remained 'miserably bad', with spelling indifferent and writing careless. Trigonometry was poor in all classes. Lessons on the practical rules of science should be provided for the benefit of boys who would never master the higher branches of mathematics or the theoretical principles of nautical astronomy. A school was properly judged by what it could do for its weakest as well as its strongest intellects, although Moseley accepted that teaching mathematics to a class of varied ability posed considerable problems.

The Lower school fared less well in the July 1843 inspection. In the third and fourth classes education had been effectively neglected with attainments in religious knowledge, arithmetic, spelling, writing and geography lamentably low. Some of the weaker boys could barely read, Moseley reported, 'of whom a considerable proportion remain in a state of gross and disgraceful ignorance.' Judged by these classes, the Lower school 'has failed in giving the common elements of an English education to one half of the boys who have resided within its walls more than three years.' Too much time was spent in the workshops on industrial training. Things were better in the first and second classes though in nearly all areas of instruction standards fell short of what was achieved in the Upper school. Even in arithmetic, for which Moseley had held out such hope with the introduction of the new methods of teaching, there were grounds for disappointment. 'I have before expressed my sense of the value and importance of that demonstrative character which the rules of arithmetic have been made to assume by the method of Pestalozzi, as introduced into these schools,' he recounted. The problem was that the boys could not work out solutions on paper when confronted with written questions. 'They are not able,' Moseley noted with consternation, 'to prove satisfactorily in writing, those operations of arithmetic which they demonstrate orally with so much facility.' The only bright spots in the Lower school were progress in singing and the introduction of a course in practical mechanics for the first class in which the theory and practical application of steam engines, water wheels, animals and human labour were all discussed. The spread of scientific knowledge was a subject dear to Moseley. This success at Greenwich demonstrated to him that 'those branches of the science of mechanics which are practically the most important, may be taught as parts of a system of elementary education.'[3]

'I fear that in some respects, and particularly in the recommendations which accompany my report, I may have exceeded the limits of my duty as inspector,' Moseley divulged in a private letter to the Admiralty on 15 August 1843. His work in the last six months had been far greater than anything he had anticipated when he agreed to chair the commission of enquiry. His subsequent inspections of the schools had required, among other arduous tasks, the perusal of a thousand examination papers so as to form an accurate opinion of academic standards. He had acted throughout 'under a deep — almost an oppressive — sense of the responsibility which rested upon me.' 'I need not describe to you the state of disunion, indeed of discord, in which I found the institution,' he recalled, 'not only as to the individuals in whose charge it was placed but as to the two systems of instruction in operation in it.' Moseley had been amazed at 'how much jealousy exists at Greenwich in respect of the strict observance on the part of everybody of the precise limits of his duty.' Since the schools had no academic Principal to whom an appeal in academic matters could be made, much of the burden of regulating the differences between the teaching staff had fallen upon him. 'I have been perpetually appealed to by the masters for advice and instructions,' he reflected.[4] In such circumstances he had been unable to limit himself to the duty of inspection.

It was indeed impossible to avoid being drawn into the intrigues at Greenwich and Moseley, rightly, was given much credit by both the Admiralty and the Committee of Council for his capacity to suggest and advise while retaining the distance appropriate to his office. He inspected the schools again in January 1844, by which time, perhaps inevitably, some voices were being raised in protest at aspects of his recommendations. From the Upper school, Graham wrote to Stopford in November 1843 pointing out that the inspector's proposals were 'quite impracticable as well as unsuitable to the school.' Stopford agreed and informed Herbert at once that there was 'much good reasoning' in the headmaster's reservations.[5] Moseley also upset Stopford by suggesting a lack of vigilance among the drill-serjeants thereby implicitly criticising the Governor and Rouse in the exercise of their disciplinary responsibilities. 'I do not accept this,' Stopford wrote indignantly to the Admiralty. 'I deny too the competence of Moseley to form valid opinions on such matters as boys' discipline out of school, when he can make only temporary visits and gather information from quarters which cannot give him sufficient facts or detail.' Stopford, of course, merely restated the time-honoured complaint of all educational institutions against those authorised to visit and to give opinions. He was, he assured Herbert, quite capable of censuring any of his staff, if necessary, 'without the intervention of the Rev. Mr. Moseley.'[6]

Stopford and Rouse equally objected to Moseley's suggestion that the railings should be raised at the front of the schools so as to prevent absconding. Regardless of the expense entailed, this would disfigure the buildings and give the schools the character of a prison. In any case, as Stopford was frank enough to admit, resourceful boys with local knowledge would always find alternative means of escape if determined to do so. Finally, Stopford was livid in July 1844 that an accusation of excessive physical punishment made against one of the drill-serjeants by the mother of a boy should have been made to Moseley rather than to Rouse as the proper channel of authority. This was not the inspector's business. Moseley 'has clandestinely been informed of it by some means or other from persons supposed to belong to the asylum.'[7] By the summer of 1844 Moseley clearly knew a great deal, for some perhaps too much, about the daily life of the Greenwich schools. On 5 December 1844 Stopford was ordered by the Board of Admiralty to make available to Moseley all notes of evidence relating to the beating, including the testimony of the hospital Matron who had witnessed its immediate effects.

The Admiralty had no intention of setting aside its inspector's recommendations and was anxious to implement almost all the proposals for improvement which Moseley had identified since March 1843. It was naturally concerned at the continuing animosity among academic and naval staff at Greenwich which Moseley had found so considerable as to highlight in his official reports. On 5 June 1843 Stopford was ordered to impress upon all staff at the institution that there must be an end to 'those feelings of jealousy and irritation which appear unhappily to have existed for some time among them. The respect of the boys for those placed over them cannot but be diminished by their observation of these differences.'[8] Stopford wrote accordingly to Rouse, Riddle, Graham and Irvine four days later. 'Due courtesy towards each other is to be observed in all written or verbal correspondence between the Superintending Lieutenant and the masters,' he warned. 'No air of superiority is to be assumed which is always offensive and will not be tolerated.'[9] Even Moseley's observation that the boys were insufficiently respectful towards their teachers in the playgrounds was to be acted upon. Henceforth boys would touch their caps on the approach of a master, the Admiralty decided, and prompt attention would be given to any complaints from masters about out of school behaviour.

Recommendations on discipline were also adopted. The Admiralty informed Stopford that it approved the checks on corporal punishment which Moseley suggested. Only the headmasters and the Lieutenant Superintendent should have authority to use rods or canes and all other physical constraints were to be banned. Instead, detentions, copying written passages and withholding privileges were to be employed for unruly boys, while in the case of those of weak intellect punishments of all sorts should be sparingly applied. The headmasters of the Upper and Lower schools submitted a revised punishment schedule, as requested, in August 1844. Library facilities for both boys and masters were to be extended. Wednesday afternoon remedial classes were introduced in October 1843 such as Moseley had urged for all boys unable to progress in the schools after six months in one of the lower classes. In July 1844 an extra assistant master was appointed for the Upper school in line with Moseley's assessment of staffing needs. At the same time, models of steam engines were being constructed such as would enable classes in practical mechanics to commence.

The Admiralty was likewise swift to make improvements for the shelter and facilities available for boys on the site. Protection from the elements in winter necessitated the conversion of a spacious cellar into a reading and recreational area. Moseley had argued convincingly in the report of 24 March 1843 that only by providing such basic accommodation could boys be deterred from escaping into the town. On 5 June Herbert informed Stopford that for the health and welfare of the boys library and playroom facilities were to be constructed and a separate room was to be made available for the chaplain in which to interview and examine boys in scriptural knowledge and moral development. The estimate for building work came to over £3000 though the Admiralty had no hesitation in confirming the expenditure. In October 1843 it wrote to the hospital authorities urging the completion of the work before the cold weather set in and sanctioning more labour to be employed should this be necessary to keep to schedule. There was only one area where Moseley was unhappy about the way in which his advice was followed: in the Lower school too much time was still being spent in industrial pursuits to the detriment of progress in essential branches of elementary education. In November 1844 he still found this to be the case and complained to Herbert accordingly.

Strangest, perhaps, of Moseley's recommendations was his scheme for the introduction of paid monitors into the schools. Given that monitorial instruction was discredited in the eyes of most educationalists and HMIs by the mid 1840s, this appeared to be a reversion to outdated teaching practice. Moseley justified his proposal by insisting that the schools were understaffed and that using monitors was the only affordable solution to the problem. It would also 'supply a succession of youths qualified, eventually, to fill the situation of masters in the institution.'[10] In fact, Moseley's monitors were more akin to the category of pupil-teachers created three years later by the Minutes of the Committee of Council. He was certainly not advocating a return to methods of mutual learning; rather, he favoured the employment of boys aged 15 who had already progressed through the schools and who would be selected on the basis of their academic attainments, skills in communication and personal qualities. To launch the scheme, and to serve until suitable boys within the schools could be found, the Admiralty appointed two students from the National Training School at Stanley Grove in April 1844. Using these monitors as teaching assistants, Moseley aimed to reduce to no more than 25 the number of boys in any class under the instruction of a single teacher. His scheme operated successfully at Greenwich until superseded by the provision of regular pupil-teachers in May 1849.

Moseley's emphatic support in 1843 and early 1844 for the reforms which had been introduced at Greenwich, and his enthusiasm for further improvements, ensured that much of the work of Graham and Irvine would be continued. In such a crucial area as that of the intimate relationship necessary between teacher and pupil Moseley's philosophy was very similar to that of the two headmasters. 'There must be the separate contact of the mind of the master with the mind of the child,' he asserted, 'the separate study of it; the separate ministering to its wants, checking its waywardness, propping up, and guiding, and encouraging its first efforts.'[11] But for Graham and Irvine this vindication of their work came too late. Both had been obliged to manage their schools under the most trying conditions since the summer of 1841 and the added ordeal of the enquiry in February and March 1843 had visibly damaged their health. Irvine struggled on throughout the summer, but after 17 August 1843 increasingly the business of the Lower school passed into the hands of the second master, Hughes, who by the autumn emerged as the principal proponent of the new system and the administrative talent needed to make it work.

From the accounts of all who knew him, Hughes was a gifted teacher and, like his headmaster, committed to modern ideas about school organisation and syllabus reform. He had taught with Irvine in Dublin in the 1830s before coming to England to serve as second master at Aubin's Norwood institution. Irvine appointed him to the Lower school at Greenwich in November 1841. Throughout the enquiry he stood staunchly by Irvine and on 15 March 1843 testified most generously on the latter's behalf as a professional colleague of long standing. The enquiry also showed Hughes as a realist who was able to accept more readily than his headmaster that the experiment with masters controlling the boys out of school had not been successful and that concessions to the naval authorities needed to be made. Moseley was much impressed by Hughes and in March 1843 was willing to support a candidate for the post of third master in the Upper school solely on the basis of Hughes' recommendation. 'No-one can judge so well of a school master as a school master,' he enlightened the Admiralty, 'and Mr. Hughes appears to me a very judicious and sensible person.'[12]

Hughes set out his own blueprint for the future of the Lower school in November 1843. Responding to Stopford's request for a formal report, he displayed once more that practicality and command of detail which had earlier so impressed Irvine and Moseley. The system of separate rooms for the four classes, each with its own master, operated successfully, Hughes judged. In each, desks were arranged in semi-elliptical form, rising progressively towards the rear of the room so that the master had a view of every pupil and every pupil, in turn, could clearly see and hear the teacher when addressing the class from the front. Sometimes, as in writing classes, it was necessary for the master to pass through the rows of desks to inspect individual work. Otherwise instructions were issued to the class as a whole, such as when to produce slates or relevant books from under the desks. Boys were allocated to classes according to proficiency and this would be reviewed every four months or so by means of an examination by the headmaster.

'The *method* of communicating instruction in these schools is that comprehended under the term of the "Improved System of Elementary Education",' Hughes informed Stopford with evident pride. This was the result of his own disposition, as well as the efforts of Irvine and Graham in recent years, and it meant essentially a commitment to teaching a syllabus of 10 subjects: religious instruction, arithmetic, reading, spelling, etymology, writing, geography and the use of globes, English grammar and composition, English history and music. He stressed his support for the new techniques in teaching arithmetic and writing. In the former, skill in mental calculations took precedence over slate arithmetic. Once basic skills in subtraction, addition, division and multiplication were acquired then practical and 'mercantile' techniques were taught alongside the mathematical principles governing the function of steam engines. 'The system of Pestalozzi is made the basis of this department,' Hughes explained, and the efficiency with which this was now taught had won approval from many of the country's leading educationalists. The great virtue of Pestalozzi's method was that it proceeded by clear steps in expanding the pupils' minds by developing the power of reasoning. 'From the composition and decomposition of numbers it proceeds through a course of nicely graduated exercises to the doctrine of ratios and proportion,' he emphasised. 'It is acknowledged the best known system in elucidating fractional arithmetic.'

In teaching writing, Hughes employed 'the system of Mulhauser which has been arranged and adapted to English school use by the direction of the Committee of Council on Education.' Copy books with horizontal and diagonal lines to guide each stroke of the pen, and a similarly patterned blackboard to display each perfectly-formed letter, were the tools required. When the essentials had been mastered, children progressed to copying whole words and then sentences and paragraphs from dictation. At this stage attention was also given to the neatness of hand and the accuracy of spelling. For reading, Hughes praised the series of five books produced by the Commissioners of Education in Ireland which moved logically from an introduction to the alphabet, through phonetics and syllables, to passages and chapters of ascending difficulty appropriate for reading aloud in class. These chapters contained texts of a religious and moral character but also, in the course of teaching reading, conveyed much valuable knowledge in the fields of natural history, geography, political economy and even poetry. Volume five contained passages and chapters which dealt with scientific subjects and technology. Hughes' greatest love was geography which once again, he stressed to Stopford, should be taught according to strict method as prescribed by modern practice. He began with the exposition of the earth, land, sea and hemispheres, moved on to a consideration of the great continents and then addressed the natural divisions occasioned by mountains, rivers and other phenomena. Nations, their economies and their capitals were next discussed and then ports, harbours, bays and creeks and tides and currents. Hughes believed that no boy should leave his class without knowing 'the causes which render us a great maritime and commercial nation', and understanding the 'invincible courage which has raised us to the rank of *first* in the scale of nations.' 'From the excellence of our navy,' every boy was told, 'the British flag is feared and respected by the greatest, as well as the most remote nations of the globe.' How could Stopford or any naval officer take exception? Hughes' tactful presentation of his educational principles would ensure that he encountered few of the difficulties experienced by Irvine and Graham.

Although he recognised that Irvine and Graham had failed to

introduce into the Greenwich schools a system whereby the moral training of boys was entrusted exclusively to professional masters, Hughes supported nonetheless the reasoning which had underlain their attempt. He certainly held that it was the duty of teachers to order their own lives according to the precepts which they inculcated in their charges: 'The dullest pupil will soon *detect* and *despise* the hypocrisy that *points* one way and *moves* the other,' he reflected. 'Not only should the teacher *give* religious instruction but he should *enforce it by example.*' Hughes' concept of moral development and social training was closely bound up with an understanding of scriptural truths; for him, as of course for most men of his generation, the principles of Christian faith were indivisible from virtue and morality in society at large. True religion, he was convinced, was 'the only sheet anchor which can stay us from ship-wreck amid the storms of passion.' But there was also a discernible social role for the progressive master when tending to the developing individuals placed in his care. Steady conduct in life, a faithful and honest discharge of duty, and an acceptance of subordination were not necessarily ends in themselves; by these means 'even the humblest of the pupils may raise himself to a distinguished position in the estimation of his country.' It was a potentially disruptive message which made many early Victorians anxious about the spread of popular education and indeed alarmed men like Stopford who saw in almost everything preached by the new generation of schoolmasters an implicit challenge to the natural hierarchy of society. Hughes, however, again showed his capacity for presentation and a pragmatic ability to make his values acceptable to men of different persuasions. In his class 'every opportunity is embraced to point out those individuals of humble origin who have distinguished themselves in the annals of the British navy.'[13] No wonder Hughes impressed all those who worked with him.

While Hughes increasingly tended to Irvine's duties in the Lower school, the headship of the Upper school became vacant following Graham's death from tuberculosis early in February 1844. Graham had long been under enormous strain and by the summer of 1843 seemed barely able to perform his duties. There was no sympathy from Fisher, though, and Moseley twice felt himself obliged to defend the ailing head against the chaplain's continued sniping. In July, he responded to Fisher's accusation that boys in the Upper school were unaware of important principles of geometry by asserting that while it could be the result of 'careless teaching' it was certainly not due to Graham's ignorance of what he should have taught. Trigonometry was poorly explained to the boys, Moseley conceded; nonetheless, 'I really think that they understand the few propositions which they have been taught.'[14] In August, Fisher detected gross errors in answers on his examination scripts which could only be the product of uncomprehending tuition. Moseley replied rather feebly that the same boys had done better on a different paper marked by him. 'I mention this to show that it cannot be absolute ignorance upon Mr Graham's part,' he added, 'but something unaccountably slovenly in his method of instruction.'[15]

By then, Graham's deficiencies could have been easily accounted for and at his inspection in January 1844 Moseley reported the headmaster to be seriously ill. After his death the Admiralty acknowledged that the pressures of work and responsibility had contributed to the deterioration in Graham's health and readily agreed to pay a gratuity of £200 to his widow. 'Mr. Graham was, unsolicited by himself, appointed to the said situation, and was brought up from Scotland for the purpose of introducing and carrying into effect a new system of education,' an official at the Admiralty recollected.[16] As second master, Campbell took over as acting head and on 15 February applied for the permanent position. His presbyterianism probably weighed against him, however, and on 27 February the Rev. James Hill was appointed head of the Upper school. On 26 April 1844 the onset of tuberculosis obliged Irvine to ask for six months' leave, at which point Hughes was formally made acting head. Irvine never returned to his duties and was forced to resign due to his failed health in December 1844. As in the case of Graham, the Admiralty showed a fitting concern for impoverished dependents when Irvine was awarded one year's pay on his discharge. On 5 December Herbert informed Kay-Shuttleworth of Hughes' promotion to the headship and of the unfortunate end to Irvine's career at Greenwich. Herbert sincerely hoped that the £200 received 'will enable him to look about for another and more suitable situation without pecuniary embarrassment.'[17] It was not surprising that Moseley reckoned that 'the labours of the schoolmaster tend to shorten life.' 'The schoolmaster's is an unhealthy occupation,' he warned in 1847 when recalling his inspections of the Greenwich schools, 'and his life a precarious one.'[18]

'I believe that our labours at Greenwich have at last borne fruit and the schools there are now in a sound and still improving state,' Herbert wrote privately to Kay-Shuttleworth on 5 February 1845. 'It is to the zeal, ability and tact of Mr. Moseley that these results are mainly owing.'[19] This was undoubtedly true. Moseley had been a force for change in the schools since his first inspection in the autumn of 1842. Since then he had developed an ever greater interest in the promotion of education among the poor and in January 1844 he resigned his chair at King's College for an appointment as HMI of normal schools. The College acknowledged the post as 'an office of so much importance' and congratulated Moseley on his selection.[20] As he soon discovered, the job was not easy. Travelling over 15 miles a day across desolate country roads in all seasons led Moseley to write despairingly in March that 'this weather does not favour the labours of an inspector.'[21] He soon emerged as one of the most perceptive and influential of the Committee of Council's inspectors with a particular concern for standards in teacher training and the need to present education to working class children in ways which were comprehensible to them and allowed for their different cultural assumptions. There was too great a tendency among middle class reformers, he observed, to 'break off a fragment from our own education and give it to the poor man's child in charity.'[22]

Moseley's insistence on properly trained masters and his conviction that a special bond must be developed between the teacher and the growing pupil made him, of course, an ideal external prop for the reforms introduced by Graham and Irvine. In later decades his strong support for teacher training colleges and for a broad elementary school curriculum were, in turn, reinforced by his experience at Greenwich in the mid 1840s. His views accorded essentially with those of Graham on the skills of teaching. Some people were natural instructors, Moseley freely avowed. But for the majority, the qualities required of a good teacher needed to be learnt methodically and then practiced in a professional manner so as to excite a sense of intellectual curiosity among the young. 'If I were asked what constituted a good teacher?', he pondered in 1845, 'I should say an habitual study of the best methods and of the art of teaching.' 'And if it were enquired of me why so few good teachers were to be found?', he continued, 'I should say because so few *study* it; or look upon it, indeed, at all in the light of a proper subject of study.'[23] In 1854 Moseley drafted a syllabus for teacher training colleges which the Committee of Council adopted as the basis for future examinations.

Moseley continued to inspect the Greenwich schools until 1856 and remained broadly satisfied both with their continued progress and with the absolute standard of education which they provided. Visiting in April 1845, he was pleased to record that the curriculum of the Nautical school had been widened sufficiently to allow the ordinary branches of an English education to be covered. He was also much impressed with the state of discipline and teaching in the Upper school under Hill, who since February 1844 had clearly brought to bear the dual benefits of 'an university education with great experience in elementary instruction.' Progress in the Lower school was also remarkable: the proficiency of Hughes' class was 'not surpassed in any other elementary school in the kingdom, and an instructive example of that which may, under favourable circumstances, be achieved in elementary education.' Hughes indeed had fulfilled all his promise and his control of everything in the Lower school was plain to see. 'I believe,' Moseley wrote approvingly, 'that his eye rests upon the progress of every individual child.' Hamilton was also praised for his industry and perseverence as master of the third class where he provided daily proof that perfect harmony and order could be kept among over 100 boys without resort to any corporal punishment. Perhaps the finest achievement was that the lowest classes in each school now catered properly for the needs of their pupils and that the improvements introduced in 1841 and 1842 were no longer confined to the more able children. 'The education of every boy in the schools, down to the lowest in ability and previous acquirements, is now equally cared for,' Moseley assured the Admiralty.[24] For him this was an essential characteristic of effective popular education. He was pleased to report that such attention was still devoted to the intellectually feeble and morally wayward in 1848.

Naturally, not every problem could be solved to the inspector's satisfaction. Moseley suspected that drill-serjeants still punished boys out of school with severe beatings which they failed to report to Rouse. He regretted indeed that drill-serjeants still spent so much time with the boys since they were invariably uneducated men who were wholly untrained and in most cases utterly unable to provide any worthy example to their charges or to assist them on the path to moral Christian manhood. In 1846 he was sorry to record that boys more than ever were absconding from the schools, though he could find no reason why this should be so and suggested that the Admiralty simply regard such behaviour in recent months as anomalous. Even in academic matters, old complaints could never be entirely buried. In 1859 a later inspector revived the suggestion that too many boys were given mathematical training at the expense of their general education, even when clearly not destined for a maritime career. A Royal Commission to investigate the Greenwich hospital in 1860 broadly endorsed the view that specialisation was not appropriate for all pupils. By that time the distinction between Upper and Lower schools had been abolished and the two united into a single academy.

The Royal Hospital School at Greenwich remained a prestigious naval institution throughout the nineteenth century, raising its status and academic reputation after the reforms of the 1840s. Moseley warranted that to be so as early as 1846 when he reported that 'there existed formerly amongst the captains of Her Majesty's ships, and of merchantmen, an indisposition to take the boys, especially those of the Lower school, into their ships. They were accused of being unsteady, and of running away from their ships.' No greater proof could be provided of the transformation at Greenwich than that there had been a dramatic rise in recruitment to the navy and merchant service from the schools, he attested. 'The character of the school would thus appear to be re-established amongst that class of persons whose favourable opinion is of the first importance to their welfare.'[25] In 1861, testimony given before the Newcastle Commission confirmed that 'the Greenwich boys, who are the best educated boys, are also the most amenable to discipline, and are the most sought after by naval officers.'[26]

The Admiralty maintained the Hospital School at Greenwich until 1933, after which it was moved to a new site at Holbrook in Suffolk. Until then, it continued to take up to a thousand boys selected on the basis of their fathers' naval records and that of family distress occasioned by tragedies within the nation's general seafaring community. The school's permanent teaching establishment comprised a head and three further masters while overall supervision of the boys remained with a retired admiral who held the post of Superintendent. Regulations for entry had, outwardly, not changed greatly in a hundred years. Boys were still admitted between the ages of 11 and 14 provided that they could meet the requirements of a test in reading, writing from dictation and basic numeracy. They were to be physically fit for maritime service, however, and were now obliged, through parents or guardians, to commit themselves to service in the Royal Navy after the age of 18.

With the increasing availability of elementary education in the late nineteenth century, providing rudimentary schooling for the destitute sons of naval ratings, as the Lower school had traditionally done, became ever more redundant and the single academy from the 1860s onwards not unnaturally came to justify itself in terms of providing only for boys attracted to service careers. In fact, even as the far-reaching reforms were implemented in the 1840s questions about the future function of the Greenwich schools were already beginning to be asked. Moseley advised the Admiralty in 1845 that 'a good elementary education may now be obtained everywhere at so cheap a cost, that any person who has neglected to procure it for his child may in some degree be considered to have forfeited his claim on the public patronage.'[27] In 1848 he observed again that 'the means of education are now everywhere provided on terms which place it within the reach of every parent really desirous to secure it for his children.'[28] It was a characteristically sweeping judgment. Moseley saw the enormous strides in educational provision being made in Britain and he rightly understood his own labours at Greenwich in that context. Perhaps an institution so much involved with introducing practices of modern schooling during the 1840s was bound to alter. That it did so was, nonetheless, at least in part a response to social changes made possible by the fulfilment of many of the ambitions of those who had been determined to create at Greenwich a model for the spread of effective education to the bulk of the population.

11 • CONCLUSION

Looking back in 1848, Moseley considered 1844 to be the year in which the most memorable improvements had taken place in the Greenwich schools. Reading rooms were opened, libraries of entertaining and instructive books were provided, evening lectures to occupy the boys before bed time were introduced, syllabuses were successfully enlarged and new and efficient masters were at last installed to give effect to all that had been aspired to since 1840. In the same year, he recollected, the instances of absconding and of corporal punishment were both reduced and a proper definition of the masters' duties had removed much of the dissatisfaction felt among the naval officers. It was essential to dwell upon these facts, he mused. Reform at Greenwich, as he well remembered, had taken four years to achieve and had involved a degree of acrimony which beggared belief. Nothing but the success so evident from 1844 onwards justified the trouble which had been taken and the expense which had been incurred.

Clashes of personality clearly played a part in the troubles which afflicted the schools in the early 1840s. Graham and Irvine were both inspired by a reforming mission which left them intolerant of any opposition and dismissive of past practices. Hartnoll and Sharp made no efforts to conceal their frustrated ambitions and the resentment which they felt towards those who disturbed their comfortable routine. Rouse was known to all as a man of ungovernable temper who saw any challenge to his own opinions as an act of mutiny. At different times, the behaviour of most staff at the schools transcended the norms of professional disagreement and personal dislike and exhibited a childish petulance which astonished Moseley and bewildered the Board of Admiralty. Irvine and Rouse were the worst offenders. In November 1841 the former was overheard by several hospital staff screaming out to Hamilton: 'I desire, Sir, that you do not know such a person as Mr Rouse. Mr Rouse has nothing to do here. I don't know such a person.'[1] Earlier, Irvine had been caught erasing Rouse's initials from the discipline book which was presented every week to the Governor. Stopford was dumbfounded at the pettiness to which the headmaster had sunk. 'These little jealousies keep alive a spirit of discord,' he rebuked Irvine, 'which if not instantly suppressed will frustrate the intention of the government in the organisation of the schools.'[2] Rouse's conduct at the Festival dinner in November 1842 was likewise an appallingly infantile display. A few weeks later he was also observed shouting and thrashing the ground with his stick while in argument with the clerk of the works. That men of such seniority should so publicly compromise their dignity in pursuit of their vendettas meant that there was no hope of any working compromise emerging on how best to implement Admiralty orders.

Personal failings aside, both headmasters were dogged by poor quality staff in their efforts to bring about reform after April 1841. Graham considered Davidson, his third master, unfit to teach; Irvine felt the same about Gillespie and Willes in the Lower school. Gillespie was a sincere and hard-working man, Irvine conceded, but he lacked the ability to adjust his teaching to the differing ages of his boys. 'The peculiar mode of teaching practised by Mr Gillespie, however admirable it may be,' he concluded, 'I believe is for infant schools.'[3] Willes was much the same: he simply could not impart basic knowledge and, worse, was resistant to all advice on how he might develop his technique. Irvine reminded him in April 1842 that frequent attendance in the first class had provided every opportunity to learn from Irvine's own proficient method of instruction. Instead, 'you appear to me so attached to the exploded and most antiquated parts of the National or Bell's system that I am afraid to hope for any improvement.'[4]

In June 1842 Irvine rebuked Willes again for the fact that the boys of the fourth class were idle and, on a visit by the headmaster, were not at their desks but discovered squatting on the floor. 'What if I had had a stranger with me on entering the class?' Irvine enquired. 'What impression would have been formed?'[5] During his inspection that year Tremenheere also warned Willes that he must change his ways if he wished to remain in the profession, only to be told rudely that Willes 'had friends in Parliament and he did not care.'[6] The truth was, as Duncannon had reported to the Committee of Council in 1841, that it was very difficult to find adequately qualified masters and assistants 'notwithstanding repeated public advertisements.'[7] Even the able Campbell, who replaced Hartnoll in August 1842, had been a risky appointment. He was only 21 and, as Graham had observed apprehensively, 'has never before taught a *public class*, having previously occupied the situation of tutor in a private family.'[8]

All this would have made the burden for Graham and Irvine heavy enough even if there had been no conspiracy against them. In fact their problems were compounded by a determined attempt to undermine them from all quarters at Greenwich. Graham perhaps felt this more keenly in the face of such hostility from his own academic colleagues. From his arrival, he sensed the greatest prejudice and believed himself to be the victim of lies and outrageous misrepresentations. 'It was alleged privately, and the same allegations appeared in a local newspaper,' he complained bitterly, 'that I was a man of no education, that I was a protégé of Lord Minto who could not get me otherwise disposed of, that I was a Whig and my appointment a mere Whig job.' Other attacks in the local press were couched in abusive and satirical language such as could only destroy his reputation. Graham protested that he was a staunch Tory and that, contrary to assertion, his appointment at Greenwich owed nothing to Minto's patronage or to that of Kay-Shuttleworth. Scurrilous journalism was Hartnoll's work; the latter had also sent free copies of the newspapers to all the naval staff of the institution. Graham repeatedly advised the Greenwich schools committee in 1841 and early 1842 that in such circumstances it was impossible for him to carry out 'the new educational system.'[9]

Rouse's attempts to foil all out of school control of boys by the masters were equally pernicious. Behind his open criticism of the procedures introduced by the Greenwich schools committee lay a systematic campaign to make them inoperable by wearing down the morale of their proponents. Although he no longer controlled the boys after the summer of 1841, he was still responsible for the pensioner-labourers who cleaned the classrooms, hall and dormitories. By January 1842, Irvine insisted, this work had effectively ceased. In the dining hall an 'extraordinary quantity of filth and dirt had of late accumulated on the walls.' In the dormitories, torn hammocks were neglected while towels and clothing were untidied, commonly removed and often found littering the school premises. As for the classrooms, Irvine groaned, 'I have for a long time attended to the cleaning of the schools myself.' 'I am obliged to go round with brushes and cloths to make my own classroom habitable.'[10] This, combined with Rouse's orders to the drill-serjeants not to assist the masters in any way, however bad the boys' behaviour, amounted to a 'well laid plan for the overthrow of the system as administered by me in the Lower school.'[11]

Moseley upheld all these charges against Rouse in March 1843; there was no shortage of reliable testimony to support Irvine's accusations. The clerk of the works, Charles Lee, recalled that on an occasion when he and the hospital architect had entered the dining hall 'we found the most unpleasant smell, so much so, that it affected us both very much.' The architect felt obliged to take a glass of wine; meanwhile, Lee explained with great solemnity, 'I went home and got some brandy.' Suitably restored, the two men braved the hall again where they found in the ledges of a window 'some meat in a putrid state, which had been chewed.'[12] The walls were likewise revolting. Only after the Governor had ordered an investigation did Rouse rush in some labourers to clean up the mess. On another occasion, Moseley noted, drill-serjeants took no action when they noticed boys throwing stones at teachers in the playground and Rouse did not even report the incident to the Governor. Rouse knew exactly what he was doing in creating conditions in which control under the masters was bound to break down, at which point the Governor and Board of Admiralty would have no alternative but to turn to him to restore order in the schools. It was a measure of his success that even Irvine had felt a need to sign the letter of 2 May 1842 in which the masters requested a return to naval discipline.

Rouse was not the only naval officer conspiring against the new educational system. Stopford and Gordon were instinctively opposed to reform and perceived a threat to naval authority at every turn. Gordon, in fairness, was open and honest and confronted his opponents with all disagreements. But Stopford played his own game. Not only did he indulge Hartnoll and Sharp in their antagonism towards Graham to the point where their behaviour became a challenge to his own command but he also encouraged Fisher in the dispute with Graham over entry to the Nautical school. In January 1842 Stopford specifically gave Fisher wider powers to examine than the Greenwich schools committee had envisaged. The committee had requested that Fisher should judge the pupils of Riddle and Graham for proficiency in nautical science. 'It is my direction,' the Governor ordered, 'that Mr Fisher do not confine his examination and selection to Mr Riddle's and Mr Graham's classes but extend it to all the classes in the Upper school.'[13] In August 1842, when pressed to state his views on promoting boys from the Upper school, Stopford replied categorically to Fisher that 'I am very averse to lowering the standard for admission into the Nautical school.'[14] Stopford also consistently supported Rouse in all disagreements with Irvine and even made excuses for the former's unwavering rudeness. On many occasions both Graham and Irvine found themselves appealing to the Governor for support in the exercise of their authority while knowing very well that Stopford was unsympathetic to their goals and even in cahoot with those who wished to remove them from the schools.

Reform at Greenwich was further complicated by outside interference. While Kay-Shuttleworth was a driving force for educational change, he also politicised the process and made the Admiralty understandably wary that there was a plan afoot to transfer the schools to the control of the Committee of Council. Kay-Shuttleworth was a headstrong and impatient man who, despite occasional conciliatory remarks concerning the feelings of others, in practice made little allowance for those who did not share his opinions or whose interests required a different approach to change. Writing to his future wife, he betrayed a relentless determination to beat the Greenwich establishment into submission and to exercise his own influence. Even his closest associates at times thought Kay-Shuttleworth too impulsive. On 12 January 1842 he had to confide that 'I found my friend Eden rather too timid in the evening to unite with me in signing the papers I had prepared. I therefore signed them alone.' 'To tell you the truth,' he boasted, 'when I found myself acting alone I wrote them out in somewhat more *decisive* terms.' In the political climate of the times, with education becoming increasingly a matter for public concern, Kay-Shuttleworth was confident that his department did not need to compromise. The Admiralty could continue to oppose him if it wished, he calculated, but he was sure that even the Tory administration after August 1841 would back the Committee of Council if it came to a Commons debate. 'I have been acting with the most perfect good faith to the present government,' he postulated, 'and I do not think they would like to put me in a position which would compel me in self defence to turn my artillery against any department.'[15] To Haddington's credit, he was quick to recognise in Kay-Shuttleworth a dangerous adversary.

The Admiralty was right to believe that Kay-Shuttleworth was using the Greenwich schools for educational experimentation. In truth, such an intention was barely concealed. Duncannon told Gordon in August 1841 that he was well aware of the problems and pitfalls of which the latter so vehemently complained, but added nonchalantly: 'after all, it must be an experiment.'[16] Three months later Kay-Shuttleworth informed Haddington proudly that 'these schools will in the course of two years become models for the elementary and secondary schools of this country.'[17] Experimentation was a part of his nature. Looking back in 1860 on his career at the Committee of Council, Kay-Shuttleworth assured the Newcastle Commission that 'I regard the whole of the proceedings in relation to education as tentative.' 'Whatever may have been the principles or motives in which any scheme has originated,' he continued, 'the government have never refused to profit by the experience either of their success or failure.'[18] No wonder Haddington and Stopford were suspicious. They also distrusted Kay-Shuttleworth for the undue influence which he wielded in the appointment of teachers.

Graham and Irvine were both recommended by Kay-Shuttleworth and both were firmly supported by the Committee of Council in their reforming work. But Kay-Shuttleworth's influence extended farther. Gillespie, who joined the Lower school in 1841, had previously been a master in the parochial school at Battersea. That had brought him to Kay-Shuttleworth's notice. Additionally, he had been trained by Stow in Glasgow which gave him the final stamp of approval. In the same year Stow's imprimatur marked out his colleague, Drysdale. Again in 1841, Kay-Shuttleworth recommended Andrew Mackenzie as an assistant master. Mackenzie, like Graham, was spoken for by John Gibson; he also had attended the normal school run by the Church of Scotland. These were impressive credentials, Kay-Shuttleworth informed the Admiralty, and but for the fact that it had been impossible to interview Mackenzie in person the schools committee would have waived the requirement of three months' probation. In August 1842 Herbert recorded that he had conferred with Kay-Shuttleworth over the appointments of Campbell and Davidson to the Upper school. The establishment at Greenwich was apprehensive of all these new men. In the opinion of many naval officers they normally were given jobs because of the fashionable views on education which they mouthed rather than any innate or acquired ability to instruct or control children. Graham and Irvine were both suspected of being Kay-Shuttleworth's eyes and ears at Greenwich and the latter's journal alone contains sufficient references to information gathered from the two headmasters to indicate that those suspicions were well-founded. Gordon told Moseley bluntly in March 1843 that 'much evil has arisen from the masters having communicated with persons not belonging to the Establishment without first communicating with the Governor on matters connected with their official duties.'[19]

Naval officers, admittedly, were generally unwelcoming to any visitor at Greenwich. HMIs were distrusted as the agents of

Kay-Shuttleworth's political ambitions; only Moseley ever gained the confidence of the Admiralty with his background in nautical science, his open-mindedness and his impeccable credentials as both scholar and cleric which enabled him in the end to be his own man and to settle the status of the schools in such a way as relieved naval trepidation. Tremenheere discovered directly from Haddington how he had been regarded at Greenwich when the two men met at a house party some years after his inspections. 'I presume you are the Mr Tremenheere who would not go down to Greenwich unless he was guaranteed against interference by the Admiral?' Haddington snorted. 'We thought at first that you meant mischief,' he continued. He then added in a friendly tone: 'but it was allright.'[20] On top of a dread of having reforms forced upon them which were undesirable and inconsistent with the nature of the institution, Stopford, Gordon, Rouse and the long-serving teaching staff feared the imposition of ideas and an organisational regime which would prove unworkable. Gordon was the only man to emerge from the debacle after April 1841 with his reputation unscathed. He had predicted all along that, given the slender resources of staff available and the problem of controlling 800 boys such as the schools contained, the innovative approach by the new headmasters and the irresponsible theorising of Kay-Shuttleworth was bound to end in disaster.

* * *

Were the Greenwich schools typical of a struggle for reform in British education in the 1840s? In one way obviously they were not so. They were subject to the authority of naval officers who expected a code of discipline to be upheld and a syllabus of instruction to be adopted which was apposite for prospective mariners. Few headmasters needed to assert their claim to a professional standing as Graham and Irvine had to do. Only an implicit subordination of academic to naval sanction led Irvine to ask the Lieutenant Governor 'in what position he was to consider himself?' Apart from loathing Rouse, he resented the harsh manner in which all the naval men barked out their orders. 'No gentleman could put up with it,' he exploded angrily, 'and he could not.'[21] Victorian schoolmasters, typically, were not required to reach an accommodation with the rigours of life in the armed services.

Yet in many important ways the schools at Greenwich were entirely representative of educational developments in the 1840s. The struggle for reform there embraced the wide debate about appropriate forms of discipline for children. Graham and Irvine were typically enlightened educators and shared Thomas Arnold's outlook on the need to cast aside draconian practice from the past. Writing in 1828, Arnold was convinced that 'boys may be governed a great deal by gentle methods and kindness, and appealing to their better feelings.'[22] In the early 1840s Graham and Irvine tried to end physical punishments at Greenwich, and when their efforts failed in May 1842 and control of the boys was restored to the naval authorities Irvine commented bitterly that order, under Rouse, was now maintained 'by the worst of all means, namely *fear* — fear of corporal punishment.'[23] Passing judgment in March 1843, Moseley, of course, could not hide the fact that in the chastisement of boys even these reforming heads had at times failed to live up to their own principles. But he clearly shared their aspirations and, although upholding the notion of naval discipline in the schools, stressed that one essential of any child's education was the freedom for personal as well as academic development. In the playgrounds the boys should naturally be watched, he remarked, but only with a 'friendly surveillance.' 'The Commission wishes it to be distinctly understood,' he decreed in the final report, 'that an injudicious meddling with boys in their hours of recreation is to be reprobated.' At play, 'every boy should feel confident that whilst he is occupied cheerfully and innocently, he will not be called to account by any of his superiors.'[24]

The schools were also typical in that even amid the rancour with naval officers a defined identity for teachers was clearly in the making, consistent with the growing professionalism of schooling at the time. Teaching standards and proper training were a preoccupation with Kay-Shuttleworth; Graham and Irvine were both willing disciples and indeed held strong opinions of their own in line with what was generally regarded as good practice among progressive educationalists both in Britain and on the Continent. Graham recognised soon after his arrival in the Upper school that in Hartnoll and Sharp he had acquired colleagues of a different and, in his view, outdated persuasion. 'Their views of education and mine were totally opposed,' he reflected, 'and on their part so strong and rooted as to render it fruitless to attempt to change them.'[25] Hartnoll, for all his obstructiveness, represented a strand of opinion wedded to thorough learning, though within a narrow range. He also singled out the duties of a master as exclusively academic and thus as finished when the bell for ending lessons sounded. Hartnoll was not ignorant of reforming ideas: he simply did not approve of them. Like his headmaster, he valued classroom skills albeit differently stipulated and employed. 'Whatever weight may be attached to particular systems,' he judged, 'the only safe reliance for the transfusion of human knowledge from one mind into another is in the intellectual energies and integrity of the teacher.'[26] Hartnoll and Graham represented a clash of ideologies which underpinned their personal dislikes. From the substantive issues of such disputes emerged the model of teaching and of teachers in the mid nineteenth century.

It was, of course, Graham's vision of an expansive curriculum and a closer relationship between teacher and pupil which ultimately prevailed. The skills required for instructing the young could be reduced to scientific method and were susceptible, therefore, to careful training. 'Teaching is an *art*,' Graham argued, 'which, like every other, comes not by instinct but is acquired slowly and progressively by study and practice.'[27] Hartnoll and Sharp were from a different culture: they believed that scholarship did not require enhancement from well-practiced routine. Their world was one of men with literary aspirations and an amateurish perception of innate qualities for dealing with children. Graham was constantly anxious to prove the superiority of technique. 'I feel very desirous that *my own* mode of teaching and examining may be known to you and their Lordships,' he informed Herbert in May 1842, and was delighted to report that he had recently had the opportunity to exhibit his abilities during a visit to the Upper school by Minto and Lord John Russell. 'A young man who may know how to answer a series of *written* questions in a *private* room,' he warned, 'may be totally deficient in those qualities which the *classroom* requires.'[28] He would never appoint a master whom he had not first seen demonstrate a perfected teaching style.

All this had the authentic ring of Scottish education. To that extent, too, the Greenwich schools typify the significant external input into mid-nineteenth century English schooling. Irvine, Graham and a number of their undermasters had all been educated, and had learned their craft, outside the English system. It was not uncommon to bring masters down from Scotland to introduce reform to English schools. In 1853 Kay-Shuttleworth confirmed that 'the schools which were organised under the Poor Law Commission, the Admiralty, and other departments, were supplied with masters chiefly selected in Scotland.'[29] In 1839 and 1840 Stow could not meet Kay-Shuttleworth's demand for teachers from the Glasgow normal seminary. When he founded the training school at Battersea, Kay-Shuttleworth engaged three masters — all from Scotland. One of them, Walter McLeod, a pupil of Stow, had first come south to teach for two years at Aubin's Norwood institution. 'The Scotch schoolbooks' were employed at Norwood, Kay-Shuttleworth recorded in 1838, until such time as new ones could be written.[30] The Limehouse school of industry, another of the pauper union schools, benefited from both a Scotch master and Scotch mistress in the 1840s. The Deptford workhouse school engaged another of Stow's former pupils as headmaster. McLeod, in particular, impressed the eager Kay-Shuttleworth. He was outstanding in his conduct of Bible and scripture lessons and he implemented to the letter the strict training procedures acquired in Glasgow. Yet for all that, Kay-Shuttleworth rejoiced that 'he was always ready to adopt any of my suggestions, and had a remarkable aptitude not only in apprehending the principles of any new method, but singular skill in carrying it into practice.'[31] It was this priceless blend of professionalism and a willingness to experiment that Kay-Shuttleworth believed he had found again in Graham and Irvine.

In placing his faith so largely in men brought into England Kay-Shuttleworth did no more than reflect the received wisdom of his day. It was axiomatic that the Scots, if a little coarse, were clever. Certainly their culture set more store by a wider spread of education and their society valued more the sacrifice of those entrusted with its diffusion. 'You cannot expect that the results which have been obtained in Scotland by perseverance, since the Reformation, will be obtained excepting in generations of progress in this country,' he informed the Newcastle Commission despairingly as late as 1860.[32] Moseley reported in 1845 that the working classes in Scotland took more interest in the education of their children than their counterparts in England, that the system of parish schooling there was more proficient and that the enthusiasm and ability of teachers was significantly greater. Elizabeth Campbell, later Duchess of Argyll, impressed upon Kay-Shuttleworth in 1846 what, from her experience of philanthropic work, was the important difference: 'the *status* of a schoolmaster in Scotland is a better one in public estimation,' she concluded, 'and generally in pecuniary ways than in England.'[33] Nevertheless, bringing men from Edinburgh and Dublin to reorganise the teaching in an institution with a strong sense of identity and an existing educational pattern to match was always going to be a gamble. As a strategy it was not entirely consistent with Fleming's advice to the Admiralty in August 1840 that the important business of introducing change into the schools 'should be approached with caution.'[34]

The Greenwich schools in the 1840s fit into an identified pattern of early nineteenth century educational change whereby new curricula were frequently over-ambitious and the improvements which they were intended to achieve were unattainable in the time envisaged.[35] To that extent, the study of reform there illustrates the difficulty of implementing change, the rationale for which could often be dismissed by its opponents, and rightly so at times, as the whim of men obsessed with bold experiment and driven by subjective precepts and nebulous theories which were untranslatable into the real world of practical instruction and the physical control of rowdy children. Thomas Arnold learned his lesson in the 1820s and 1830s. 'I came to Rugby full of plans for school reform,' he rued, 'but I soon found that the reform of a public school was a much more difficult thing than I had imagined.'[36] Kay-Shuttleworth should have learned from his experiences at Norwood where, he complained in 1838, a principal obstacle to the speedy adoption of improvement was 'the fact that we have many of the old servants of the establishment about us.'[37] Again at Norwood, in 1841, he became drawn into a personal conflict between its chaplain and headmaster, the former having 'the most vexatious way of making mischief without any malevolent intention.' 'I find that I must be on horseback a little more,' he concluded, 'and frequently renew my visits to these schools.'[38] Kay-Shuttleworth's preoccupation with, yet remoteness from, the routine of Greenwich was spotted by Gordon as part of the problem in October 1841. At Norwood, Gordon complained, the Committee of Council did not insist on masters having authority over the children at all times; why then was Kay-Shuttleworth so persistent in pressing such a hopeless experiment upon the Admiralty?

Inevitably, comparisons with other schools were made and those too comprise in part a judgment on the state of early Victorian schooling. After two years on the road as an HMI, Moseley was well placed to assess how typical the standards reached at Greenwich really were. Returning to inspect the schools in April 1845, he was struck by the attention of boys during lessons, by the ease with which the masters handled their classes and by the quality of the teaching which was delivered. This was much in contrast to 'the listless and desultory characteristics of an ordinary commercial school,' he explained, 'and to the noisy mechanism of a National school.'[39] After his visit in 1846 he reported that 'the schools have attained a state second in efficiency and in reputation to no other elementary schools in this country.[40] Given Fleming's damning verdict on the education provided in 1840, Moseley's praise, merely five years later, represented a considerable accomplishment.

The 1840s was a decade of educational experiment and the naval schools were, at different times, both victims and beneficiaries of the prevailing opinion in favour of reform. Their unique record has survived and from it can be seen the pressures which were generated by change, the mistakes which were made and the enduring lessons which those involved with the development of popular education should have comprehended and respected. Addressing Newcastle as an assistant commissioner in 1860, Matthew Arnold surveyed the momentous changes of his generation and drew the contrast between the present and 20 years before. 'The day has gone by,' he declared, 'when the actual mechanism of primary schools formed the principal object of enquiries upon public education. Rival school methods have fought their fight; and at the present day we in England, at any rate, think that we know pretty well in what good school-keeping consists.'[41] Nowhere could the rival school methods have been fought out more bitterly than at Greenwich or become so interwoven with political considerations. Lost in the immenseness of its archive, the Admiralty preserved a little of the world of schools and schoolmasters at the most critical time in the creation of a national system of education in Britain.

Preserved too was the intensely human dimension. The burden of work and the anxiety of the 1843 Commission tragically broke the health of both Graham and Irvine and contributed to the former's premature death. As outsiders, both men struggled to overcome the prejudice with which they were confronted on a daily basis. Boys taunted Irvine with the nickname 'Paddy'. On one occasion in March 1842 Irvine became so demoralised before a group of unruly boys that he offered them a stick and pathetically invited them to beat him. The insults from Rouse revealed the latter's perception of the status of a common teacher in England in the 1840s. Likewise, Stopford repeatedly made it plain that the humble social origins of all the masters appointed after 1840 made them ill-suited to exercise authority and certainly unworthy of respect from naval officers.

But, amid all the tensions, there were humorous incidents which light up the characters of several of those who participated in the years of argument about how the schools should be run. Though staff railed against the appalling behaviour of the boys and complained that respectable people could no longer cross the playground free from abuse or injury, Riddle's daughters, who had grown up on the premises, remembered no greater offence to their sensibilities than that boys no longer appeared to doff their caps as had been the habit, so legend had it, in days of yore.

Gordon, when not in heated disagreements, was a jovial man who had seen sufficient of the world to place the outraged moral rectitude of idealistic and sometimes priggish schoolmasters in perspective. Called to the dormitories to witness the disgusting depravity of boys lying in the same hammock, Gordon ridiculed the complaint with the offhand quip that 'it was of no consequence since it was often done on board ship.'[42] Above all, Irvine's way of teaching was more than just eccentric. He was crude, yet many of the boys responded well to his use of vulgar language, liked him greatly and considered him a genuinely funny man who had a gift for holding their attention for long periods. Of course, there may have been more to the problems at Greenwich than was ever written down. In March 1843 Moseley assured the Admiralty in confidence that 'the Commission has carefully examined into the rumours respecting Lieutenant Rouse's moral conduct, to which its attention was verbally directed. It has not been able either to substantiate or rebut them.'[43] But there was no further clue. The Commission finished and his job at Greenwich at least partly done, Moseley discreetly allowed the veil to fall back across the lives of those who had commanded, taught and studied at the naval schools in the most important moments of their history.

NOTES

Introduction

1. T. G. Cook (ed) *Local Studies and the History of Education* (London, 1972), p xiv.
One attempt to understand the routine of an elementary school at this time
is P. and H. Silver *The Education of the Poor: the History of a National School
1824–1974* (London, 1974). Information available for the mid nineteenth
century, however, is very thin. That is also the case for E. Hopkins 'A Charity
School in the Nineteenth Century: Old Swinford Hospital School, 1815–1914',
British Journal of Educational Studies, XVII (1969), pp 177–192. Another
contribution is D. K. Jones 'Socialization and Social Science: Manchester
Model Secular School 1854–1861', in P. McCann (ed) *Popular Education and
Socialization in the Nineteenth Century* (London, 1977), pp 111–139. See also B.
Madoc-Jones 'Patterns of Attendance and their Social Significance: Mitcham
National School 1830–39', in McCann (ed) *op. cit.* pp 41–66; and R. Pallister
'The Determinants of Elementary School Attendance about 1850', *The Durham
Research Review*, V (1969–70), pp 384–398. The Hazelwood and King's Somborne
schools in the 1840s are discussed in W. A. C. Stewart and W. P. McCann *The
Educational Innovators 1750–1880* (London, 1967), pp 98–135. A general study
on this theme is P. Gardner *The Lost Elementary Schools of Victorian England:
the Peoples' Education* (London, 1984)

Chapter 1

1. These figures are from R. Aldrich *An Introduction to the History of Education*
(London, 1982), pp 15–16. There is a large bibliography on the development
of English schooling in the early and mid nineteenth century among the
most valuable of which are M. Sturt *The Education of the People: a History of
Primary Education in England and Wales in the Nineteenth Century* (London,
1967); J. Hurt *Education in Evolution: Church, State, Society and Popular Education
1800–1870* (London, 1971); J. M. Goldstrom *Education: Elementary Education
1780–1900* (Newton Abbot, 1972); B. Simon *The Two Nations and the Educational
Structure 1780–1870* (London, 1974); D. K. Jones *The Making of the Education
System 1851–1881* (London, 1977); and J. Roach *A History of Secondary Education
in England 1800–1870* (London, 1986)

2. The effects of industrialisation and rapid urbanisation on the progress of national
education have proved controversial among historians. See in particular E. G.
West *Education and the Industrial Revolution* (London, 1975); E. G. West 'Resource
Allocation and Growth in early Nineteenth-Century British Education', *Economic
History Review*, XXIII (1970), pp 68–95; J. S. Hurt 'Professor West on early

161

Nineteenth-Century Education', *Economic History Review*, XXIV (1971), pp 624–632, reprinted in M. Drake (ed) *Applied Historical Studies: an Introductory Reader* (London, 1973), pp 93–105; and E. G. West 'The Interpretation of early Nineteenth-Century Education Statistics', *Economic History Review*, XXIV (1971), pp 633–642. See also D. A. Reeder (ed) *Urban Education in the Nineteenth Century* (London, 1977); and the authoritative M. E. Bryant *The London Experience of Secondary Education* (London, 1986)

3.   Report by Hedley, 1861, Parliamentary Accounts and Papers, XXI (1861) part II

4.   Arnold to Hawkins, 29 December 1839, in A. P. Stanley *The Life and Correspondence of Thomas Arnold* (London, 1881), vol II, pp 153–4

5.   English public schools have received a good deal of scholarly interest. Among the most illuminating studies covering the mid nineteenth century are T. W. Bamford *Rise of the Public Schools: a Study of Boys' Public Boarding Schools in England and Wales from 1837 to the Present Day* (London, 1967); A. C. Percival *Very Superior Men: some early Public School Headmasters and their Achievements* (London, 1973); B. Simon and I. Bradley (eds) *The Victorian Public School* (London, 1975); and J. R. de S. Honey *Tom Brown's Universe: the Development of the Victorian Public School* (London, 1977)

6.   Jones *The Making of the Education System* pp 11–12

7.   The best study of English education before the nineteenth century is R. O'Day *Education and Society 1500–1800* (London, 1982)

8.   Report by Watkins, 26 February 1845, P.P. XXXV (1845)

9.   Newcastle Commission Report, 1861, P.P. XXI (1861) part I

10.   Aldrich *op. cit.* p 72

11.   Report by Moseley, February 1845, P.P. XXXV (1845)

12.   Evidence of Girdlestone, 1861. Appendix to Report by Cumins, P.P. XXI (1861) part III

13.   Report by Watkins, March 1846, P.P. XXXII (1846)

14.   Report by Tremenheere, 21 August 1841, P.P. XXXIII (1842)

15.   Report by Bellairs, February 1845, P.P. XXXV (1845)

16.   Report by Moseley, 23 February 1846, P.P. XXXII (1846)

17.   The history of the teaching profession in the early and mid nineteenth century is covered in E. B. Castle *The Teacher* (Oxford, 1970); H. C. Dent *The Training of Teachers in England and Wales 1800–1975* (London, 1977); and C. More *The Training of Teachers, 1847–1947: a History of the Church Colleges at Cheltenham* (London, 1992). See also M. Seaborne 'Early Theories of Teacher Education', *British Journal of Educational Studies*, XXII (1974), pp 325–339

18.   Reports by Hedley and Wilkinson, 1861, P.P. XXI (1861) parts II and III respectively

19.   Evidence of the Bishop of St. David's, May 1859, P.P. XXI (1861) part V

20.   Quoted in P. Horn *Education in Rural England 1800–1914* (London, 1978), p 152

21.   Evidence of Watkins, 7 December 1859, P.P. XXI (1861) part VI

22.   Report by Watkins, 1845, P.P. XXXII (1846)

23.   Report by Arnold, June 1860, P.P. XXI (1861) part IV

24.   Report by Cumin, 1861, P.P. XXI (1861) part III

25.   Report by Noel, 1841, P.P. XX (1841)

26.   Report by Moseley, 1846, P.P. XXXII (1846)

27.   Developments in Scottish education in the early and mid nineteenth century are covered in R. D. Anderson *Education and Opportunity in Victorian Scotland* (Oxford, 1983); W. M. Humes and H. M. Paterson (eds) *Scottish Culture and*

Scottish Education 1800–1980 (Edinburgh, 1983); and R. D. Anderson *Education and the Scottish People 1750–1918* (Oxford, 1995)

28. Aldrich *op. cit.* p 77
29. J. H. Hinton *The Case of the Manchester Educationists, Part II. A Review of the Evidence taken before a Committee of the House of Commons, in relation to a scheme of Secular Education* (London, 1854), p 99
30. Report by Cumin, 1861, P.P. XXI (1861) part III
31. He changed his name on marriage in 1842. However for the sake of consistency I have referred to him as Kay-Shuttleworth throughout. Kay-Shuttleworth's career is well analysed in F. Smith *The Life and Work of Sir James Kay-Shuttleworth* (London, 1923); and in Stewart and McCann *op. cit.* pp 179–197. More recently, his career has been reassessed by D. G. Paz 'Sir James Kay-Shuttleworth: the Man behind the Myth', *History of Education*, XIV (1985), pp 185–198; and by R. J. W. Selleck *James Kay-Shuttleworth: Journey of an Outsider* (London, 1994). Many of Kay-Shuttleworth's own writings on education are reproduced in T. R. Tholfsen (ed) *Sir James Kay-Shuttleworth on Popular Education* (New York, 1974)
32. Evidence of Chester, 2 December 1859, P.P. XXI (1861) part VI
33. The most comprehensive study of the work of the Committee of Council and its HMIs is N. Ball *Her Majesty's Inspectorate 1839–1849* (Birmingham, 1963). See also A. S. Bishop *The Rise of a Central Authority for English Education* (Cambridge, 1971); N. Ball *Educating the People: a Documentary History of Elementary Schooling in England, 1840–1870* (London, 1983); J. Alexander and D. G. Paz 'The Treasury Grants, 1833–1839', *British Journal of Educational Studies*, XXII (1974), pp 78–92; and D. G. Paz 'Working-Class Education and the State, 1839–1849: the Sources of Government Policy', *Journal of British Studies*, XVI (1976), pp 129–152
34. The evolving culture of education in the nineteenth century is dealt with in D. Newsome *Godliness and Good Learning: Four Studies on a Victorian Ideal* (London, 1961); J. M. Goldstrom 'The Content of Education and the Socialization of the Working-Class Child 1830–1860', in McCann (ed) *Popular Education and Socialization in the Nineteenth Century* pp 93–109; P. Horn *The Victorian and Edwardian Schoolchild* (Gloucester, 1989); L. Rose *The Erosion of Childhood: Child Oppression in Britain 1860–1918* (London, 1991); and E. Hopkins *Childhood Transformed: Working-Class Children in Nineteenth-Century England* (Manchester, 1994)
35. See D. Leinster-Mackay *The Educational World of Edward Thring* (London, 1987)
36. Minutes of the Committee of Privy Council, P.P. XX (1841)
37. Quoted in Percival *op. cit.* p 196
38. Quoted in Bryant *op. cit.* p 157
39. Report by Watkins, 1845, P.P. XXXII (1846)
40. Report by Moseley, February 1845, P.P. XXXV (1845)
41. Reports by Allen, 1842, P.P. XXXIII (1842) and 24 February 1846, P.P. XXXII (1846)
42. Minutes of the Committee of Privy Council, P.P. XX (1841)
43. Report by Tremenheere, 20 March 1843, P.P. XL (1843)
44. Minutes of the Committee of Privy Council, P.P. XX (1841). An account of Pestalozzi's influence in Britain is provided in K. Silber *Pestalozzi: the Man and his Work* (London, 1960), pp 278–315; and in Stewart and McCann *op. cit.* pp 136–154
45. Report by Watkins, March 1846, P.P. XXXII (1846)
46. Report by Moseley, 1846, P.P. XXXII (1846)

47. Report by Allen, 24 November 1840, P.P. XX (1841)
48. Quoted in Sturt *op. cit.* p 25. Lancaster's career is most comprehensively covered in M. Dickson *Teacher Extraordinary: Joseph Lancaster 1778–1838* (Lewes, 1986). See also J. R. Carr 'Lancasterian Schools: a Reappraisal', *The Durham Research Review*, V (1969–70), pp 427–436
49. Quoted in Report by Tremenheere, 1 July 1842, P.P. XL (1843)
50. Report by Hodgson, 1861, P.P. XXI (1861) part III
51. Report by Cook, 20 May 1848, P.P. L (1847–8)
52. Report by Moseley, 1846, P.P. XXXII (1846)
53. Report by Watkins, March 1846, P.P. XXXII (1846)
54. Report by Tremenheere, 1 July 1842, P.P. XL (1843)
55. Arnold to Pasley, 15 April 1835, in Stanley *Life of Arnold* vol I, p 358
56. Report by Moseley, 1846, P.P. XXXII (1846)
57. Report by Watkins, 26 February 1845, P.P. XXXV (1845)
58. Report by Cook, January 1845, P.P. XXXV (1845)
59. Evidence of Davids, 3 June 1859, P.P. XXI (1861) part V
60. Report of Cumin, 1861, P.P. XXI (1861) part III
61. Evidence of Chester, 4 January 1860, P.P. XXI (1861) part VI
62. The growing political dimension to educational development is covered in D. G. Paz *The Politics of Working-Class Education in Britain 1830–50* (Manchester, 1980) and D. A. Reeder *Educating our Masters* (Leicester, 1980). See also R. Johnson 'Educational Policy and Social Control in early Victorian England', *Past and Present*, 49 (1970), pp 96–119; P. Hollis (ed) *Pressure from Without in early Victorian England* (London, 1974) and a valuable specific study by D. Fraser 'Education and Urban Politics c.1832–1885', in D. A. Reeder (ed) *Urban Education in the Nineteenth Century* pp 11–25
63. The spread of schooling into rural areas in the mid nineteenth century is explained in P. Horn *Education in Rural England* and in excellent local studies by R. R. Sellman *Devon Village Schools in the Nineteenth Century* (Newton Abbot, 1967) and M. J. G. Gray-Fow 'Squire, Parson and Village School: Wragby 1830–1886', in P. Scott and P. Fletcher (eds) *Culture and Education in Victorian England* (Cranbury, N.J., 1990), pp 162–173
64. Report by Allen, 23 January 1845, P.P. XXXV (1845)
65. Report by Moseley, 1847, P.P. L (1847–8)
66. Report by Morell, July 1848, P.P. L (1847–8)
67. Changing educational values in the early and mid nineteenth century are examined in P. Gordon and D. Lawton *Curriculum Change in the Nineteenth and Twentieth Centuries* (London, 1978) and P. Gordon and J. White *Philosophers as Educational Reformers: the Influence of Idealism on British Educational Thought and Practice* (London, 1979). See also J. Roach *Public Examinations in England 1850–1900* (Cambridge, 1971)
68. Report by Arnold, 1861, P.P. XXI (1861) part IV
69. Report by Morell, July 1848, P.P. L (1847–8)
70. Report by Allen, 29 January 1847, P.P. XLV (1847)
71. Dent *op. cit.* pp 10 and 14
72. Report by Moseley, 1844, P.P. XXXV (1845)
73. Report by Gibson, 30 June 1842, P.P. XXXIII (1842)
74. Report by Morell, July 1848, P.P. L (1847–8)
75. F. Harrison *Autobiographic Memoirs* (London, 1911), vol I, p 33
76. Hurt 'Professor West on early Nineteenth-Century Education', in M. Drake (ed) *Applied Historical Studies* p 98
77. Evidence of Scott, 6 July 1859, P.P. XXI (1861) part V
78. Quoted in Report by Wilkinson, 1861, P.P. XXI (1861) part III

79. Camps to Allen, 6 February 1844, enclosed in Report by Allen, P.P. XXXV (1845)
80. Evidence of Penrose, 7 June 1859, P.P. XXI (1861) part V
81. Evidence of Zincke, 13 June 1859, P.P. XXI (1861) part V

Chapter 2

1. Memorandum by Seymour, 11 June 1842, Admiralty Records, Public Record Office, London, ADM 1/5519
2. For a general history of the institution see H. D. Turner *The Cradle of the Navy: the Story of the Royal Hospital School at Greenwich and at Holbrook, 1694–1988* (York, 1990). Pp 55–76 cover in outline the years 1842 to 1890
3. Le Geyt to London, 31 October 1843, ADM 66/72
4. Le Geyt to Baldwin, 22 November 1842, ADM 66/72
5. Le Geyt to Baldwin, 11 March 1843, ADM 66/72
6. Memorandum by Keats, 21 February 1831, ADM 80/71
7. Le Geyt to Wilks, 21 October 1842, ADM 66/72
8. Fleming to More O'Ferrall, 7 August 1840, Ministry of Education Records, P.R.O. London, ED 17/4
9. ibid
10. Kay-Shuttleworth to Russell, 11 October 1839, *Papers of Sir James Kay-Shuttleworth*, John Rylands Library, Manchester, 202:1839
11. Kay-Shuttleworth to Russell, 29 October 1838, *Papers of Lord John Russell*, P.R.O. London, PRO 30/22/3B
12. Kay-Shuttleworth to Janet Shuttleworth, 1 February 1842, *Kay-Shuttleworth papers*, 220:1841
13. Stow to Kay-Shuttleworth, 1843, *Kay-Shuttleworth papers*, 269:1843
14. Report by Tremenheere, 9 September 1840, ED 17/4. A memorandum dated 18 December 1840, written by the chaplain of the schools in response to Tremenheere's report, gives a brief account of how monitorial instruction was introduced: 'The Lower school was first organised by a person from Dr Bell's central school in Baldwyn's Gardens who was supposed to be perfectly conversant with the National System of Education, and who continued to be master of this school for 10 years. This system has ever since been continued, and also the books which he introduced.' *Papers of the Reverend George Fisher*, National Maritime Museum, Greenwich, FIS/32
15. Report by Tremenheere, 9 September 1840, ED 17/4
16. Kay-Shuttleworth to Admiralty, 1 December 1840, ED 17/4
17. Minto to Adam, 6 December 1840, ADM 7/601
18. Barrow to Duncannon, 14 December 1840, ED 17/4
19. Minto to Adam, 6 December 1840, ADM 7/601
20. Memorandum by Fisher, 18 December 1840, *Fisher papers*, FIS/32
21. Minto to Adam, 6 December 1840, ADM 7/601
22. Duncannon to Admiralty, 20 January 1841, ED 17/4

Chapter 3

1. Kay-Shuttleworth to Haddington, 28 October 1841, ADM 7/601
2. Evidence of Campbell, 4 March 1843, ADM 1/5532
3. Graham to Herbert, 23 May 1842, ADM 7/601
4. Kay-Shuttleworth to the Commission, 7 March 1843, ADM 1/5532
5. Kay-Shuttleworth to Irvine, 11 February 1841, ADM 1/5532
6. Hamilton to Irvine, 8 March 1842, ADM 1/5532
7. Evidence of Hughes, 15 March 1843, ADM 1/5532

8. Tremenheere to Irvine, 7 March 1843, ADM 1/5532
9. Irvine to the Commission, 4 March 1843, ADM 1/5532
10. Quoted in Bamford *Rise of the Public Schools* p 13
11. F. Miles and G. Cranch *King's College School: the First 150 Years* (London, 1979) pp 18–19
12. Dobson to Stopford, 3 November 1841, ADM 65/108
13. Rouse to Stopford, 6 November 1841, ADM 65/108
14. Locker and Hope to Herbert, 25 February 1843, ADM 65/29
15. Evidence of Domville, 1 March 1843, ADM 1/5532
16. Hospital report, 8 November 1839, ADM 80/71
17. Report by Rouse, 1841, ADM 1/5533
18. Greenwich schools committee report, 7 May 1841, ADM 7/601; and Kay-Shuttleworth to Fisher, 8 May 1841, *Fisher papers*, FIS/32
19. Kay-Shuttleworth to Haddington, 28 October 1841, ADM 7/601
20. Irvine to Moseley, 4 April 1843, ADM 1/5532
21. Graham to Stopford, 16 May 1842, ADM 66/12
22. Report by Tinling, April 1848, Minutes of Committee of Privy Council, P.P. L (1847–8)
23. Irvine to Kay-Shuttleworth, 25 May 1841, ADM 1/5508
24. Graham to Kay-Shuttleworth, 1841, ADM 1/5508
25. Kay-Shuttleworth to Haddington, 28 October 1841, ADM 7/601
26. Irvine to Stopford, 20 January 1843, ADM 7/601
27. Kay-Shuttleworth to Haddington, 28 October 1841, ADM 7/601
28. Graham to Kay-Shuttleworth, 1841, ADM 1/5508
29. Graham to Stopford, 16 May 1842, ADM 66/12
30. Irvine to Stopford, 20 January 1843, ADM 7/601
31. Kay-Shuttleworth to Admiralty, 11 January 1842, ADM 7/601

Chapter 4

1. Irvine to Kay-Shuttleworth, 25 May 1841, ADM 1/5508
2. Irvine to Stopford, 20 January 1843, ADM 7/601
3. Kay-Shuttleworth to Admiralty, 13 May 1841, ADM 7/601
4. Journal of Kay-Shuttleworth, 28 June 1841, *Kay-Shuttleworth papers*, 219:1841
5. Gordon to Minto, 16 July 1841, ADM 1/5508
6. Journal of Kay-Shuttleworth, 29 June 1841, *Kay-Shuttleworth papers*, 219:1841
7. Journal of Kay-Shuttleworth, 1 July 1841, *Kay-Shuttleworth papers*, 219:1841
8. Duncannon to Admiralty, 7 July 1841, ADM 1/5508
9. Minute by Minto on Duncannon to Admiralty, 7 July 1841, ADM 1/5508
10. Jones to Royal Naval School, 15 August 1837, ADM 1/5532. A biographical sketch of Rouse is given in Turner *The Cradle of the Navy* pp 48–50
11. Evidence of Gordon, 25 February 1843, ADM 1/5532
12. Report by Rouse, 1841, ADM 1/5533
13. Journal of Kay-Shuttleworth, 6 July 1841, *Kay-Shuttleworth papers*, 219:1841
14. Journal of Kay-Shuttleworth, 7 July 1841, *Kay-Shuttleworth papers*, 219:1841
15. Minto to Pechell, 11 July 1841, ADM 1/5508
16. Minto to Duncannon, 19 July 1841, ADM 1/5508
17. Memorandum by Minto, 23 July 1841, ADM 1/5508
18. Journal of Kay-Shuttleworth, 3 July 1841, *Kay-Shuttleworth papers*, 219:1841
19. Wharncliffe to Kay-Shuttleworth, 20 December 1841, *Kay-Shuttleworth papers*, 241:1841
20. Kay-Shuttleworth to Morpeth, 7 September 1841, *Kay-Shuttleworth papers*, 233:1841
21. Graham to Stopford, 16 May 1842, ADM 66/12

22. Graham to Kay-Shuttleworth, 1841, ADM 1/5508
23. Kay-Shuttleworth to Herbert, 16 October 1841, ADM 7/601
24. Kay-Shuttleworth to Haddington, 28 October 1841, ADM 7/601
25. Gordon to Stopford, 12 October 1841, ADM 7/601
26. 'In Sir Robert Stopford you will find I think a much more agreeable Governor than Sir James Gordon,' second-lieutenant John Huskisson from the Mediterranean fleet off Beirut wrote to his sister, Mary Ann, who still lived with their parents in the hospital grounds, on 25 August 1841; 'he was generally liked very much on this station.' *Papers of Captain Thomas Huskisson*, N.M.M. HUS/1
27. Minto to Stopford, 31 January 1841, *Papers of Admiral Sir Robert Stopford*, N.M.M. STO/5
28. Minto to Stopford, 13 March 1841, *Stopford papers*, STO/5
29. Stopford to Herbert, 14 October 1841, ADM 7/601
30. Lee to Lethbridge, 23 December 1841, ADM 65/108
31. Kay-Shuttleworth to Herbert, 16 October 1841, ADM 7/601
32. Hall and de Morgan to Admiralty, 15 November 1841, ADM 7/601
33. Minute by Haddington, December 1841, ADM 7/601
34. Riddle to Stopford, 31 December 1841, ADM 7/601
35. Kay-Shuttleworth to Admiralty, 12 January 1842, ADM 7/601
36. Minute by Haddington, 31 December 1841, ADM 7/601

Chapter 5

1. Miles and Cranch *op. cit.* p 54
2. Bamford *Rise of the Public Schools* p 178
3. Hartnoll to Greenwich schools committee, 20 March 1841, ADM 7/601
4. Hartnoll to Cowper, 25 March 1841, ADM 7/601
5. Hartnoll to Dalmeny, 1 April 1841, ADM 7/601
6. Hartnoll to Admiralty, 9 August 1841, ADM 7/601
7. Graham to Stopford, 4 May 1842, ADM 66/12
8. Lethbridge to Graham, 24 November 1841, ADM 66/24
9. Hartnoll to Stopford, 11 October 1841, ADM 7/601
10. Kay-Shuttleworth to Admiralty, 11 January 1842, ADM 7/601
11. Graham to Stopford, 11 April 1842, ADM 66/12
12. Stopford to Herbert, 11 April 1842, ADM 66/12
13. Stopford to Herbert, 28 March 1842, ADM 1/5533
14. Stopford to Herbert, 16 April 1842, ADM 66/12
15. Hartnoll to Herbert, 15 February 1842, ADM 7/601
16. Hartnoll to Stopford, 14 April 1842, ADM 7/601
17. Graham to Stopford, 17 March 1842, ADM 65/111
18. Hartnoll to Stopford, 21 March 1842, ADM 65/111
19. Hartnoll to Stopford, 14 April 1842, ADM 7/601
20. Graham to Herbert, 2 May 1842, ADM 7/601
21. Fisher to Stopford, 21 April 1842, *Fisher papers*, FIS/32
22. Graham to Stopford, 26 April 1842, ADM 1/5533
23. Graham to Stopford, 4 May 1842, ADM 66/12

Chapter 6

1. Rouse to the Commission, February/March 1843, ADM 1/5532
2. Evidence of Gordon, 28 February 1843, ADM 1/5532
3. Evidence of Huskisson, 28 February 1843, ADM 1/5532
4. Evidence of Gordon, 28 February 1843, ADM 1/5532

5. Evidence of Huskisson, 28 February 1843, ADM 1/5532
6. Minute by Rouse, on Rouse to Irvine, 28 February 1842, ADM 1/5532
7. Hamilton to Irvine, 8 March 1842, ADM 1/5532
8. Irvine to Stopford, 9 March 1842, ADM 1/5532
9. Rouse to Stopford, 11 March 1842, ADM 1/5532
10. Sulivan to Rouse, 11 March 1842, ADM 1/5532
11. Stopford to Irvine, 14 March 1842, ADM 1/5532
12. Minute by Rouse, on Aylmer to Rouse, 1 April 1842, ADM 1/5532
13. Irvine to Stopford, 1 April 1842, ADM 1/5532
14. Evidence of Gillett, 27 February 1843, ADM 1/5532
15. Evidence of Rouse, 15 March 1843, ADM 1/5532
16. Evidence of Lethbridge, 25 February 1843, ADM 1/5532
17. Irvine to Gordon, 13 May 1842, ADM 1/5533
18. James to Stopford, 13 May 1842, ADM 1/5533
19. Minute by Rouse, 4 April 1842, on Hartnoll to Graham, 4 April 1842, ADM 7/601
20. Memorandum by Stopford, 10 February 1842, ADM 80/71
21. Stopford to Herbert, 10 February 1842, ADM 66/12
22. Stopford to Haddington, 13 February 1842, ADM 66/12
23. Stopford to Herbert, 5 April 1842, ADM 66/12
24. Memorandum by Herbert, undated, ADM 7/601
25. Herbert to Stopford, 11 April 1842, ADM 65/111
26. 6 masters to Stopford, 2 May 1842, ADM 7/601
27. Irvine to Gordon, 13 May 1842, ADM 1/5533
28. Evidence of Willes, 25 February 1843, ADM 1/5532
29. Evidence of Kay, 1 March 1843, ADM 1/5532
30. Evidence of Denison, 28 February 1843, ADM 1/5532
31. Evidence of Kay, 1 March 1843, ADM 1/5532

Chapter 7

1. Irvine to Stopford, 18 May 1842, ADM 1/5532
2. Irvine to Stopford, 11 June 1842, ADM 66/12
3. Stopford to Herbert, 11 June 1842, ADM 66/12
4. Stopford to Irvine, 1 September 1842, ADM 66/12
5. Stopford to Haddington, 13 February 1842, ADM 66/12
6. Duncannon to Admiralty, 14 March 1842, ADM 7/601
7. Haddington to Duncannon, 18 March 1842, ADM 7/601
8. Evidence of Willes, 21 February 1843, ADM 1/5532
9. Evidence of Rouse, 15 March 1843, ADM 1/5532
10. Irvine to Stopford, 5 November 1842, ADM 1/5532
11. Evidence of Lee, 15 March 1843, ADM 1/5532
12. Irvine to Stopford, 5 November 1842, ADM 1/5532
13. Stopford to Irvine, 7 November 1842, ADM 66/12
14. Stopford to Herbert, 26 December 1842, ADM 66/12

Chapter 8

1. Graham to Herbert, 14 June 1842, ADM 1/5533
2. Graham to Herbert, 14 July 1842, ADM 7/601. Fisher disparaged Graham's teaching by informing the Governor that in the July examination he found only 8 of Graham's pupils fit for the Nautical school but had passed a further 14 under protest since the classes in the Upper school would be impossibly large if this additional transfer was not made. Fisher to Stopford, 30 August 1842, *Fisher papers*, FIS/33

3. Graham to Stopford, 24 September 1842, ADM 7/601
4. Moseley to the College Council, 9 August 1832, *Archive of King's College, London*, in letters: M32
5. Moseley to Riddle, 13 December 1842, ADM 1/5532
6. Moseley to Riddle, 27 December 1842, ADM 1/5532
7. Moseley to Admiralty, January 1843, ADM 1/5532. This document is undated. Its content and conclusions are reproduced and printed in Appendix B to a report from Moseley to the Admiralty in 1846 in P.P. XXXII (1846) where it is incorrectly dated as January 1842. Since the document describes classes conducted by Campbell as second master in the Upper school, who was not appointed until August 1842, the correct date must be January 1843
8. Seymour to Herbert, 15 January 1843, ADM 1/5532
9. Irvine to Fisher, 30 December 1842, *Fisher papers*, FIS/33
10. Fisher to Stopford, 17 March 1842, *Fisher papers*, FIS/32
11. Irvine to Fisher, 30 December 1842, *Fisher papers*, FIS/33
12. Tremenheere to Admiralty, 7 January 1843, ADM 1/5532
13. Seymour to Herbert, 15 January 1843, ADM 1/5532
14. Moseley to Admiralty, 6 April 1843, ADM 1/5532. Although the inspection occurred early in February 1843 Moseley was too preoccupied with the Commission of Enquiry later that month and in March to complete his report on the Lower school before April. When printed, the date of the report was incorrectly given as 6 April 1842. That this was a printing error is plain from the fact that in the report Moseley refers the Admiralty to his recent report on the discipline of the Greenwich schools which he wrote on 31 March 1843
15. Major to Smith, 18 September 1840, *KCL archive*, in letters: M24
16. Quoted in Miles and Cranch *op. cit.* p 52
17. Rouse to Stopford, 19 January 1843, ADM 66/12
18. Hospital commissioners to Herbert, 11 February 1843, ADM 66/3
19. Herbert to Moseley, Webster and Hastings, 18 February 1843, ADM 7/601

Chapter 9

All evidence taken by and papers submitted to the Commission of Enquiry were filed in box ADM 1/5532. The references in this chapter are all to that source.

1. Evidence of Irvine, 20 February 1843
2. Evidence of Hamilton, 20 and 21 February 1843
3. Evidence of Howcroft, 22 February 1843
4. Evidence of Gordon, 25 February 1843
5. Evidence of Graham, 4 March 1843
6. Evidence of Campbell, 4 March 1843
7. Evidence of Stopford, 4 March 1843
8. Rouse to Stopford, 7 January 1843
9. Evidence of Aylmer, 27 February 1843
10. Rouse to the Commission, 27 February 1843
11. Evidence of the boys, 15 March 1843
12. Evidence of Willes, 25 February 1843
13. Evidence of Hamilton, 28 February 1843
14. Evidence of Irvine, 28 February 1843
15. Memorandum by Irvine, February 1843
16. Irvine to the Commission, 4 March 1843
17. Hamilton to Irvine, 5 March 1843
18. Evidence of Hughes, 15 March 1843

19. Evidence of Huskisson, 28 February 1843
20. Hamilton to Irvine, 5 March 1843
21. Evidence of Harris, 25 February 1843
22. Evidence of Fisher, 28 February 1843
23. Evidence of Huskisson, 28 February 1843
24. Commission Report, 24 March 1843
25. Commissioners to Herbert, 24 March 1843

Chapter 10

1. Report by Moseley, 31 March 1843, ADM 1/5532
2. Stopford to Herbert, 2 August 1843, ADM 66/12
3. Reports by Moseley, 1 August 1843, P.P. XXXVIII (1844)
4. Moseley to Admiralty, 15 August 1843, ADM 1/5532
5. Graham to Stopford, 7 November 1843, and Stopford to Herbert, 10 November 1843, ADM 66/12
6. Stopford to Herbert, 5 February 1844, ADM 66/12
7. Memorandum by Stopford, 1 July 1844, *Fisher papers*, FIS/34
8. Admiralty to Stopford, 5 June 1843, ADM 65/29
9. Stopford to Rouse, Riddle, Graham and Irvine, 9 June 1843, ADM 66/12
10. Report by Moseley, 12 January 1844, P.P. XXXVIII (1844)
11. Quoted in D. Layton *Science for the People: the Origins of the School Science Curriculum in England* (London, 1973), p 83
12. Moseley to Admiralty, 31 March 1843, ADM 1/5532
13. Memorandum by Hughes, 13 November 1843, ADM 65/111
14. Moseley to Fisher, 12 July 1843, *Fisher papers*, FIS/33
15. Moseley to Fisher, 2 August 1843, *Fisher papers*, FIS/33
16. Barrow to Stopford, 21 February 1844, ADM 65/30
17. Herbert to Kay-Shuttleworth, 5 December 1844, *Kay-Shuttleworth papers*, 287:1844
18. Report to Moseley, 1847, P.P. L (1847–8)
19. Herbert to Kay-Shuttleworth, 5 February 1845, *Kay-Shuttleworth papers*, 291:1845
20. Council meeting minutes, 12 January 1844, *KCL archive*, KA/C/M4
21. Moseley to College Secretary, 13 March 1844, *KCL archive*, in letters: M34
22. Report by Moseley, 1847, P.P. L (1847–8)
23. Report by Moseley, 8 March 1845, P.P. XXXV (1845)
24. Report by Moseley, 18 April 1845, P.P. XXXV (1845). Moseley continued to take a close interest in appointments at the schools. On the occasion of a vacancy in the Lower school in 1848 he wrote curtly to Fisher: 'Why have you passed over Mr McDougall? Will you be good enough to send me the testimonials? Oblige me with an answer if possible by return of post.' Fisher replied coldly that he had already sent the papers to Moseley at the Privy Council Office and had nothing to say other than that 'Mr Hughes and myself gave his testimonials & etc. the best consideration we were able.' Moseley to Fisher and Fisher to Moseley, 17 February 1848, *Fisher papers*, FIS/35
25. Report by Moseley, 1846, P.P. XXXII (1846)
26. Report by Cumin, P.P. XXI (1861) part III
27. Report by Moseley, 18 April 1845, P.P. XXXV (1845)
28. Report by Moseley, 19 July 1848, P.P. L (1847–8)

Chapter 11

1. Rouse to Stopford, 20 November 1841, ADM 1/5532
2. Stopford to Irvine, 27 September 1841, ADM 1/5532

3. Irvine to Stopford, 20 January 1843, ADM 7/601
4. Irvine to Willes, 29 April 1842, ADM 1/5532
5. Irvine to Willes, 26 June 1842, ADM 1/5532
6. Irvine to Moseley, 4 April 1843, ADM 1/5532
7. Minutes of Committee of Council, 23 June 1841, P.P. XXXIII (1842)
8. Graham to Herbert, 31 August 1842, ADM 1/5533
9. Graham to Herbert, 23 May 1842, ADM 7/601
10. Irvine to Stopford, 18 January 1842, ADM 1/5532
11. Irvine to Stopford, 11 June 1842, ADM 66/12
12. Evidence of Lee, 28 February 1843, ADM 1/5532
13. Stopford to Fisher, 15 January 1842, *Fisher papers*, FIS/32
14. Stopford to Fisher, 24 August 1842, *Fisher papers*, FIS/32
15. Kay-Shuttleworth to Janet Shuttleworth, 12 January 1842, *Kay-Shuttleworth papers*, 220:1841
16. Duncannon to Gordon, 1 August 1841, ADM 7/601
17. Kay-Shuttleworth to Haddington, 28 October 1841, ADM 7/601
18. Evidence of Kay-Shuttleworth, 26 January 1860, P.P. XXI (1861) part VI
19. Evidence of Gordon, 4 March 1843, ADM 1/5532
20. E.L. and O. P. Edmonds (eds) *I Was There: the Memoirs of H. S. Tremenheere* (Eton, 1965), p 52
21. Evidence of Gordon, 4 March 1843, ADM 1/5532
22. Arnold to Blackstone, 28 September 1828. Quoted in Stanley *Life of Arnold* vol I, p 218
23. Irvine to Stopford, 20 January 1843, ADM 7/601
24. Commission Report, 24 March 1843, ADM 1/5532
25. Graham to Stopford, 26 April 1842, ADM 1/5533
26. Hartnoll to Greenwich schools committee, 20 March 1841, ADM 7/601
27. Graham to Herbert, 14 June 1842, ADM 1/5533
28. Graham to Herbert, 2 May 1842, ADM 1/5533
29. J. P. Kay-Shuttleworth *Public Education as affected by the Minutes of the Committee of Privy Council from 1846 to 1852 with suggestions as to future policy* (London, 1853), p 61
30. Kay-Shuttleworth to Russell, 29 October 1838, *Russell papers*, PRO 30/22/3B
31. Quoted in Smith *Life and Work of Sir James Kay-Shuttleworth* p 58
32. Evidence of Kay-Shuttleworth, 26 January 1860, P.P. XXI (1861) part VI
33. Campbell to Kay-Shuttleworth, 22 January 1846, *Kay-Shuttleworth papers*, 294:1846
34. Fleming to More O'Ferrall, 7 August 1840, ED 17/4
35. Roach *A History of Secondary Education in England* p 71
36. Quoted in Stanley *Life of Arnold* vol I, p 163
37. Kay-Shuttleworth to Russell, 29 October 1838, *Russell papers*, PRO 30/22/3B
38. Journal of Kay-Shuttleworth, 6 July 1841, *Kay-Shuttleworth papers*, 219:1841
39. Report by Moseley, 18 April 1845, P.P. XXXV (1845)
40. Report by Moseley, 1846, P.P. XXXII (1846)
41. Report by Arnold, June 1860, P.P. XXI (1861) part IV
42. Evidence of Gordon, 4 March 1843, ADM 1/5532
43. Commissioners to Herbert, 24 March 1843, ADM 1/5532. Whatever the nature of Moseley's informal enquiries, Rouse remained superintending officer at the schools until his retirement in 1863

BIBLIOGRAPHY

UNPUBLISHED MATERIAL

1. *Official Papers*

MINISTRY OF EDUCATION RECORDS (Public Record Office, London)
Minutes and Reports of the Committee of Privy Council on Education, 1839–1899:
ED 17/

ADMIRALTY RECORDS (Public Record Office, London)
Series:
ADM 1/
ADM 7/
ADM 65/
ADM 66/
ADM 80/

2. *Private Collections*

(a) *In the Public Record Office, London*
Papers of Lord John Russell   PRO 30/22/

(b) *In the National Maritime Museum, Greenwich*
Papers of Admiral Sir Robert Stopford   STO/
Papers of Captain Thomas Huskisson   HUS/
Papers of the Reverend George Fisher   FIS/

(c) *In the John Rylands Library, Manchester*
Papers of Sir James Kay-Shuttleworth

(d) *At King's College, London*
Archive of King's College:
In letters/
College Council Minutes/

(e) *At the Royal Society, London*
Papers and correspondence relating to:
Reverend Henry Moseley
Reverend George Fisher
Professor Augustus de Morgan
J. H. Hartnoll

PUBLISHED MATERIAL

1. *Documentary Sources*

Parliamentary Accounts and Papers
Hansard (Parliamentary Debates)
Navy List
The Times

2. *Secondary Sources*

Adams, F., *History of the Elementary School Contest in England* (London, 1882)

Adkins, T., *The History of St. John's College Battersea* (London, 1906)

Aldrich, R., *Sir John Pakington and National Education* (Leeds, 1979)

Aldrich, R., *An Introduction to the History of Education* (London, 1982)

Alexander, J. and Paz, D. G., 'The Treasury Grants, 1833–1839', *British Journal of Educational Studies*, XXII (1974), pp 78–92

Allen, A. O., *John Allen and his Friends* (London, 1922)

Allport, D. H. and Friskney, N. J., *A Short History of Wilson's School* (London, 1987)

Anderson, R. D., *Education and Opportunity in Victorian Scotland* (Oxford, 1983)

Anderson, R. D., *Education and the Scottish People 1750–1918* (Oxford, 1995)

Archer, R. L., *Secondary Education in the Nineteenth Century* (London, 1921)

Armytage, W. H. G., *Four Hundred Years of English Education* (Cambridge, 1964)

Arnold, M., *Schools and Universities on the Continent* (London, 1868)

Auchmuty, J. J., *Sir Thomas Wyse, 1791–1862; the Life and Career of an Educator and Diplomat* (London, 1939)

Baines, E., *Letter to the Right Honourable Lord Wharncliffe, Chairman of the Committee of Council on Education, on Sir James Graham's Bill for Establishing Exclusive Church Schools built and supported out of the Poor's Rates, and discouraging British Schools and Sunday Schools* (London, 1843)

Baines, E., *Letters to the Right Honourable Lord John Russell on State Education* (London, 1846)

Baines, E., *An Alarm to the Nation, on the Unjust, Unconstitutional, and Dangerous Measure of State Education proposed by the Government* (London, 1847)

Baines, E., *A Letter to the Most Noble the Marquis of Lansdowne, President of the Council, on the Government Plan of Education* (London, 1847)

Baines, E., *Education Best Promoted by Perfect Freedom, not by State Endowments* (London, 1854)

Baines, J. M. and Conisbee, L. R., *The History of Hastings Grammar School 1619–1956* (Hastings, 1956)

Ball, N., *Her Majesty's Inspectorate 1839–1849* (Birmingham, 1963)

Ball, N., 'Elementary School Attendance and Voluntary Effort before 1870', *History of Education*, II (1973), pp 19–34

Ball, N., *Educating the People: a Documentary History of Elementary Schooling in England, 1840–1870* (London, 1983)

Bamford, T. W., *Rise of the Public Schools: a Study of Boys' Public Boarding Schools in England and Wales from 1837 to the Present Day* (London, 1967)

Bamford, T. W., *Thomas Arnold on Education* (Cambridge, 1970)

Bamford, T. W., 'Thomas Arnold and the Victorian Idea of a Public School', in Simon, B. and Bradley, I. (eds) *The Victorian Public School* pp 58–71

Barnard, H. C., *A History of English Education from 1760* (London, 1947)

Behlmer, G. K., *Child Abuse and Moral Reform in England 1870–1908* (Stanford, 1982)

Bell, A., *An Experiment in Education made at the Male Asylum at Egmore, near Madras* (London, 1805)

Best, G. F. A., 'The Religious Difficulties of National Education in England, 1800–1870', *Cambridge Historical Journal*, XII (1956), pp 155–173

Binns, H. B., *A Century of Education: being the Centenary History of the British and Foreign School Society 1808–1908* (London, 1908)

Bishop, A. S., *The Rise of a Central Authority for English Education* (Cambridge, 1971)

Bradley, A. G., Champneys, A. C. and Baines, J. W., *A History of Marlborough College* (London, 1923)

Briggs, A., 'The Study of the History of Education', *History of Education*, I (1972), pp 5–22

Bryant, M. E., *The London Experience of Secondary Education* (London, 1986)

Burgess, H. J., *Enterprise in Education: the story of the work of the Established Church in the Education of the People prior to 1870* (London, 1958)

Butterfield, P. H., 'The Educational Researches of the Manchester Statistical Society, 1830–1840', *British Journal of Educational Studies*, XXII (1974), pp 340–359

Carr, J. R., 'Lancasterian Schools: a Reappraisal', *The Durham Research Review*, V (1969–70), pp 427–436

Castle, E. B., *The Teacher* (Oxford, 1970)

Cawley, E. H., *The American Diaries of Richard Cobden* (Princeton, 1952)

Chapman, C. R., *The Growth of British Education and its Records* (Dursley, 1991)

Clarke, H. L. and Weech, W. N., *History of Sedbergh School 1525–1925* (Sedbergh, 1925)

Coleman, B. I., 'The Incidence of Education in mid-century', in Wrigley, E. A. (ed), *Nineteenth-Century Society* (Cambridge, 1972), pp 397–410

Combe, G., 'On Secular Education', *Westminster Review*, (1852); reprinted in Reeder, D. A., *Educating Our Masters* pp 43–68

Connell, W. F., *The Educational Thought and Influence of Matthew Arnold* (London, 1950)

Cook, T. G. (ed), *Local Studies and the History of Education* (London, 1972)

Cruickshank, M., 'David Stow, Scottish Pioneer of Teacher Training in Britain', *British Journal of Educational Studies*, XIV (1965–6), pp 205–215

Curtis, S. J., *History of Education in Great Britain* (Cambridge, 1948)

Davies, W., *The Curriculum and Organisation of the County Intermediate Schools 1880–1926* (Cardiff, 1989)

Davis, S. E., *Educational Periodicals during the Nineteenth Century* (Washington, 1919)

Dent, H. C., *The Training of Teachers in England and Wales 1800–1975* (London, 1977)

Dickson, M., *Teacher Extraordinary: Joseph Lancaster 1778–1838* (Lewes, 1986)

Digby, A. and Searby, P., *Children, School and Society in Nineteenth-Century England* (London, 1981)

Dobbs, A. E., *Education and Social Movements 1700–1850* (London, 1919)

Donajgrodzki, A. P. (ed), *Social Control in Nineteenth-Century Britain* (London, 1977)

Drake, M. (ed), *Applied Historical Studies: an Introductory Reader* (London, 1973)

Draper, F. W. M., *Four Centuries of Merchant Taylors' School 1561–1961* (Oxford, 1962)

Dunford, J. and Sharp, P., *The Education System in England and Wales* (London, 1990)

Dunn, H., *National Education, the Question of Questions* (London, 1838)

Edmonds, E. L., *The School Inspector* (London, 1962)

Edmonds, E. L. and Edmonds, O. P., 'Hugh Seymour Tremenheere, Pioneer Inspector of Schools', *British Journal of Educational Studies*, XII (1963–4), pp 65–76

Edmonds, E. L. and Edmonds, O. P. (eds), *I Was There: the Memoirs of H. S. Tremenheere* (Eton, 1965)

Ellis, A. C. O., 'Influences on School Attendance in Victorian England', *British Journal of Educational Studies*, XXI (1973), pp 313–326

Farrar, P. N., 'American Influence on the Movement for a National System of Elementary Education in England and Wales 1830–1870', *British Journal of Educational Studies*, XIV (1965–6), pp 36–47

Fisher, G. W., *Annals of Shrewsbury School* (London, 1899)

Fletcher, J., 'Moral and Educational Statistics of England and Wales', *Journal of the Statistical Society of London*, X (1847), pp 193–242

Fletcher, J., 'Moral and Educational Statistics of England and Wales', *Journal of the Statistical Society of London*, XII (1849), pp 151–176 and 189–335

Forrester, E. G., *A History of Magdalen College School, Brackley, Northamptonshire 1548–1949* (Buckingham, 1950)

Fox, C. et als., *Education* (Truro, 1977)

Fraser, D., 'Education and Urban Politics c.1832–1885', in Reeder, D. A. (ed), *Urban Education in the Nineteenth Century* pp 11–25

Frith, S., 'Socialization and Rational Schooling: Elementary Education in Leeds before 1870', in McCann, P. (ed), *Popular Education and Socialization in the Nineteenth Century* pp 67–92

Gardner, P., *The Lost Elementary Schools of Victorian England: the Peoples' Education* (London, 1984)

Gathorne-Hardy, J., *The Public School Phenomenon, 597–1977* (London, 1977)

Goldstrom, J. M., *The Social Content of Education, 1808–70; a study of the Working Class School Reader in England and Ireland* (Shannon, 1972)

Goldstrom, J. M., *Education: Elementary Education 1780–1900* (Newton Abbot, 1972)

Goldstrom, J. M., 'The Content of Education and the Socialization of the Working-Class Child 1830–1860', in McCann, P. (ed), *Popular Education and Socialization in the Nineteenth Century* pp 93–109

Gordon, P., *The Victorian School Manager: a study in the Management of Education 1800–1902* (London, 1974)

Gordon, P. and Lawton, D., *Curriculum Change in the Nineteenth and Twentieth Centuries* (London, 1978)

Gordon, P. and White, J., *Philosophers as Educational Reformers: the Influence of Idealism on British Educational Thought and Practice* (London, 1979)

Grant, A. C., 'A Note on "Secular" Education in the Nineteenth Century', *British Journal of Educational Studies*, XVI (1968), pp 308–317

Gray, I. E. and Potter, W. E., *Ipswich School 1400–1950* (Ipswich, 1950)

Gray-Fow, M. J. G., 'Squire, Parson and Village School: Wragby 1830–1886', in Scott, P. and Fletcher, P. (eds), *Culture and Education in Victorian England* (Cranbury, N.J., 1990), pp 162–173

Green, J. A., *Life and Work of Pestalozzi* (London, 1913)

Grier, R. M., *John Allen: a Memoir* (London, 1889)

Grounds, A. D., *A History of King Edward VI Grammar School Retford* (Worksop, 1970)

Hake, G., *Memoirs of Eighty Years* (London, 1892)

Harries, R., Cattermole, P. and Mackintosh, P., *A History of Norwich School: King Edward VI School at Norwich* (Norwich, 1991)

Harrison, F., *Autobiographic Memoirs* Volume I (London, 1911)

Heeney, B., *Mission to the Middle Classes: the Woodard Schools 1848–91* (London, 1969)

Hennock, E. P., *Fit and Proper Persons: Ideal and Reality in Nineteenth-Century Urban Government* (London, 1973)

Hill, A., *Hints on the Discipline Appropriate to Schools* (London, 1855)

Hill, C. P., *A History of Bristol Grammar School* (London, 1951)

Hill, F., *National Education: Its Present State and Prospects* Volumes I and II (London, 1836)

Hinder, E. F., *The Schoolmaster in the Gutter* (London, 1883)

Hinton, J. H., *The Case of the Manchester Educationists. A Review of the Evidence taken before a Committee of the House of Commons in Relation to the State of Education in Manchester and Salford* (London, 1852)

Hinton, J. H., *The Case of the Manchester Educationists, Part II. A Review of the Evidence taken before a Committee of the House of Commons, in relation to a scheme of Secular Education* (London, 1854)

Hollis, P. (ed), *Pressure from Without in early Victorian England* (London, 1974)

Honey, J. R. de S., *Tom Brown's Universe: the Development of the Victorian Public School* (London, 1977)

Hook, W. F., *On the Means of rendering more Efficient the Education of the People: a Letter to the Lord Bishop of St. David's* (London, 1846)

Hopkins, E., 'A Charity School in the Nineteenth Century: Old Swinford Hospital School, 1815–1914', *British Journal of Educational Studies*, XVII (1969), pp 177–192

Hopkins, E., *Childhood Transformed: Working-Class Children in Nineteenth-Century England* (Manchester, 1994)

Horn, P., *Education in Rural England 1800–1914* (London, 1978)

Horn, P., *The Victorian and Edwardian Schoolchild* (Gloucester, 1989)

How, F. D., *Six Great Schoolmasters* (London, 1904)

Hughes, K., *The Victorian Governess* (London, 1993)

Humes, W. M. and Paterson, H. M. (eds), *Scottish Culture and Scottish Education 1800–1980* (Edinburgh, 1983)

Hurt, J., *Education in Evolution: Church, State, Society and Popular Education 1800–1870* (London, 1971)

Hurt, J. S., 'Professor West on Early Nineteenth-Century Education', *Economic History Review*, XXIV (1971), pp 624–632

Hurt, J. S., 'Drill, Discipline and the Elementary School Ethos', in McCann, P. (ed), *Popular Education and Socialization in the Nineteenth Century* pp 167–191

Hutton, T. W., *King Edward's School Birmingham 1552–1952* (Oxford, 1952)

Hyndman, M., *Schools and Schooling in England and Wales: a Documentary History* (London, 1978)

Johnson, R., 'Educational Policy and Social Control in Early Victorian England', *Past and Present*, 49 (1970), pp 96–119

Johnson, R., 'Administrators in Education before 1870: Patronage, Social Position and Role', in Sutherland, G. (ed), *Studies in the Growth of Nineteenth-Century Government* pp 110–138

Johnson, R., 'Educating the Educators: "Experts" and the State 1833–9', in Donajgrodzki, A. P. (ed), *Social Control in Nineteenth-Century Britain* pp 77–107

Johnson, R., *The Blue Books and Education, 1816–1896: the Critical Reading of Official Sources* (University of Birmingham, Centre for Contemporary Cultural Studies)

Jones, D. K., 'Working-Class Education in Nineteenth-Century Manchester: the Manchester Free School', *The Vocational Aspect*, XIX (1967), pp 22–33

Jones, D. K., *The Making of the Education System 1851–1881* (London, 1977)

Jones, D. K., 'Socialization and Social Science: Manchester Model Secular School 1854–1861', in McCann, P. (ed), *Popular Education and Socialization in the Nineteenth Century* pp 111–139

Judges, A. V., 'James Kay-Shuttleworth, Pioneer of National Education', in Judges, A. V. (ed), *Pioneers of English Education* (London, 1952), pp 104–127

Kay, J., *The Education of the Poor in England and Europe* (London, 1846)

Kay, J., *The Condition and Education of Poor Children in English and in German Towns* (London, 1853)

Kay-Shuttleworth, J., *Public Education as affected by the Minutes of the Committee of Privy Council from 1846 to 1852 with Suggestions as to Future Policy* (London, 1853)

Kay-Shuttleworth, J., *Four Periods of Public Education as reviewed in 1832, 1839, 1846, 1862* (London, 1862)

Kay-Shuttleworth, J., 'A Sketch of the History and Results of Popular Education in England', (1866) reprinted in Reeder, D., *Educating Our Masters* pp 69–90

Kay-Shuttleworth, J., *Memorandum on Popular Education* (London, 1868)

Lancashire Public School Association, *National Education not necessarily Governmental, Sectarian or Irreligious* (London, 1850)

Lancaster, J., *Improvements in Education, as it respects the Industrious Classes of the Community* (London, 1803)

Lawrence, E. (ed), *Friedrich Froebel and English Education* (London, 1952)

Lawrence, P. S. H. (ed), *The Encouragement of Learning* (Salisbury, 1980)

Lawson, J., *The Endowed Grammar Schools of East Yorkshire* (York, 1962)

Lawson, J., *A Town Grammar School through six centuries: a History of Hull Grammar School against its local background* (Oxford, 1963)

Lawson, J. and Silver, H., *A Social History of Education in England* (London, 1973)

Layton, D., *Science for the People: the Origins of the School Science Curriculum in England* (London, 1973)

Leetham, C. R., *Ratcliffe College 1847–1947* (Leicester, 1950)

Leinster-Mackay, D., *Cross Pollinators of English Education: Case Studies of three Victorian School Inspectors* (Leeds, 1986)

Leinster-Mackay, D., *The Educational World of Edward Thring* (London, 1987)

Liebschner, J., *Foundations of Progressive Education: the History of the National Froebel Society* (Cambridge, 1991)

Lubenow, W., *The Politics of Government Growth: early Victorian Attitudes towards State Intervention 1833–1848* (Newton Abbot, 1971)

Ludlow, J. M. and Jones, L., *Progress of the Working Class 1832–1867* (London, 1867)

McCann, P. (ed), *Popular Education and Socialization in the Nineteenth Century* (London, 1977)

McCann, P., 'Popular Education, Socialization, and Social Control: Spitalfields 1812–1824', in McCann, P. (ed), *Popular Education and Socialization in the Nineteenth Century* pp 1–40

MacDonagh, O., *Early Victorian Government 1830–1870* (London, 1977)

Maclure, J. S. (ed), *Educational Documents: England and Wales 1816 to the Present Day* (London, 1965)

Mack, E. C., *Public Schools and British Opinion 1780 to 1860* (London, 1938)

Madoc-Jones, B., 'Patterns of Attendance and their Social Significance: Mitcham National School 1830–39', in McCann, P. (ed), *Popular Education and Socialization in the Nineteenth Century* pp 41–66

Mains, B. and Tuck, A., *Royal Grammar School Newcastle upon Tyne: A History of the School in its Community* (London, 1986)

Maltby, S. E., *Manchester and the Movement for National Elementary Education 1800–1870* (Manchester, 1918)

Mangan, J. A., 'Athleticism: a case study of the Evolution of an Educational Ideology', in Simon, B. and Bradley, I. (eds), *The Victorian Public School* pp 147–167

Mangan, J. A., *Athleticism in the Victorian and Edwardian Public School* (Cambridge, 1981)

Mann, H., *Report of an Educational Tour in Germany, and parts of Great Britain and Ireland* (London, 1846)

Mann, M. T. P., *Life of Horace Mann* (Boston, 1888)

Marsden, W. E., *Unequal Educational Provision in England and Wales: the Nineteenth-Century Roots* (London, 1987)

Martin, C., *A Short History of English Schools 1750–1965* (Hove, 1979)

Maxwell-Lyte, H. C., *A History of Eton College 1440–1898* (London, 1899)

Miles, F. and Cranch, G., *King's College School: the First 150 Years* (London, 1979)

More, C., *The Training of Teachers, 1847–1947: A History of the Church Colleges at Cheltenham* (London, 1992)

Morley, J., *The Struggle for National Education* (London, 1873)

Mumford, A. A., *The Manchester Grammar School 1515–1915* (London, 1919)

Murray, A. L., *The Royal Grammar School Lancaster: A History* (Cambridge, 1951)

Newsome, D., *Godliness and Good Learning: Four Studies on a Victorian Ideal* (London, 1961)

O'Day, R., *Education and Society 1500–1800* (London, 1982)

Oldham, J. B., *A History of Shrewsbury School 1552–1952* (Oxford, 1952)

Ollard, R., *An English Education: a Perspective of Eton* (London, 1982)

Pallister, R., 'Workhouse Education in County Durham: 1834–1870', *British Journal of Educational Studies*, XVI (1968), pp 279–291

Pallister, R., 'The Determinants of Elementary School Attendance about 1850', *Durham Research Review*, V (1969–70), pp 384–398

Pallister, R., 'Educational Capital in the Elementary School of the mid Nineteenth Century', *History of Education*, II (1973), pp 147–158

Pallister, R., 'The Use of Public Funds for Education in England before 1839', *The Durham and Newcastle Research Review*, IX (1980), pp 145–153

Parkin, G., *Edward Thring: Life, Diary and Letters* (London, 1900)

Pattison, M., *Memoirs* (London, 1885)

Paz, D. G., 'Working-Class Education and the State, 1839–1849: the Sources of Government Policy', *Journal of British Studies*, XVI (1976), pp 129–152

Paz, D. G., *The Politics of Working-Class Education in Britain, 1830–50* (Manchester, 1980)

Paz, D. G., 'Sir James Kay-Shuttleworth: the Man behind the Myth', *History of Education*, XIV (1985), pp 185–198

Pearce, E. H., *Annals of Christ's Hospital* (London, 1901)

Percival, A. C., *Very Superior Men: some early Public School Headmasters and their Achievements* (London, 1973)

Perkin, H., *The Origins of Modern English Society 1780–1880* (London, 1969)

Phillips, F. R., *Creating an Education System for England and Wales* (Lampeter, 1992)

Platts, B., *A History of Greenwich* (Newton Abbot, 1973)

Playfair, L., 'National Education', (1870) reprinted in Reeder, D., *Educating Our Masters* pp 127–149

Pritchard, F. C., *The Story of Westminster College 1851–1951* (London, 1951)

Reeder, D. A. (ed), *Urban Education in the Nineteenth Century* (London, 1977)

Reeder, D. A., *Educating Our Masters* (Leicester, 1980)

Rich, R. W., *The Training of Teachers in England and Wales during the Nineteenth Century* (Cambridge, 1933)

Rivington, S., *The History of Tonbridge School from its Foundation in 1553 to the Present Date* (London, 1898)

Roach, J., *Public Examinations in England 1850–1900* (Cambridge, 1971)

Roach, J., *A History of Secondary Education in England, 1800–1870* (London, 1986)

Roach, J., *Secondary Education in England 1870–1902: Public Activity and Private Enterprise* (London, 1991)

Robson, A. H., *The Education of Children Engaged in Industry in England 1833–1876* (London, 1931)

Rose, L., *The Erosion of Childhood: Child Oppression in Britain 1860–1918* (London, 1991)

Russell, R. (ed), *Early Correspondence of Lord John Russell 1805–1840* (London, 1913)

Sanderson, M., 'Literacy and Social Mobility in the Industrial Revolution in England', *Past and Present*, 56 (1972), pp 75–104

Sanderson, M., 'The National and British School Societies in Lancashire 1803–1830: the Roots of Anglican Supremacy in English Education', in Cook, T. G. (ed), *Local Studies and the History of Education* pp 1–36

Sandford, F., *Reports on Elementary Schools 1852–1882 by Matthew Arnold* (London, 1889)

Scott, P. and Fletcher, P. (eds), *Culture and Education in Victorian England* (New Jersey, 1990)

Scrimgeour, R. M. (ed), *The North London Collegiate School 1850–1950: A Hundred Years of Girls' Education* (Oxford, 1950)

Seaborne, M., 'Early Theories of Teacher Education', *British Journal of Educational Studies*, XXII (1974), pp 325–339

Searby, P. (ed), *Educating the Victorian Middle Class* (London, 1982)

Selleck, R. J. W., *James Kay-Shuttleworth: Journey of an Outsider* (London, 1994)

Sellman, R. R., *Devon Village Schools in the Nineteenth Century* (Newton Abbot, 1967)

Senior, N. W., *Suggestions on Popular Education* (London, 1861)

Silber, K., *Pestalozzi: The Man and his Work* (London, 1960)

Silver, H., *The Concept of Popular Education: A study of Ideas and Social Movements in the Early Nineteenth Century* (London, 1965)

Silver, H., *Robert Owen on Education* (Cambridge, 1969)

Silver, H., 'Ideology and the Factory Child: Attitudes to Half-Time Education', in McCann, P. (ed), *Popular Education and Socialization in the Nineteenth Century* pp 141–166

Silver, H., *Education as History: Interpreting Nineteenth and Twentieth Century Education* (London, 1983)

Silver, P. and Silver, H., *The Education of the Poor: The History of a National School 1824–1974* (London, 1974)

Simon, B., *The Two Nations and the Educational Structure 1780–1870* (London, 1974)

Simon, B. and Bradley, I. (eds), *The Victorian Public School* (London, 1975)

Smith, F., *The Life and Work of Sir James Kay-Shuttleworth* (London, 1923)

Smith, F., *A History of English Elementary Education 1760–1902* (London, 1931)

Stanley, A. P., *The Life and Correspondence of Thomas Arnold* Volumes I and II (London, 1881)

Staunton, H., *The Great Schools of England* (London, 1865)

Steedman, C., Urwin, C. and Walkerdine, V. (eds), *Language, Gender and Childhood* (London, 1985)

Stephens, M. D. and Roderick, G. W., *Post School Education* (London, 1984)

Stewart, W. A. C., *Progressives and Radicals in English Education 1750–1970* (London, 1972)

Stewart, W. A. C. and McCann, W. P., *The Educational Innovators 1750–1880* (London, 1967)

Stone, L., 'Literacy and Education in England 1640–1900', *Past and Present*, 42 (1969), pp 69–139

Sturt, M., *The Education of the People: A History of Primary Education in England and Wales in the Nineteenth Century* (London, 1967)

Sutherland, G., *Elementary Education in the Nineteenth Century* (London, 1971)

Sutherland, G. (ed), *Studies in the Growth of Nineteenth-Century Government* (London, 1972)

Sutherland, G. (ed), *Matthew Arnold on Education* (London, 1973)

Sylvester, D. W., *Robert Lowe and Education* (Cambridge, 1974)

Tholfsen, T. R. (ed), *Sir James Kay-Shuttleworth on Popular Education* (New York, 1974)

Thomas, A. W., *A History of Nottingham High School, 1513–1953* (Nottingham, 1957)

Thomas, B., *Repton 1557–1957* (London, 1957)

Trimmer, S., *A Comparative View of the New Plan of Education Promulgated by Mr Joseph Lancaster* (London, 1805)

Turner, H. D. T., *The Royal Hospital School, Greenwich* (London, 1980)

Turner, H. D., *The Cradle of the Navy: the story of the Royal Hospital School at Greenwich and at Holbrook, 1694–1988* (York, 1990)

Tylecote, M., *The Mechanics' Institutes of Lancashire and Yorkshire before 1851* (Manchester, 1957)

Vance, N., 'The Ideal of Manliness', in Simon, B. and Bradley, I. (eds), *The Victorian Public School* pp 115–128

Varley, B., *The History of Stockport Grammar School* (Manchester, 1957)

Vaughan, C. J., *A Letter to the Viscount Palmerston M.P. on the Monitorial System of Harrow School* (London, 1854)

Vaughan, R., *The Age of Great Cities: or Modern Society viewed in its Relation to Intelligence, Morals, and Religion* (London, 1843)

Vincent, D., *Literacy and Popular Culture: England 1750–1914* (Cambridge, 1989)

Ward, G., 'The Education of Factory Child Workers 1833–1850', *Economic History*, III (1935), pp 110–124

Ward, J. T. and Treble, J. H., 'Religion and Education in 1843: Reaction to the "Factory Education Bill"', *Journal of Ecclesiastical History*, XX (1969), pp 79–110

Wardle, D., *Education and Society in Nineteenth-Century Nottingham* (Cambridge, 1971)

Watson, J. and Gregory, K., *In the Meantime: a book on Greenwich* (Greenwich, 1988)

Waugh, H. L., *George Watson's College: History and Record 1724–1970* (Edinburgh, 1970)

Webb, R. K., 'A Whig Inspector', *Journal of Modern History*, XXVII (1955), pp 352–364

West, E. G., *Education and the State: a Study in Political Economy* (London, 1965)

West, E. G., 'Resource Allocation and Growth in Early Nineteenth-Century British Education', *Economic History Review*, XXIII (1970), pp 68–95

West, E. G., 'The Interpretation of Early Nineteenth-Century Education Statistics', *Economic History Review*, XXIV (1971), pp 633–642

West, E. G., *Education and the Industrial Revolution* (London, 1975)

West, E. G., 'Literacy and the Industrial Revolution', *Economic History Review*, XXXI (1978), pp 369–383

Whiteside, L., *A History of the King's Hospital* (Dublin, 1975)

Woodard, N., *Public Schools for the Middle Classes: a Letter to the Clergy of the Diocese of Chichester* (London, 1851)

Wyse, T., *Education Reform; or the Necessity of a National System of Education* (London, 1836)

INDEX